THE LIBERATORS

THE LIBERATORS

*A Study of Independence Movements in
Spanish America*

by
IRENE
NICHOLSON

FREDERICK A. PRAEGER, Publishers
New York · Washington

BOOKS THAT MATTER

Published in the United States of America in 1969
by Frederick A. Praeger, Inc., Publishers
111 Fourth Avenue, New York, N.Y. 10003

© 1968 in London, England by Irene Nicholson

Library of Congress Catalog Card Number: 69-19554

Printed in Great Britain

To the memory of my father
PERCY MERWYN NICHOLSON
of
WILLIAMSON, BALFOUR AND COMPANY LTD
CHILE

ACKNOWLEDGEMENTS

My thanks are due to the Arts Council of Great Britain for a grant made to me during the writing of this book; to the Venezuelan, Chilean, and Argentine Embassies in London, to Mr. C. L. Pountney of the Anglo-Chilean Society, to Miss Barbara Jenkins of the Canning House Library, and to my local branch of the Barnes Public Library for making books readily available to me; to Gwyneth and Ricardo Pérez in Chile, Antonio Vargas Macdonald and Alvaro Matute in Mexico, and Alberto Palaus and Peter Day in London for tracing specialized material; and to Dr. Harold Blakemore for generously finding time out of a busy University term to read the typescript and make valuable suggestions.

Thanks are also due to the following sources for the illustrations:

Dr. Humberto F. Burzio, Director of the *Museo Histórico Nacional*, Buenos Aires, for permission to reproduce the portraits of San Martín and O'Higgins and Mr. Hugh Lyall for arranging to have these photographed;

The Rt. Hon. the Earl of Dundonald for permission to reproduce the portrait of Admiral 10th Earl of Dundonald when Lord Cochrane and for the photograph by Morgan-Wells;

The *Instituto Nacional de Antropología e Historia*, Mexico, and the artist, for permission to reproduce slides of Juan O'Gorman's portraits of José María Morelos in Chapultepec Castle;

Sir John Walker of the Hispanic and Luso-Brazilian Councils, Canning House, London, for permission to photograph and reproduce the portrait of Simón Bolívar and the portrait of Andrés Bello which appeared in the Councils' Diamante XVI booklet on *Londres en la vida y la obra de Andrés Bello*, by Pedro Grases and *Andrés Bello in Chile* by Victor Santa Cruz;

Dr. Pedro Grases for permission to reproduce the above.

NOTE

Where already existing English versions of Spanish texts have been cited, emendations have been made to bring the translated style into conformity with modern usage. Quotations from Pilling's version of Mitre's biography of San Martín have particularly been altered in this way though without, I hope, destroying the unique flavour of this classic translation. Translations from Miranda, Bolívar, and other protagonists have been made direct from the originals. Bolívar's documents are quoted not by page numbers but according to Lecuna's numbering in his Spanish-language compilations and (where they exist) in the numbering of his English editions.

EXTENT OF THIS BOOK

This study deals only with Spanish America, extending from the Río Grande on the U.S. border to Tierra del Fuego on the verge of the Antarctic. It does not embrace the independence history of the Spanish Antilles, that is, the Dominican Republic and Cuba, which occurred later and needs treatment on its own. Nor does it include Portuguese-speaking Brazil which is in some ways a case apart.

The book is not intended as a catalogue of events but as an analysis of the thoughts and emotions that caused them. Rather than attempt a complete history of campaigns, battles, changing frontiers, and diplomatic exchanges, of which full and detailed accounts are available in books listed in the Bibliography, it selects those examples that can best throw light on the underlying motives of the independence movement.

It proceeds beyond the fighting stage and examines post-independence trends of thought; but here the amount of material is so vast that it has been necessary to be even more selective. The last chapter especially makes no attempt to be more than a very partial study of a complex problem. It is included as an indication of the ways in which the independence wars have provided and can continue to provide the basis for a cohesive Spanish American cultural unit exercising its own influence on the total world scene.

CONTENTS

13

Contents

PART THREE

THE AFTERMATH OF INDEPENDENCE

ILLUSTRATIONS

MAPS

PROLOGUE

The Nature of the Spanish American Independence Movement

Atlantic
Ocean

Rio Grande

Gulf of Mexico

Caribbean Sea

Magdalena R.

Apure R. Orinoco R.

Amazon R.

Pacific

Ocean

Andes

Paraná R.

Uruguay R.

Atlantic

Ocean

0 200 400 600 800 1000
Miles

Cape Horn

1. Relief map of the region from the Río Grande to Cape Horn

PROLOGUE

Spanish America has been called the graveyard of ideals, but this is unjust to her liberators. Not often in history have men fought against such odds to establish a new era and a new society. Portraits of them, with their aristocratic features, their Napoleonic poses, the sashes and medals and the strong thrust of their thighs, seem suspiciously bombastic as though something about their courage and sincerity had to be underscored. This was never so, for the fact is that these men succeeded in changing the face of two-thirds of a hemisphere. If many of their aims are unrealized yet, they exist in the constitutions and in the minds of the spiritual descendants of Bolívar, San Martín, and Morelos.

The overt purpose was to free the area from Spanish domination; but already in the early stages, which began as a loyalist outbreak in support of Spain against Napoleon, it was clear that the real aim was deeper. It arose out of hatred for the dictatorial powers and the pomp Napoleon represented, and love for freedom as symbolized by that pathetically inadequate figurehead, Ferdinand VII. The loyalist uprising soon became an instrument of rebellion, and the struggle then variously took on aspects of civil war, of nationalistic jingoism, of economic protest, of agnosticism or of adherence to the Roman Catholic faith, of reversion to kingship or—conversely—support for the new democratic ideals to which the French revolution had given passionate expression. But the many reverses would never have been overcome, and spirits would have faltered long before the end, if behind these shifting purposes there had not been an unflinching desire to see the victory of liberalism and a new kind of society established on earth.

Destruction and division could never have provided the necessary driving force. The wars, that were one war only though they spread over the most diverse theatres and threw up leaders who found more than a little difficulty in tolerating each other's foibles, nevertheless gathered into comradeship the intellectuals, aristocrats, lawyers, prairie-men, poets, and traders that made up the heterogeneous population. Those of European blood had inherited the burning conviction of Columbus that he had been elected by God for a high task, to unlock the keys of the Atlantic and draw the Indies into the civilized world.[1] It was their faith in the capacity of man to achieve absolute goodness on earth that gave the liberators their quality of genius. Their actual achievements, in terms of effectual freedoms, were as nothing compared with the object lesson they afforded—frail and vulnerable to criticism as they in many ways were: for they proved that ideals can transcend personal quarrels, pomp and bombast and vanity— and indeed most of the weaknesses that flesh is heir to. It was what they aspired to be, not what they were, that made them great.

Regarded as a civil war, the independence conflict was unique. It was not the struggle of one tribe or social groups against another as we see happening in Africa today. Nor was it, like the American War of Independence or the crisis caused by the rebel Smith government in Rhodesia, the result of a clash of ideals between settlers and their blood-relatives in the parent country, for the split between liberals and autocrats was as bitter in Spain as it was in the colonies. Still less could it be called a rebellion of conquered against conqueror; for the Indians, when they fought at all (which, because of their marginal participation in life as a whole, was seldom), weighed in for the most part on the Creole side. Trained within codes of loyalty to Inca or *cacique*, they sympathized with devotion to Ferdinand. Not that they knew any-

[1] Columbus quoted by Bello, Andrés, *Obras Completas*, vol. xix, p. 482.

thing about him, but they had an inborn liking for authority and the divine right of kings. When the Ferdinand issue became obsolete they were prepared to take their orders from the Creoles on the spot. They had always liked their hierarchies to be tangible.

Here rather was a war in which one whole continent and half of another struggled to break free from what was believed to be the petrification of Europe and her ancient institutions, but which had at the base of its social pyramid a far more autocratic and rigid hierarchy than Europe had known for a long time.

The Creoles of the New World liked to assert that even as early as the end of the fifteenth century Europe had lost her moral and political equilibrium, that only the discovery of the western hemisphere, where the fountain of eternal youth was to be found, had saved her from total destruction. The decrepit civilization of the Old World was thought to have drawn fresh youth and strength from the virgin soil of America, where Rousseau's noble savage could live and labour according to natural law.[1] But a strange and, to the people of the Americas, an unexpected thing happened. The Spanish Empire fell, it is true; but Europe, so spurned for an ankylosed old laggard, remained. This old-fashioned, over-populated, suffocated area continued to produce its share of science, art, philosophy, and good government, whereas Latin America remained undeveloped scientifically, technologically dependent on the great powers, and shaken by political upheavals. Why? Not, certainly, because moral, intellectual, or artistic qualities were inferior. Something else had gone amiss. Too many tares had been sown with the good seed.

The picture of the western hemisphere as virgin and unspoiled was, as we now know, a false one. The colonists overlooked the fact that the New World was exceedingly old. To them the natives were little better than animals; and even though their great lords such as Moctezuma, Cuauhtémoc, and Atahualpa were respected and their fabulous cities admired, it was patently obvious that a

[1] See Pilling, William, *The Emancipation of South America*, p. 6. This is a condensed English version of the history of San Martín written by Bartolomé Mitre, First Constitutional President of the Argentine Republic. It was published in London in 1893 and is a classic of its kind.

continent newly discovered to Europe could have no history worth troubling about.

From the earliest days the discoverers and colonizers of these lands were torn by two contrary desires: greed for gold, which represented power; and the longing for Utopia, which meant, at the time, Christianity in the form the friars conceived it. Intense greed and liberalism thus grew up side by side and could find no way of coexisting without unbearable tensions. From the days of Cortés to the last of the viceroys these were ever-present if often muted.

The *conquistadores* were ruthless men bent on acquiring gold and power for themselves and for the Spanish Crown; yet they were convinced that they had come to plant the True Cross in barbarian lands. The friars who followed them were disinterested evangelists who cared for the indigenous peoples as if they had been their own kin. They learned their languages, and made experiments in setting up communities where it was hoped that the love of God and good husbandry would be practised in fruitful partnership. The Kingdom of Heaven was to be established on earth.

An ambivalent attitude toward the Indians was thus established from the beginning, and régimes of violence and of love had for three centuries to maintain an uneasy confrontation, sometimes one and sometimes the other gaining the upper hand according to the wisdom or follies of the viceroys and church dignitaries sent out to rule them. Greed and utopian dreams grew side by side, and it became clear that sooner or later one would inevitably choke the other. Which was to win? This was the burning question and it remains open to this day. It explains the fascination utopian schemes have always held for Latin Americans. It also explains the Creole pride that grew up to counteract what seemed to be the arrogance of Spain.

The *conquistadores* maintained the traditions of the Spanish *hidalgo* and tended naturally to conservatism and autocracy. The friars on the other hand identified themselves first with the pure Indian population and later with the various castes or grades of *mestizo*, which were looked down on by the very Spaniards who had begotten them in lust. Cortés, it is true, had an aristocratic Indian mistress whom there is every reason to suppose he loved and who was afterwards a devoted wife to one of his captains. In most cases, however, the *conquistadores* felt no shame for their lust but did feel it, hypocritically and illogically, for their progeny. The more autocratic members of the Church agreed with the more ruthless of the *conquistadores* in regarding the Indians as animals. It thus became pardonable and even natural to desire creatures who were sub-human, and, in doing so, to perpetuate a half-species for whom nobody need feel responsible because it was by definition outside the human family. The attitude bred insufferable arrogance and lack of conscience; and both among the victims and the perpetrators it harboured jealousy of caste against caste, race against race.

The tensions thus created caused ominous rumblings in the eighteenth century but the volcano did not erupt until the early nineteenth. The liberation of Spanish America is usually supposed to have been accomplished with the formation of the several republics in the eighteen-twenties and with the wars of Dominican and Cuban independence considerably later; but, though there have been dormant periods, the injustices that caused the movement and violent outbreaks to remedy them have continued to our day. Perhaps the ideals that guided the leaders were from the first too contradictory, or insufficiently clearly defined, ever to have been wholly fulfilled. Broadly they were: freedom; unity within the area; national and economic independence; religious tolerance (though—and to many it did not seem a contradiction in terms—such tolerance was intended at first to fit only within the Roman Catholic Church); and sociological improvement of outcast communities.

The philosophy that informed the liberators was based on the new concept of the rights of man, and hopes were at first pinned on the French revolution (which sadly let the liberators down), on the American revolution, and on *Habeas Corpus* in some kind of modernized form. Equality, and emancipation from the stranglehold of unfair privileges accorded to small sectors of the community, became—as Mitre said—'an entirely fresh field for experiment in the development of the physical and moral faculties of man'.[1] The written charters were noble and in theory as perfect as the impatient idealists of the movement could have wished; but the codes laid down came to differ from the ways in which a country was actually governed, until in the end the gap became so wide that it ceased any longer to be heeded. Freedom of the Press was abused or sidestepped, and every kind of law-breaking was tolerated.

Neither in Spanish America nor elsewhere has it ever been easy to define what freedom means. The liberators were certainly not simple xenophobes satisfied to give their countries a name, a flag, and a measure of pride. On a deeper level they were realistic enough to know that the right of the mass to impose its will can have only one result: the triumph of the lowest common denominator of a country's intelligence. They were more inclined to the ancient Greek concept of a free man, whose aim it was to be the best possible kind of human being and who was distinguished from the slave not merely legally but in essence.

From the Age of Enlightenment onward, freedom in the New World was opposed by vested interests embalmed within the sarcophagus of an exclusive aristocracy. The heritage of the Inquisition was a drag even upon the progressive mentality of Charles III and his advisers. Across the ocean Indian cultures had evolved a peculiar absolutism of their own. When the two joined, autocracy was reinforced. Yet both Spaniards and Indians were at heart lovers of freedom. Free people had been caught within a barricade of repression which had to be violently torn down. Add the sharp contrasts of the geography of the New World, and there is the perfect setting for a drama which has been acted out since time immemorial both within societies and within man himself, in which some kind of police force or gestapo is pitted against freedom of conscience and of action.

Unfortunately in Spanish America, once the impulse given by the first liberators had petered out, freedom had a way of

[1] Pilling, W., p. 4.

accelerating down a path to licence, and licence to despotism. Experience showed that freedom required regulating, even (if need be) by enlightened despotism. But such words as 'despot', 'élite', 'autocracy', became bogeys and opposition became concentrated upon the form rather than the inner cause of repressive power.

Spanish America set out to solve an insoluble problem and wondered why it failed. It tried to create a free social order before it had created a free spiritual climate. It put the cart before the horse. Yet the liberators were spiritually-minded men who knew that the struggle they undertook had its battleground within men's minds. The realization they came to, one by one, was too painful to be followed to its conclusion; and laws and constitutions were drawn up which were implemented or broken according to whim. The beauty of the language—and the Spanish language is finely tempered to rhetoric and poetry—was of no avail.

Unity proved no easier to attain than freedom. Bolívar was one of the first men to conceive of a united brotherhood of nations, but he died disappointed, his Gran Colombia fragmented into a number of relatively weak nations which have failed to coalesce even in our own age of international blocs or racio-political groupings. Even the cultural unity that might have emerged out of the use of a common language has been bedevilled, first by lack of communications and later by the intrusion of foreign influence in some areas (such as the *pochismo* or Americanized Spanish used along the Mexican northern border). Andrés Bello's dream of preserving the classical purity of Spanish has been no more realizable than Bolívar's of a united republic.

The petty nationalisms that have sundered Spanish America have been the ultimate and most ironic betrayal not only of Bolívar himself but of many who in his day had no hesitation in crossing frontiers to help the common cause. Even in spite of an inherent antipathy between Argentines and Chileans, the Argentine José de San Martín collaborated with Bernardo O'Higgins to free Chile and then went on to join forces with Bolívar's armies in the north-west. It was a mixed Peruvian-Colombian army that won the battle of Ayacucho and freed Upper Peru, which, when it became the new republic of Bolivia, was presided over by the Venezuelan Sucre. Miguel Santamaría, a Mexican, was at one time a congressman of Gran Colombia and Secretary of the Congress of Cúcuta. Vicente Rocafuerte of Ecuador, an enemy of the self-appointed Mexican emperor Iturbide, served in the Mexican diplomatic service. An early Mexican foreign minister was José Cecilio del Valle of Honduras. The list could be extended. Foreigners were seldom regarded as intruders though they were often punctilious and delicate enough to imagine that they might be—there are cases of men refusing office in a foreign country lest they should seem impostors. Though regional variations were respected, it was accepted in those days that all were first and foremost Americans.

The situation would be different today, and the present failure of Latin America to work as one unit really does verge upon disaster. At a meeting of foreign ministers of the Latin American Free Trade Association on December 10, 1966, the Chilean Gabriel Valdés Subercaseaux reminded his colleagues that the United States had promised publicly that it will reach the moon in 1970, that the Soviet Union had similar aspirations, and yet Latin America could not promise, another three years ahead, in 1973, to initiate a process of common tariff agreements which is the essence of the Treaty of Montevideo signed in 1960. Obviously no one will doubt, said Valdés Subercaseaux, that it is much more difficult to reach the moon than to initiate a process of common tariff agreements among countries that, ever since Bolívar, San Martín, Sucre, and other liberators did so, have been making constant promises to achieve unity. In other words the United States might reach the moon after six years' effort, and Latin Americans, after 160 years of wanting to do so, would not have begun to initiate a process of re-unification by economic and commercial means. It all seemed very dispiriting to the Chilean Foreign Minister who was not, as he admonished his friends and colleagues, prepared to admit that feats involving concessions to national pride may be more difficult than technological ones, even when the latter have the improbable appearance of science fiction!

Thinking in terms of a single large unit—call it Andean, Colombian, or what you will—has not come easily to the common run of Spanish Americans, who have preferred to sacrifice Bolívar's great vision on the altar of local, national independence (even, as in the case of Bolivia, when the nation's boundaries have neither geographical nor ethnic logic). Not only that, but from the start the new nations were fragmented in the name of the supposedly republican principle of federalism as opposed to centralism. It was fortunate that this issue, which today looks more administrative than political and which is holding up the development of some areas where local *caciques* still rule at the point of a gun, should have become one of the main bones of contention between conservatives and liberals; and still more so that centralism should have been associated with conservatism. The issue looks even sillier as communications become more rapid and the world shrinks in effective size. We now have a situation in which, in the name of constitutional purity and liberalism, a sophisticated central government (such as Mexico's) does not dare to impose its will upon the federal states even when the latter are flagrantly violating constitutions.

The first fondness for federalism arose because of the sharp, sudden topographical differences that abound on the continent. Plainsmen felt themselves culturally and economically superior to mountain dwellers; and even the Creoles, separated from the Indians or coastal Africans by race, were no less remote from one another by virtue of the varying customs imposed by climate. Communications were so bad as to reinforce these local differences. *Serrano*, *llanero*, were words spat out as reciprocal insults, and each province built up a body of tradition and an aristocracy of its own. There was no psychological basis for centralism; nor was there, for that matter, for republicanism.

Though the one monarchy that was established in the Americas as a direct result of the independence wars—that of Iturbide's in Mexico—was a failure, it was never proven whether some form

27

of limited monarchy (with the Crown as a buffer between anarchists and exponents of the strong arm) might not have been a more practical solution for these countries than a democracy that has rarely been effective. No monarchy would have aroused greater chauvinism than exists in many countries in spite of an early desire for such unifying institutions as free trade. Nor would any limited monarchy have vested such limitless powers in one man as some presidents possess.

At the outset the rebels had no particular prejudice against dictators and even gave the name officially and proudly to some of the liberators. Only later did hatred for the very name obscure the real issue—whether the countries were to receive an enlightened government in whatever form, or one centred in those class privileges and racial antagonisms which seemed doomed to dominate many aspects of life. 'A people that oppresses another cannot itself be free,' said a direct descendant of Inca Túpac Yupanqui in 1810. He might have added that his axiom was true within nations as well as among them.

While economic betterment was not the liberators' foremost aim, it was certainly hoped to correct the unfairness of prohibitions imposed upon the colonies in matters of trade, and especially to prevent profits from agriculture and mining from going abroad. Prohibited crops were soon flourishing in the newly liberated countries; but another kind of economic colonialism arose with the conversion of the area into a source of supply—a storehouse of raw materials—that could be drawn on by the richer countries who took their shares without a thought for the economic well-being of the producers. This point has been made much of by left-wing Latin Americans, and little credit has been given to those foreign enterprises that quite soon after independence took heavy financial risks in order to build railways and open up new sources of wealth which the countries themselves could not have done until much later. In spite of the glaring examples of exploitation and monopolistic practice that still need to be corrected, it is doubtful whether national entrepreneurs are necessarily fairer than foreign ones.

If economic pressure does not force the countries to unity, which would open bigger markets and allow planning on a supranational scale, it is difficult to see what will; especially since countries that have shown sporadic signs of prospering have tended after a time to lapse into conditions not very much better than they had been in a few decades previously, thus perpetuating the vicious circle. An English visitor, Theodore Child, wrote of Argentina in 1890 in terms that exactly apply to the situation in many Latin American countries today. 'Owing to the lamentable want of public morality south of the equator,' he said in his smugly Anglo-Saxon way, 'and to the cynicism of the political vultures who make it their business to prey upon their fatherland, it is always a painful task to speak about the administration of the South American republics.' His regret was the more heartfelt because he knew the Argentines to be richly gifted by nature, energetic, full of youth and promise, and endowed with natural wealth. He sighed for the hundreds of thousands of 'simple-minded workers' who had become the victims of dishonest politicians. The commercial and economic crisis they had created would, he calculated with remarkable optimism, take fully ten years of national effort to remove. He noted that the most important newspaper, *La Prensa*, continued to reveal abuses and scandals and to warn the Argentines of the wrath to come. When, he wondered rhetorically, would the turning point be reached and the tide of misfortune retreat?[1]

What Child failed to notice was that economic discussions generated less heat in Argentina than religious or philosophical ones, the priority of Spanish American values being firmly in the tradition of the land of Cervantes. But curiously enough, in spite of the strongly liberal tendency of the freedom movement, its religious aim was at first to conserve the ultra-right-wing Roman Catholic Church. The natural laws propounded by the men of the enlightenment were believed to have come from God. Now God's representative on earth was the Catholic Church. It followed that liberalism must give support to a body that had instituted the

[1] Child, Theodore, *The Spanish American Republics*, p. 435.

Inquisition and was at the time of independence taking strong measures to suppress free thought in Spain, as a Spanish priest, Blanco White, testified.[1] In some countries, notably Mexico, the anomaly was later over-compensated and there was bitter persecution of the clergy. Either way the Church-State relationship was delicate enough to rouse fanatical feelings on both sides. As zeal and tempers rose, ideals were readily set aside.

The aim of helping the poor sectors of the community was less important than is usual in revolutions, though it was one that had been dear to the early friars and to men like Pedro Gante and Vasco de Quiroga. There was, nevertheless, considerable concern for the wretched state of the Indians, and this led to a pride in the Indian heritage which became linked with a type of chauvinism that was very distant from the friars' early intentions. In practice the liberation movement favoured the upper classes and little was done for the marginal sections of the community although certain tithes and forced labour were abolished. A more practical result could hardly have been expected until the gap between upper and lower orders had been bridged by the creation of a middle class, and this began to emerge only with industrialization in more advanced areas, especially in Argentina, Chile, and Mexico.

In contrast to the nineteenth century, the present one has seen a more urgent drive toward a higher standard of living. The economists have reverted to the dream that impelled Bolívar, of creating a great Andean (or Colombian, or Spanish American) republic. They take this view not idealistically but convinced that only economic integration will save the mass of Indian and *mestizo* peasants from being relegated indefinitely to a marginal existence. They believe, too, that only economic integration will ever put an end to the lawless *coups* that topple governments one by one and give the area a reputation for instability to say the least, if not for downright contempt of order. 'Even supposing that an honest president be elected,' said Child in 1892, '. . . how can we control his entourage? How can one or even a few honest men cure the

[1] See Blanco y Crespo, alias Blanco White or Leucadio Doblado, *Letters from Spain*, 1822.

mass of their Creole countrymen of their traditional and secular dishonesty? . . . The whole apparatus of republicanism in these countries is a farce, and in spite of sonorous speeches of after-dinner orators, they have not yet begun to enjoy even the most elementary political liberty. . . .'[1]

There was from the beginning much flaunting of law in the name of lawfulness; much violence, though it may have been unavoidable if the liberators were to achieve their immediate ends (there are signs that some of them hated it, and even Bolívar's controversial 'War to the Death' decree should not be taken altogether at its face value, as we shall presently see); much ambivalence and conflict in the lesser aims, however unequivocal the greater. The independence movement reflects acutely and painfully the recurring human situation. The ends were made to justify the means and men steered a perilous course between compromise and intolerance. Like the jagged shapes of its mountains and cacti, human conflicts tended in Spanish America to become acutely sharpened.

Except in the minds of Europeans who think of a people in perpetual feast and *siesta*, nothing in this continent has ever been easy. The earth is too extremely tropical, or too extremely desert, or too high, or too low, for ready cultivation; water is too plentiful or too scarce; the mines too remote or the veins too tangled for metals to be extracted without great labour; the forests too dense and varied in their timbers to be easily exploited; the oceans, with their hurricanes and cyclones, too treacherous to invite fishermen to venture far from their coasts. There are too many faults in the crust of the earth, too many tremors.

The idea of the land as a cornucopia is only one of the misconceptions that foreigners have about Mexico specifically, about Spanish America in general. Foreign misunderstanding of the area has been so widespread as to appear almost deliberate. Europeans think of Spanish Americans as by definition shiftless, unreliable, and unduly given to killing one another. If Spanish Americans express the same opinion of us, they are met with the rebuke that

[1] Child, Theodore, p. 435.

they never had a philosophy and therefore can have nothing but subjective opinions. This kind of attitude impedes a proper understanding of the way in which Spanish American history has unfolded, the kind of trends that we may expect in future, and a constructive analysis of failures. The present situation of this area, with its high population growth, its efforts to industrialize, and its restless intelligentsia ready to experiment with almost any political chimera that might by some off chance provide a solution to problems of poverty and inequality, is seldom studied in the historical setting but only from the point of view of the countries that have had the good luck to develop (industrially speaking) earlier, and have imposed upon the world not only their special system of economics but their views upon what constitutes a worthy or an unworthy character. A man is considered shiftless because he puts happiness before industry, feckless because he spends his last peso on some trivial piece of fun (though how a forty-hour-week, betting, smoking Britain can uphold this kind of puritan morality any longer, it is difficult to see).

In our history books Latin America has never received the attention it deserves. Its heroes are scarcely known. Bolívar yes— but mainly because Bolivia, which took Bolívar's name at its independence, serves as a perpetual memorial to his achievements whereas other heroes who have no such memorial have failed to attract the attention of any but the student of Latin America.

The emancipation wars were often cruel and primitive—such faults being common to either side—but they were also noble, courageous, and in many ways extraordinarily sophisticated. It is therefore odd that this piece of history should have been so neglected since. During the wars of independence, and for some time before, Spanish America was being wooed, cajoled, and planned for by most of the great powers. Britain, France, the United States, and Catherine the Great's Russia all played a part in encouraging Miranda, the 'precursor' of independence; and many British soldiers distinguished themselves during the fighting phase. Spanish Americans were transported hither and thither in British warships which seemed at times to have become a shuttle

1. Simón Bolívar. El Libertador de America.
Oil painting, copy. Original by Efrén Apesteguía

2. General José de San Martín. Oil painting by the General's daughter, Mercedes de San Martín de Balcarce, Paris, 1856. Unsigned, probably copied from a daguerreotype taken in Paris in 1848

service for their exclusive benefit. The leaders were sucked into the American War of Independence, the French revolution, and Napoleon's battles. They could be excused for thinking—sometimes cynically—that they were being ground between wheels they could do little to control. If the Latins were accused of duplicity, personal ambition, and self-seeking, they might have retaliated that this was no more than the pot calling the kettle black. It is, as a matter of fact, surprising that they managed to keep their tempers, to cling to their admiration for French theories, British common sense, and American experimentalism as well as they did.

Long after Europe had grown tired of them they continued to admire the more liberal of Old World institutions and to make experiments in adapting them to their own needs. But except during the bizarre incident when Napoleon III wished an unwanted emperor upon Mexico, they were—after independence— cold-shouldered, written out of history, and left to the mercies of the Americans and the Monroe Doctrine.

The United States came to believe, as Britain did in the early nineteenth century and forgot afterwards, that control of the western hemisphere was of the utmost importance if the balance of power was to be maintained in the east. Preoccupation with two world wars and heavy commonwealth commitments have limited Britain's capacity to pay attention to the Americas in the last decades; and since 1939 the United States has gained a dominant hold not only on hemisphere trade but also on the political and cultural scenes (though there have been times when three or four of the larger Latin American countries have been able to hold their own against extreme pressure from the colossus).

In the next few decades Spanish America will either grow into maturity or explode into anarchy. The pressures within and without it, and its extraordinary energies, make any mid-term impossible. 'You shall be what you must be; if not you shall be nothing,' said San Martín;[1] and one can scarcely imagine Spanish America coming, after all its tribulations, to nothing. The continent has a magnetic quality of its own, and both by its age and

[1] *Serás lo que debes ser; y si no, no serás nada.*

its youthfulness imposes its style on newcomers. For the independence fighters—even for some of the foreign mercenaries among them, let alone for the people born and bred there—the continent became the new loyalty.

Not the whole hemisphere, but that part of it populated by Spain, was the hero of the nineteenth-century drama we are to study. The almost impregnable spine of the Cordillera; the endless plains where cattle and horses pastured so freely that they were counted not in heads but in thousands; the earthquake-shaken coastlands where cataclysms drew men together against Nature's gruesome caprices; its jungles and deserts: all these, not to mention the beauty of its flora and fauna, had conquered the conquerors. Domingo Faustino Sarmiento, author of a famous study of the Argentine *gaucho,* noted even that the atmosphere is so charged with electricity that if one rubs a piece of cloth it sends off sparks like a cat's hair stroked the wrong way. He paid tribute to the musical temperament of the Argentines in city and pampa alike.[1] Their musicality is closely interlocked with the landscape and the sentiments it evokes. The music of the cattle drovers of the plains is typified in the songs of the *arrieros*:

> *Sorrows and cattle travel together.*
> *The sorrows are ours, the cattle belong to others . . .*
> *Transfixed by the magic of the trails, the drover goes . . .*[2]

and by the nostalgic tunes played on a shin-bone flute in the high Andes where the air is so rarefied that it generates a heady intoxication. The music is at one not only with this solitary landscape but with the native Indian psychology as it mixes with the Spanish. There is a style in the Creole adaptation of European dress to the needs of living days in the saddle and of bedding under the stars. There is no detail of the *gaucho*'s, the *huaso*'s, or the *charro*'s accoutrements that is accidental to the conditions in which they are used.

[1] Sarmiento, Domingo Faustino, *Facundo,* pp. 37 *et seq.*
[2] Song recorded by 'The Four Guaranis', *Musique Folklorique d'Amérique Latine,* Editions de la Boîte a Musique (B.A.M. LD 302), Paris, 1953.

There was style in the decorations instituted by the liberators, such as the seven-rayed star which was the badge of Bolívar's order conferred on a life basis only and thus meeting democracy half way, but entirely aristocratic in its heraldry (were not the ancient knights of the Sun the embodiment of gods?). This union of democracy and aristocracy became a feature of Spanish American life; for no democrat on this continent, from the humblest Indian to the Liberator himself, wanted to be one of a crowd. Democracy became an aggregate of aristocrats; or, looked at in reverse, the aristocrats were compelled for their survival to learn the lore of the *huaso* and the *roto*. Toughness and courtesy were not incompatible; they were twin virtues. The Mexican Indian is gentle but he is also hardy. The songs of the Guaraní-speaking Paraguayans are sweet and run softly off musical tongues, but these same people have a reputation for being indomitable fighters. There is a lesson to be learned from a rag-and-bone man, physically a stinking old pariah, who, when he collected his load of junk, touched his cap invariably in regal thanks. This kind of behaviour is not exceptional.

There is a unique quality in the New World version of baroque, which is less heavily planted upon earth than that of Moorish Spain, full of a sultry Indianness, as if the continent's dark and impenetrable but sinuous vegetation had congealed in delicate gesso curlicues. The domestic architecture, on the other hand, was adapted to the simplicity of the life of ranging cattlemen and rich but earth-soiled miners. The very buildings that became famous because historic acts of independence took place in them—in provincial towns like Tucumán, Cúcuta, and Dolores Hidalgo—have the functional dignity which the liberators must have hoped would continue to inform the builders of the new nations and which is wholly 'modern' in spirit. Post-Bauhaus idiom blends with it so well that in Spanish America modern architecture need never look self-conscious as it so often does in Europe. The simple façade, flush with the street and with its typical long, barred windows, of the house in which Bolívar was born, testifies to the attitude to wealth of aristocrats who were so certain of their lineage that they had no need for show. Humboldt noted that rich families were prouder of their mules than of personal finery. Banquets were splendid, but ordinarily the upper classes lived frugally and were the better able to endure hardships when war forced rough conditions upon them. Much of the antagonism felt by the liberators toward France, in spite of the attraction of its revolutionary doctrines, came from an innate mistrust of good and easy living which Spanish Americans regarded as soft.

Thus through the different requirements of climate, altitude, and flora, a single indefinable style persists so that one cannot—presented with an engraving or a photograph—make the mistake of transporting a scene from the New World to the Old. Even importations from Europe underwent marked transformation; and it must be emphasized that this characteristic style is worlds apart from the usual European conception of what Spanish America typically is—florid and not a little effeminate.

In spirit and in blood, then, the conquerors became one with the indigenous peoples; and the halfcastes became an amalgam not only of race but of two ways of life—two ways so different that they can hardly be said to have conflicted, for there was scarcely so much as a confrontation between them. It was impossible for European Spaniards to understand what the trouble was about, impossible for them to realize even that they did not understand. They could not comprehend the pride of the Creole in having been born in the New World, of the *mestizo* for the very fact of *mestizaje*. Indian and Spaniard had not mingled but had fused to create a new psychology and a new thought. The independence wars were fought in order to bring a new social order into being.

PART ONE

Antecedents

2. Map of the region showing viceroyalties and other Spanish administrative divisions

CHAPTER I

EARLY CAUSES

1. Dissatisfaction with Spanish Rule

The independence movement had two impulses: one from without, given by Spain's enemies with intent to crush her; and one from within, arising from the great mass of Indians, *mestizos*, and Creoles who had gradually been acquiring an identity that was not Spain's though it owed much—and continues to do so—to that empire of Moors and Roman Catholics, *hidalgos*, lawyers, and adventurers. The Indians were the least involved of the three main sections of the Spanish-American population, the Spanish Creoles the most. But the Indians and *mestizos* did play an important part, even if only as underdogs whom the Creoles ostensibly championed.

Almost from the time the *conquistadores* first stepped onto New World soil there had been contradictory tendencies of arrogant cruelty to the native races, and of the love for them manifested in the work of the friars; of Spanish lordship and inter-Spanish jealousies as between the Crown and the conquerors, between those born in Spain and those born in the New World, between the lawmakers and the gold-seekers, between those who believed prehispanic cultures to be the work of the devil and those who saw through the human sacrifices and other degenerations to a deep and perhaps already long-lost philosophy not really so very far removed from Christianity (if vestiges of it had not still existed, Christianity would never have taken root so quickly nor mingled in such an intricate way with the old gods).

Many pious duties imposed upon the *conquistadores* amounted to no more than the shallowest appeasement of conscience. Such, for example, was the *requerimiento*, which every conqueror was supposed to read to the heathen natives before taking military action against them. It was a history and summary of the Christian faith seen strictly through the eyes of Spanish Catholicism. Having heard the garbled version of the faith, the natives were supposed immediately to pledge obedience to the Pope and to the King of Castile. If they did not, violence would be unleashed against them. Since at times the document was not even translated into the native tongue, it was a little difficult for the Indians to make up their minds on the subject. In any case, even if they agreed with certain statements about one God who was Lord of the Universe, they could hardly be expected to accept the implication that the deity was entirely on the side of Spain.

In spite of such pantomimes, those who formulated many of the early laws relating to the Indians, especially the Laws of Burgos (1512), were doing their best to establish fair treatment. It was, for example, laid down that if at any future date the Indians proved capable of self-government, they should be allowed to exercise it. A treatise by Matías de Paz 'concerning the Rule of the King of Spain over the Indies' affirmed that it was unjust for Christian princes to make war on infidels merely to amass wealth, though it was legitimate to do so for the purpose of spreading the faith. Pope Paul III declared in Rome in 1537 that the Indians were 'truly men' and that they were not only capable of receiving the Christian faith but desirous of doing so. They should therefore, he said, be converted by preaching and by 'good and holy living'.[1] Examples not far removed from sainthood were given by such men as Bartolomé de las Casas, one of the staunchest champions of the Indians. But in spite of such pronouncements as Pope Paul's, repression, persecution, and exploitation of labour were rife. Taxes were high. Slavery existed though it masqueraded under legal forms. There was poverty, and there was hunger. A vast chasm separated the mental outlook of conqueror and

[1] A full account of efforts to ameliorate the lot of the Indians is given by Lewis Hanke in *The Spanish Struggle for Justice in the Conquest of America*.

conquered, the one firmly embedded in doctrines of the Catholic Church, the other as equally devoted to a religion which (debased as it might have become) contained at its root an extraordinarily complete guide to man's way of redemption from folly. The fact that the two modes of thought were by no means dissimilar in their essence did nothing to make the outer forms less inimical one to the other. If there were some, even at that decayed moment of aboriginal history, who understood the message of Quetzalcoatl and the deep philosophical content of such languages as Quechua, Maya, and Nahuatl; and if there were some among the friars who sought to penetrate through dogma to the meaning of Christ's words; the fact remained that in both cases the outer interpretations were the general ones, and that these were incompatible.

Besides Christianity, the Old World had also brought to the New a host of technical innovations ranging from the domestication of animals to the use of mercury for extracting silver from rock. As it scattered the cupolas of its churches like bright marigolds in the most remote corners of the land, it gave the *coup de grâce* to an ancient civilization that was by then too full of bloodshed and too topheavy with bureaucratic controls to have lasted much longer anyway.

Both the good and the bad in Spanish dominion led inevitably to unrest—unrest *against* arbitrary repressions, and *toward* a fuller expression of identity by the new breed of men that was arising from the mingling of blood and ideas.

In 1494 the Treaty of Tordesillas had determined the spheres of influence of Castile and of Portugal in the New World, Portugal's share including the whole of Brazil to the east of a line running through the town of São Vicente but excluding the lands known as the *Banda Oriental*, now Uruguay and the southern portions of Brazil. Even at the time this high-handed sharing out of the new territories had unfortunate results. Castile and Portugal squabbled over a line that had no geographical features to define it, and the Portuguese explored and occupied lands regardless of legal rights. Although the town of Buenos Aires came into being because a

Spanish soldier, Alejo García, marched from there to Potosí in Upper Peru in search of the Sierra de la Plata—a legend that turned out actually to be true (the mountains held not only silver but mercury as well)—its formal establishment in 1535 was an attempt by Spain to stem Portuguese advance. The natives were so hostile, however, that the settlement had to be abandoned; and it was not until 1580, by which time communication between Upper Peru and Paraguay had been firmly established, that Juan de Garay laid the foundations of the City of Trinidad, which was to become Buenos Aires and the resplendent capital of a province. By 1617 administrative units had been established both there and in Paraguay, and there was a temporary *Audiencia* in Buenos Aires in 1661. A later precaution of the same kind was the conversion of Buenos Aires into a viceregal capital in 1776, with sway over La Plata, the vast area from Upper Peru to Patagonia. In the meantime Spain had put up trade barriers against other European nations, including Britain.

The empire was so enormous that it had to be carved into units which proved difficult to manage efficiently. After the conquest of Mexico by Hernán Cortés between 1519 and 1521, and that of Peru by Francisco Pizarro between 1532 and 1535, Viceroyalties were established in New Spain, which is now modern Mexico, in 1535; and in Peru in 1542. Under them were lesser divisions known as presidencies or captaincies-general. New Spain, for example, held sway over Nueva Galicia, later (1786) the *Intendencia* of Guadalajara and now west Mexico; and it had also some measure of control over the captaincy-general of Guatemala which included most of modern Central America, and of Santo Domingo which embraced the Spanish West Indies. The Viceroyalty of Peru was responsible for the Presidency of Cuzco and for the remote and in those days unimportant Captaincy-general of Chile, which had been conquered by Pedro de Valdivia between 1540 and 1553. Between 1536 and 1538 the lands about Bogotá in present-day Colombia were conquered by Gonzalo Jiménez Quesada who gave them the name of The New Kingdom of Granada. This became the Viceroyalty of New Granada which was established in 1717, abolished seven years later, but restored in 1741, with jurisdiction over Colombia, Ecuador, and Venezuela. In 1617 the territory of Paraguay was divided into two departments called *gobernaciones*. One, Paraguay itself, was ruled from Asunción, and the other was the La Plata area with Buenos Aires as its capital; but Buenos Aires was too important for so humble a role and eventually, as we have seen, became a viceregal seat.

In 1528, apart from the administrative divisions within the Spanish Empire, Spain had ceded Venezuela to the German bankers, Welser. This firm, together with Ambrose Alfinger who provided three ships for the enterprise, instead of opening up the lands for colonization and agriculture as they had agreed, proceeded to search for El Dorado which, had it been found, might have proved a less arduous means of fortune-making. Their methods were ruthless, they waged constant war against the Indians, and in 1547 the concession was revoked—Alfinger having in the meantime died in Colombia of wounds received in combat.

Exploits of this kind, shady though they were, did much to rouse European interest in the economic development of lands with obvious mining and agricultural potential. Soon after the founding of Buenos Aires, Spain closed the port in order to protect imperial interests and all trade had to go through Lima on the Pacific—a three months' journey from the La Plata estuary in those days, three thousand miles overland. Merchandise bound for the colonies traversed the Atlantic, crossed the Isthmus of Panama and was shipped down the Pacific coast to Lima, whence it was sent by mule to Potosí. Atlantic and southern Pacific provinces had to buy at five or six hundred per cent above the original cost. At the European end of the trade routes, Seville and later Cádiz were the only ports from which ships were allowed to sail with cargo for the colonies or which were empowered to land cargo from them. Direct trade among the colonies was forbidden.

The closure of Buenos Aires as a port caused immediate trouble from contraband trade between the La Plata colonies and Europe —particularly Portugal and Britain. Holland, too, was an important rival to Spain, especially after the founding of the West India

Company which received its charter in 1621 and was rich enough to maintain a private and formidable navy. To be protected against pirates, Spanish merchant ships had to sail twice yearly in convoys shepherded by warships, a measure which placed a heavy burden on the Spanish exchequer, on manpower, and on shipping, and was an important contributory cause of the downfall of the empire. Measures taken to prevent smuggling were also unexpectedly damaging to Spain, especially the prohibition of tobacco cultivation in Venezuela and—in 1605—the depopulating of the coast of Hispaniola (the island now shared between Haiti and the Dominican Republic), which was left to be ravaged by pirates and the French.

The extent of Spain's jealous guarding of her trade can be gauged from the fact that repressive policies were adopted even during the enlightened reign of Philip II. He was so suspicious of the Flemish engineers who thought of cutting a canal from Atlantic to Pacific that he forbade anyone to mention the subject on pain of death. He placed the same penalty on anyone navigating Central American rivers, some of which—draining variously to Atlantic and Pacific—nearly met at the watershed and were thus a temptation for surreptitious traders wishing to cross from ocean to ocean.

Spain's trading policy, mistaken as it turned out to be, was hallowed by tradition and seemed sensible at the time. It was followed also by Britain when it established such privileged organizations as the East India Company, thus reserving to the Crown all authority over trade and condemning the providers of the merchandise to a position of subservience.

Not until 1777 was Buenos Aires reopened to traffic with Spain and her dependencies, but contraband with Britain continued, causing considerable unrest and vociferous demands for free trade. These demands grew out of the Spanish attitude to the colonies, which was described by a British naval officer and Fellow of the Royal Society, Basil Hall, in his log of a voyage along the coast of Chile, Peru, and Mexico between 1820 and 1822:

'The sole purpose for which the Americas existed was held to be that of collecting together the precious metals for the Spaniards; and if the wild horses and cattle which overrun the country could have been trained to perform this office the inhabitants might have been altogether dispensed with, and the colonial system would then have been perfect. Unfortunately, however, for that system, the South Americans . . . finding that the Spaniards neither could nor would furnish them with an adequate supply of European products, invited the assistance of other nations. To this call the other nations were not slow to listen, and in process of time there was established one of the most extraordinary systems of organized smuggling which the world ever saw . . . conducted by the Dutch, Portuguese, French, English, and latterly by the North Americans. . . . Along with the goods no small portion of knowledge found entrance, in spite of the increased exertions of the Inquisition. . . . Many foreigners, too, by means of bribes and other arts, succeeded in getting into the country, so that the progress of intelligence was encouraged, to the utter despair of the Spaniards, who knew no other method of governing the colonies but that of brute force.'[1]

Free trade and free intellectual discussion, which together with dissatisfaction due to racial discrimination had been causing unrest since the early seventeenth century, were thus two of the chief aims of independence. In 1609 free and enslaved Negroes on the Gulf coast of Mexico chose the Day of the Kings to initiate an uprising that was a kind of independence movement in embryo, for they planned to kill all Spaniards and to set up a monarchy of their own. The Viceroy sent a military expedition to round up the ringleaders hiding in the hills and forests about Mount Orizaba.

Some fifteen years later there was another uprising in Mexico, this time significantly not by Negroes or slaves but by Creoles. Unrest mounted steadily until 1643 when a picaresque Irish adventurer called Lampart—who claimed to be a natural son of Philip III and thus half-brother of the reigning Philip IV—

[1] Quoted by Pilling in a footnote, p. 477.

conceived the quixotic notion that he was 'King of America and Emperor of Mexico'. It was quite usual for the early rebels—radical though they might be—to wish to set up kingships and viceroyalties (in 1711 a mulatto was proclaimed king of Venezuela, and in 1730 there was a movement to make Mexico independent from Spain under an Austrian prince). In those days the concept of popular rule had not been born.

Lampart, an impecunious teacher living on the bounty of his pupils, had false papers prepared for him in order to give credence to his cause. He wanted to abolish taxes, establish free trade with all countries except Spain, suppress slavery, and help the natives to shake off the Spanish yoke. Disingenuously he confided his plan to an army officer who denounced him to the Holy Office. This semi-lunatic who yet anticipated many of the aims of independence, who had claimed that he could 'easily become king of Mexico because no one had a right to the throne but the man the people wanted', and who had written to the rulers of France, England, and Portugal, and to the Pope himself, asking for help, was condemned to being burned at the stake but committed suicide before sentence could be executed. He was accused of anti-Church activities; of resorting to astrology and occultism; of using 'herbs' (possibly mezcaline, peyote, or Mexican 'magic' mushrooms) in order to foretell the future, a practice much frowned on since it was invading the province of God; of effecting cures with the aid of the devil; and of being a follower of—among others—Calvin, Pelagius, Huss, and Luther. Mad as the story sounds, it showed which way the wind was blowing.

In 1692 the maize crops were destroyed by floods and there was serious rioting in Mexico City. 'Death to the Viceroy and to all who defend him!' men cried. 'Death to the Spaniards who are eating our maize!' A fitting prelude to the shouts of Hidalgo's rabble armies in 1810.

Unrest was not confined to Mexico. In 1730, in Cochabamba, Upper Peru, 2,000 *mestizos* staged an armed protest against a poll tax, and the Spaniards were forced in self-defence to pass a law allowing only Creoles (not European-born Spaniards) to be elected as officers of justice. In 1749 an armed insurrection of Venezuelan Creoles was directed against a commercial monopoly held by the Compañía Guipúzcoana of Caracas, which had begun its career by boosting Venezuela's economy by guarding the coastlands against smugglers, but which had soon fallen into abusive practices and was finally dissolved in 1788.

One of the most threatening insurrections was that of José Gabriel Condorcanqui (said to have been the illegitimate son of a Spanish friar and an Indian). He had been educated at the famous college of San Borja in Cuzco and was tall, well built and well mannered, brave but uncontrollably violent. His blind hatred of all Spaniards made it impossible for him to distinguish between Creoles and peninsulars, and he made enemies of both. He took the name Túpac Amaru which means 'the gifted one' in the Quechua tongue. In 1579 an Inca of that name had been beheaded for rebelling against Spanish rule. Condorcanqui also called himself Marquis of Oropesa, a title granted by Philip II to the Inca line. In 1780 he gathered over 60,000 badly armed Quechua Indians and gained control of parts of southern Peru, Upper Peru (Bolivia), and Argentina. His troops were composed of hardy mountain dwellers accustomed to running long distances and— like the soldiers of the Chaco in our century—chewing *coca* leaves to stave off hunger. With these sturdy followers he reached the gates of Cuzco; and his cousin, Diego, occupied adjoining areas. A contemporary newspaper account describes him in his moment of near-triumph, clad in a blue velvet suit embroidered with gold, a red velvet cloak, a three-cornered hat, and a kind of sleeveless surplice richly embroidered. Round his neck, on a golden chain, hung an image of the Sun, symbol of the Incas. Two henchmen are described as 'looking as though they might be English',[1] but whether any Englishmen were actually implicated in his plot is not known.

In spite of his bravado the Spanish cavalry was too much for him and within six months, early in 1781, the rebellion was quelled. Condorcanqui was forced to witness the execution of his

[1] Arciniegas, G., p. 199.

wife, children, and closest followers before he himself had his tongue cut out and his limbs torn asunder by wild horses.

Stormy, romantic, and bloody as this uprising was, it had in the end less political significance than an event that occurred at the same time in Lima, where a leading intellectual, José Baquíjano, was chosen to deliver a welcoming address to the Viceroy, Agustín Jaúregui, who had arrived there the year before. Baquíjano's sponsors could not have anticipated that he would use this formal and courteous occasion to launch a bitter attack on the Spaniards, accusing them of bringing nothing but hunger and death to the Indians, and warning that if individual human lives were not respected the body politic would rot. The authorities were properly incensed. They seized and destroyed all copies of the address and made certain that Baquíjano was defeated in his bid for the rectorship of San Marcos University. Henceforth the intellectual firebrand found it expedient to keep his subversive views to himself, but he continued to influence thought within the Masonic lodges, and he had the support of other intellectuals such as Hipólito Unánue who contributed to the scientifically orientated *Mercurio Peruano*, founded the first school of medicine in Peru, and later became his country's first Treasury Minister. It was men of this stamp who inspired the liberal movement which by 1808, simultaneously with the liberation uprisings throughout Spanish America, had found a mouthpiece in the volatile but unreliable Manuel Lorenzo de Vidaurre (whose *Plan del Perú* demanded that the Spanish Cortes give the colonies at least a measure of autonomy).

The authorities were not insincere in their belief that Baquíjano, Unánue and their kind were deliberately and maliciously whipping up Indian resentment against European rule. Though many of the physical conditions under which the labouring classes worked were deplorable even by the standards of their day, there was every reason to believe that conditions had been still worse in Inca times. Food was now relatively plentiful, wars were less frequent, and good wool was available for clothing. In spite of this the Quechuas wanted to be free from white domination, to

48

3a. General Bernardo O'Higgins. This picture, signed by Juan Cabral, 1909, is a copy in oils of the original portrait by José Gil de Castro, which is in Chile. It was specially copied by Cabral for the Museo Histórico Nacional, Buenos Aires

3b. Admiral 10th Earl of Dundonald when Lord Cochrane. Oil painting by Peter Stroehling (from the collection of the Rt. Hon. the Earl of Dundonald)

4b. Andrés Bello. Attributed to Raymond Quinsac Monvoisin, now in the Biblioteca Nacional, Caracas, Venezuela

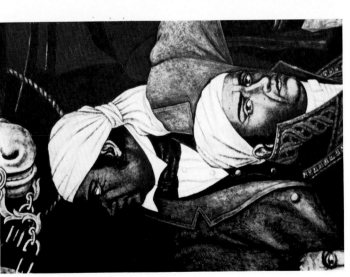

4a. José María Morelos painted from two angles by Juan O'Gorman, from a mural in the Mexican National Historical Museum, Chapultepec Castle

re-establish an Inca government, and to revert—as the Spaniards saw it—to primitive customs. Material hardships had been their lot ever since they could remember, and they did not resent these so much as the degradation of being forced to toil for alien masters. Under a system called *mita* they were legally obliged to work in the mines where they received half the wage of field workers and were therefore constantly in debt to their employers. Some Indians became *pongos* or menial servants to the governors of provinces, for which compulsory service they were paid with food and essential clothing.

The governors, or *corregidores*, were owners of tracts of land known as *encomiendas* or *repartimientos*, which had been given to them in the first place so that they might exercise paternal protection over the Indians. They were also able to collect the tribute of eight dollars for every Indian between eighteen and twenty-five years old, this being payable to the Spanish Crown. But the system was naturally abused. General William Miller, an Englishman who after fighting against Napoleon went to the Río de la Plata provinces in 1817 and later saw service at the battles of Junín and Ayacucho (he was upward of ten years with the South American independence armies), tells us that not only were dying mules, damaged goods, and other worthless articles forced upon the Indians at double or treble the value of the best commodities of the same kind, but razors upon men who had no beards, silk stockings, velvets, and other luxuries on barefoot Indians who did not even know their use.[1] Some *corregidores*, too, forced Indians to pay tribute money before they were eighteen and on into old age. The Crown was kept ignorant of such extortions.

Natives were forbidden to cultivate certain crops or to weave cloth except for personal use. They were not allowed to study science but only Latin grammar, ancient philosophy, theology, and civil and canonical jurisprudence. (In some countries the legacy of anti-science is being combated today but the results of this policy are still felt. Educational systems, fortified by social

---

[1] Miller, John, vol. 1, p. 6.

prejudice, lay undue stress on law at the expense of practical skills and laboratory research which are urgently needed.)

For a long time Spain had had reason to fear the power of the Franciscans and Jesuits, who had tried to establish model colonies in various parts of the hemisphere. In Chile Capuchin missions actually for a time tamed the wild Araucanian Indians and they also worked in the Orinoco valley and in Nueva Granada. In the La Plata region the Jesuits ruled over a state within a state, an area extending through parts of present-day Uruguay, Paraguay, and Argentina and populated by somewhere near a hundred thousand Indians. Such a large measure of ethical and social order and such an exemplary economic system were established that the Crown accused the Church of meddling in the affairs of Mammon, of establishing a monopoly over the lucrative *yerba maté* trade, of maltreating the Indians and of enslaving them (this was pure hypocrisy: the fact was that the Creoles could not entice the contented Indians away from the attractive conditions of the missions).

Spain expelled the Jesuits from the South American colonies in 1766–7 and, as the anti-clerical Domingo Faustino Sarmiento pointed out with wicked glee (conveniently forgetting that the expulsive measures were so strong as to amount to homicide), by independence times no trace of their good work remained. This proved to the not always very logical Sarmiento that the Jesuit experiment was rotten and he made the somewhat fanciful suggestion that the special breed of men, the *gauchos*, were the wandering residue of the Jesuit colonies left to fend for themselves on the pampas.[1] If there were any truth in this, then it would have to be admitted that though cruelty flourished among them so also did crude honour and compassion, a rough, practical philosophy, and a love of music and Nature. The *gauchos* were far from being wholly reprehensible.

The position of the reforming Jesuit communities was so invidious that on the one hand in Paraguay the patriot José de Antequera and his pupils, who founded the *communeros* party,

[1] Sarmiento, D. F., *Conflicto y Armonías de las Razas en América*, p. 87 *et seq.*

opposed them for being representatives of authoritarian and therefore anti-liberal, anti-progressive Church interests; whereas in Mexico on the other hand the Jesuits were accused of the opposite crime, disloyalty to the Crown. Partly as a result of their expulsion from New Spain in 1767, partly because of Indian unrest, an abortive independence movement broke out in Patzcuaro. The ringleaders were hanged, whipped, banished, or imprisoned for life.

It is known, says Sarmiento airily, that the Jesuits were socialist philosophers who in Europe wanted to order society in accordance with their own interpretation of Christian maxims. It perfectly fitted their convenience, then, when in America they found themselves in a position to mould the lives of savages. The souls of the aborigines being so crushed that they could scarcely have a desire of their own—says Sarmiento with all the prejudice of a non-Catholic in a predominantly Catholic country—the Order could easily impose its will. Work was communal, but when it came to the point of sharing its fruits, those who profited were not the farmers but the Jesuits, who, it went without saying, kept the accounts.[1]

Sarmiento's views were not new. Well before his birth in 1811 similar accusations had caused the Jesuit communities in Spain and Portugal, as well as in the Americas, to be suppressed one by one. In the latter part of the eighteenth century, refugee members of the Order formed a solid body of anti-royalist opinion in the other countries of western Europe. A curious situation was thus created in that some influential Jesuits, from within the reputedly diehard Roman Church, on the whole favoured some kind of democratic rule in the Americas, as the friars had always done; whereas on the opposite side of the religious-philosophical fence the Masons—also working against Spain and for the independence of Spanish America—were far from averse to some kind of modified monarchic form. This confusion of ideologies was never to be disentangled. It would have been convenient to think in terms of monarchy versus democracy, conservatism versus liberalism,

[1] *Ibid.*

black versus white; and many tried to see things in this way. But they were naïve. In a hemisphere of rough pragmatism the reality was not at all so neatly logical.

2. THE EUROPEAN SETTING

Such was the situation in the New World. In the Old, the Spanish Empire had already by the beginning of the eighteenth century begun to collapse under its own weight. The difficulty of maintaining maritime and legal connections with the colonies was great; and the gold flowing in from the Indies, far from being an unmixed blessing, created a maladjustment between its currency and that of other countries in Europe.[1]

There were also confusing new alignments of nations and shifts of traditional loyalties. In the closing years of the seventeenth century intrigue had centred on the possible successor to the Emperor Charles II, the 'bewitched', whose long reign had been harassed by attacks from Louis XIV of France. Charles's two marriages were childless; and the second, to Mariana of Neuburg, daughter of the Elector Palatine, so infuriated the French that they declared war on Spain, invaded Catalonia, and in 1697 captured Barcelona. When the resulting Treaty of Ryswick was signed, the leading candidates for the Spanish throne were Prince Joseph Ferdinand of Bavaria, great-grandson of Philip IV, whose claim was supported by the British and Dutch; the Archduke Charles of Austria; and Philip of Anjou, grandson of Louis XIV, who seemed to be eligible since his grandmother the Infanta María Teresa's dowry had never been paid in full, and for that reason (according to the French) she had not forfeited her rights to the succession.

In a will dated November 1698 Charles appointed Joseph Ferdinand his heir, but the young prince died the following year leaving the Austrian and French candidates to fight things out between them. Charles, half Austrian himself, hated Germany and

---

[1] See especially Parry, J. H., *The Spanish Seaborne Empire.*

was easily persuaded to name the Duke of Anjou his heir. When he died on November 1, 1700, the Duke became Philip V and the French House of Bourbon secured its hold upon Spain. In May 1702 Britain and the Emperor Joseph simultaneously declared war on France, and for eleven years there was no peace in Europe. The Emperor Joseph died in 1711 and was succeeded by his brother the Archduke Charles, the defeated candidate for the Spanish throne. Europe's two great maritime nations, Britain and Holland, could on no account allow Austria and Spain to unite. Therefore they would espouse the Bourbon cause only on condition that Philip V should renounce all claim to the French throne, thus preventing a union of the two crowns. This agreement, embodied in the Treaty of Utrecht (1713), put an end to the war of the Spanish succession. The Spanish House of Habsburg had been liquidated and for a time the European domain of Spain shrunk to include only Castile and Aragon.

From this time forward French influence upon the wealthier Creoles became strong. Scions of aristocratic families and of the new and rich mine owners completed their educations in France and came under the influence of such subversive thinkers as Voltaire, Montesquieu, and Rousseau. Freemasons advised the Bourbon kings, especially Charles III who imported ideas of the new enlightenment and a taste for critical analysis into the very citadel of the Inquisition. Not only Jesuits, but also Jews, who had been expelled from Spain in 1492 and later from Portugal, were a focus for dissatisfaction with the old order.

In spite of the wise counsellors with whom Charles III surrounded himself, and some astute viceroys such as Count Revillagigedo in Mexico, he had many enemies inside his own country. From without he was threatened by the growing strength of Britain whose traders (as we have already seen) were a constant threat to Spain's overseas economy. Powerful fleets were massed by Spain to confront Britain during the War of Jenkins's Ear (1739–41) and the Seven Years' War (1756–63), but they could not prevent the British from occupying Havana and Manila. (Under the Treaty of Paris, Britain later gave up her claims to both these strategic points and received Florida and Minorca instead.)

During the War of Jenkins's Ear, Admiral Vernon and Commander Anson worked in a pincer movement, the former in the Caribbean and Mexican Gulf, the latter in the Pacific. They had hoped to join forces at Panama and thus to separate North from South America and, with the help of the Indians (who would be provided with arms), to destroy the Spanish Empire. Even if Spain's overseas possessions remained intact, at least—they had hoped—its ports would be opened to British trade. Rydjord[1] quotes Bernard Moses as saying that the War of Jenkins's Ear occupied 'a place midway between the raids of the earlier freebooters and the later more elaborately prepared attempts to supplant Spanish power in America'. The war seemed to reflect the double nature of Britain's attitude to independence in Spanish America, an attitude on the one hand unashamedly mercenary and on the other almost quixotically idealistic, especially when it fired individual adventurers to take up arms in remote corners of the new continent.

The British by this time had reason to suppose that the desire for independence was strong enough in the Americas to justify their intervention—the more so since as early as 1742 Mexican rebels had asked Sir Robert Walpole for support in forming an independent kingdom under an Austrian prince, Britain's reward to be a monopoly of Mexican trade. Walpole had lent a favourable ear to this request but was out of office before he could take action; and the proposal, reconsidered by Lord Newcastle, came to nothing.[2]

Charles III was forced to recognize his dependence upon the French branch of the dynasty; and, by signing (in 1761) the famous 'family compact', he united the Bourbons against the British. It was logical, therefore, for him to support Britain's rebel colonists in North America even when his adviser, the Count of Aranda, warned him that the breakaway of New England from

[1] Rydjord, John, p. 52.
[2] *Ibid.*, p. 51.

Britain's empire would establish a dangerous precedent for New Spain. So it came about that Spain and France found themselves aligned on the side of the American colonists against Britain.

To protect New Spain from the Anglo-Saxons to the north, France ceded Louisiana to the Spaniards. It had even been planned (such were the diabolical machinations of the politicians) to turn this fertile area, including the Mississippi delta, into a desert in order to create a no-man's-land between Mexico and the British, who were justly regarded as the arch-enemy. With footholds on the Mosquito Coast of Honduras, on Campeche in the Yucatán Peninsula, and in Jamaica, they were in an ideal strategic position, at any time they wished, to cut communications between Mexico and the mother country.

In 1765, just when Benjamin Franklin was appealing to the British Parliament for more enlightened treatment of the English colonists, Mexicans were in Madrid protesting against the discrimination exercised against Creoles. Finding that they were making no impression on the Spanish authorities, the Mexicans crossed the border to enlist the help of French revolutionaries, especially one, D. Guiller, who if the plan he propounded to them could be made to succeed was to be given a dukedom and hereditary governorship of Veracruz. Once again Spaniards in London got to hear of the plan, and Lord Weymouth, who had by then replaced Lord Shelburne as Secretary of State, was obliged to retreat as diplomatically as he could from an embarrassing situation. Had the plot succeeded, the advantages to Britain would have been considerable.[1]

If Charles III had been ill-advised not to heed Aranda's caution, he was probably wise to have nothing to do with a monarchical plan of Aranda's whereby one infante was to be made King of Mexico, one King of Peru, and a third 'King of the Mainland', Charles himself to retain the overall rule as Emperor.

Charles IV, who ascended the throne in 1788, showed less perspicacity when he united with the British against France, thereby losing Santo Domingo. The uneasy alliance was severed in 1796

---

[1] Rydjord, J., p. 60 *et seq.*

when Spain again joined with France and—managing somehow always to be on the losing side—conceded another and richer island, Trinidad, to the British. Britain's defeat of the united forces of France and Spain at Trafalgar in 1805 persuaded Spain for a time to throw in her lot with Britain, but this alliance was broken by Napoleon whose aggressiveness became the immediate cause of open rebellion in Spanish America.

Much of this is to anticipate. In 1750 the precursor of all the independence movements in the Hispanic New World had been born. By 1785 he was in London plotting a rebellion on a larger scale than had yet been envisaged. The machinations of the powers and the dissatisfaction of the colonies finally coalesced into so explosive a compound that nothing could now prevent the disintegration of the Spanish Empire overseas.

CHAPTER II

FRANCISCO DE MIRANDA

1. MIRANDA'S EARLY BACKGROUND

Sebastián Francisco de Miranda y Ravelo had a way of entangling himself in every war that happened to be going on. At various times he fought for Spain, for the United States, and for France. Spain and France branded him as a traitor, Catherine of Russia courted him, and the British paid him to keep them informed of events across the Atlantic. His enemies condemned him as an unscrupulous adventurer; his admirers applauded his courage, integrity, and knowledge. One thing is certain: he was the link joining European and U.S. interests with the aspirations of his own people to freedom—whatever that word might be made to mean. He was a bridge flung between two worlds and poised as shakily as some liane or rope trapeze-work across an Andean torrent. It must often have seemed to him that he was no more than a strategic prize in a power game fought high above his head. But he kept his sense of purpose and won his posthumous victory even though betrayed by Bolívar and the younger generation of liberators whom he had inspired. If two and a half centuries of dissatisfaction with Spanish rule had not driven Creoles and Indians alike to the limits of their patience, the fame of this courtier, intriguer, and not inconsiderable soldier could never have survived his ignominious death in a Spanish jail. As it was, posterity awarded him the proud title of '*El Precursor*'. He was the initiator of independence.

Miranda left a mass of autobiographical material. Sixty-three folio tomes of diaries, letters, memoranda, and newspaper cuttings were discovered in 1922 by W. S. Robertson in possession of the third Lord Bathurst in Cirencester. These were deposited with the *Academia Nacional de la Historia* in Caracas and published by the Venezuelan government. They form the basis of a number of books by Robertson himself, who has also drawn on Foreign Office archives and on the testimony of Miranda's eminent friends in all parts of the world, especially in the U.S.A., Britain, and France.

In the late eighteenth century and the early nineteenth, Caracas was one of the most active and dynamic cultural centres in the Americas, its pre-eminence contested only by Lima and Mexico City. It was here that Spanish genius, which had languished since its golden age, became revitalized by contact with other forms and situations. It was here that two liberators—Miranda and Bolívar—and their intellectual successor, Andrés Bello, were nurtured. Here the emancipation movement was conceived and American thought given its distinctive shape. In this rich city of Caracas, Miranda was born in 1750 of well-to-do parents. Though he lived almost entirely in exile from his native soil, he was to become the moving spirit of the intellectual movement toward liberation in Caracas.

After passing through Santa Rosa and Caracas universities, he went at the age of twenty-one to Spain where he bought a commission in the army. Three years later the Moroccan Sultan, Sidi Mohamed, demanded that the Spanish army and all Christians be evacuated from his Muslim domain. The Spaniards refused to go. Whereupon he besieged Melilla, a strong point on the Moroccan coast where Miranda was initiated into the bestialities of war. Angered at not gaining a speedy victory, Sidi Mohamed had one of his own generals executed and ordered the hands of an artillery-man to be amputated. Once three bullets ripped Miranda's trousers so that he narrowly escaped death; but what most horrified him was witnessing the throats of soldiers slit with brutal casualness by the Moors. These events made such a profound impression on him that they must have contributed to his vacillations and apparent cowardice in later years, particularly when he was being repulsed from his own Venezuelan soil. He was courageous, but was never one to bring suffering upon himself or his compatriots if to do so seemed mere foolhardiness. Antagonism from superior officers was also making him over-conscious of the inferior status accorded to Creoles in Europe. Personal extravagances, coupled with the financial insecurities of a young soldier of fortune in a foreign land, were leading him to value himself highly, sometimes aggressively so, in terms of hard cash. Such were the less attractive sides of a personality that endeared itself to many for its intelligence, firmness, and devotion.

A thorn in his flesh at this time was his commanding officer, an Irishman by the name of Count Alexander O'Reilly, who accused him of dressing in a way unbefitting an officer and of embezzle-ment. In 1776, therefore, Miranda snatched the opportunity of escaping from him by enlisting in a Spanish expedition that was being dispatched by Charles III to the Caribbean, there to aid the United States by attacking British possessions. Passing through Gibraltar, which under the Treaty of Utrecht was now British territory, he acquired a liking for English ways, and henceforth his Anglophile tendencies were to bedevil his relations with Spain. In Cádiz he met an influential English business man, John Turn-bull, and probably outlined to him plans for the liberation of Spanish America; but his schemes were still unknown to the Spanish authorities, and on reaching Havana he so impressed General Juan Manuel de Cagigal, presently to become Captain-General of Cuba, that he was entrusted with negotiating the exchange of British and Spanish prisoners. This task gave him the opportunity of obtaining information about British naval strength in the Caribbean and of laying the foundations for an information dossier embracing the whole American continent. His findings were to become available to the British and were paid for by them in a somewhat erratic manner. Britain was not, however, by any means as ungenerous as Miranda sometimes liked to suppose.

On Cagigal's expedition of 1782 to the Bahamas, Miranda was among those who entered New Providence, the capital, with the triumphant armies of Spain, but on his return to Havana he found himself temporarily under ignominious arrest. It must be admitted that the Spaniards had a case against him, for it appears that he was already corresponding with dissatisfied Venezuelans including Juan V. Bolívar (father of the Liberator) and Martín de Tobar whose friends nicknamed him the Venezuelan Cato. These people were keeping him up to date with the situation in Caracas. They informed him of the 'regrettable condition' of the whole province and of the tyrannies of the Intendant—one by the name of Gálvez —who 'seems to have come here only to torment us like a modern Lucifer . . . crueller than Nero and Philip II rolled into one'. This man, they said, treated Americans of whatever rank or lineage as if they were low slaves: 'he has just sent an order to all governors that no American gentleman may travel abroad without the king's permission'. It stung these haughty Creoles that they were compelled to live 'in a dishonourable prison . . . treated worse than Negro slaves, whose masters trust them more'. No recourse seemed left to them but to cast off such insufferable and base oppression, and they looked to Miranda, the motherland's 'eldest son', to restore their tottering self-respect. They regarded him as their elder brother, and 'on bended knees and with open arms' they begged him to save them for the love of God:

'The least sign from you will find us ready to follow you as our leader to the end, and to shed the last drop of our blood for causes that are great and honourable. . . . We do not want to take a single step except in your advice, and we shall not do so; for we have placed all our hopes in your good judgment. . . . We send you . . . the information which we think necessary so that in our name and that of our entire province you may make compacts or contracts with our full power and consent. Also, if you judge it convenient, you may negotiate with foreign powers in order to release us from this accursed captivity.'[1]

This flattering letter naturally encouraged Miranda to believe that he had the full support not only of the intellectuals but of all freedom-loving Venezuelans. The very receipt of it might be considered technical treachery, since he was still serving under the Spanish flag. In his role of trusted officer in the Spanish army he

[1] Miranda, F. de, *Archivos del General*, vol. 15, p. 68.

personally received the surrender of the British garrison at
Pensacola; in his role of Creole conspirator he was laying his first
plans for freeing the whole Hispano-American world. He knew
that in this latter task the British would have to take a leading role.

The curious situation in which a Spanish officer lately fighting
against the British at the side of the rebellious colonies could
without a scruple become so identified with British methods can
be better understood if we remember that a Creole American was
interested not so much in nations as in ideas, and was prepared to
find sympathetic souls on whichever side they might be. Miranda's
loyalty was to freedom, wherever he might find it, and armies in
any case in those days were largely mercenary.

In April 1783 hostilities between Britain and the U.S.A. came to
an end. Miranda was allowed his freedom and used it to tour
America as a neutral observer. In Philadelphia he saw Washington
received as triumphantly as 'the Redeemer entering Jerusalem'. A
letter of recommendation from Cagigal, who still thought highly
of him, opened the way to a private interview with Washington,
but neither Washington nor Lafayette, whom he might also have
been expected to admire, lived up to his ideas of what a liberating
hero should be.

He met many influential Americans, including Alexander
Hamilton, Henry Knox, and John Quincy Adams (the latter said
of him that he knew more about the American War of Independence than any U.S. statesman); but he was not entirely uncritical
of the country which had become the standard-bearer of Western
freedom. People of such low calibre, he noted acidly, had been
given legislative office, that after a two-hour debate one of them
did not know what the motion before the house actually was.
Putting his finger on the Achilles heel of the United States, he asked:

'Why, in a democracy whose basis is Virtue, is there no place
assigned to it? On the contrary all the dignity and powers are
given to Property, which is the blight of such a democracy.
Another point is the contradiction I noticed between admitting as
one of the rights of mankind that of worshipping a Supreme being
in the manner and form in which it may please one, yet afterwards

excluding a man from office if he did not profess Christianity. These are certainly grave solecisms.'[1]

It has been supposed that Miranda was irreligious, but he never attacked faith in God, only the absurdities of sectarianism and clerical dogmatism. In this he was a true forerunner of the anticlerical movement among Spanish American intellectuals, particularly Mexicans. He disliked public confession of sin and the puritanical New England Sabbath, but he praised the tolerance that brought New England into being. Like many lapsed Catholics he found he had no desire to rid himself of belief in the basic doctrines of the faith, especially in the mystery of the Trinity or in the Creed. He was even anxious to have his illegitimate child, Leander, baptized in the Catholic Church.

Miranda preferred Yale, perhaps because its President eulogized him, to Harvard which, he judged, was better equipped to train clergymen than citizens, and he deplored the fact that it had no professors of living languages.

While in the U.S.A. he was able to meet such eminent British intellectuals as Joseph Priestley (who had emigrated) and Lord Shelburne to whom Priestley had acted as librarian. He was inclined to attribute any virtues he saw in the United States, such as the industrious habits of the people of New England, to the fact that British institutions had been transplanted to American soil. He had already sensed, probably, that the United States had proprietary designs upon the whole hemisphere. These had been expressed as early as 1786 by Thomas Jefferson, who wrote that the United States confederacy should be thought of as 'the nest from which all America, North and South, should be peopled'; and who expressed his fear that Spain might prove too 'feeble' to hold her colonies until 'our population' (the U.S.A.) could gain it from them 'piece by piece'.

In view of this barefaced statement of U.S. aims in Spanish America, it is interesting to recall Count Aranda's prophecy made at the time of the Treaty of Paris in a memorandum to Charles III. The independence of the British colonies, which had just been

[1] Quoted by Herníquez-Ureña, P., p. 95.

recognized, seemed to him to give food for thought and grounds for fear. The new republic of federated states had been born a pigmy; but the time would come, Aranda predicted, when she would grow into a colossus whose chief aim would be self-aggrandisement.

Miranda kept his eyes and ears well open while in America. His interests were broad and he wanted to make them more so, for he believed that a forceful personality could be formed only by delving into 'the great book of the universe' and studying 'the most wise and virtuous societies that compose it—their laws, governments, agriculture, police, commerce, military art, navigation, science, and art'.[1]

The man who could write thus was being accused by Spain of being godless and a treacherous intriguer. Treacherous to Spain he undoubtedly was. In 1784 he betook himself to London where his arrival caused a stir among those who had been following events in the Spanish colonies. Thus the *Political Herald and Review*:

'That jealousy which confined the appointments of government in Spanish America to native Spaniards, and established other distinctions between these and their descendants on the other side of the Atlantic, has been a two-edged sword, and cut two ways. If it has hitherto preserved the sovereignty of Spain in those parts, it has sown the seeds of a deep resentment among the people. Conferences are held, combinations are formed in secret among a race of men whom we shall distinguish by the appellation of Spanish Provincials. The example of North America is the great subject of discourse, and the grand object of imitation. In London, we are well assured, there is at this moment a Spanish American of great consequence and possessed of the confidence of his fellow-citizens, who aspires to the glory of being the deliverer of his country. . . . This gentleman, having visited every province in North America, came to England, which he regards as the mother country of liberty, and the school for political knowledge.'[2]

It was all very flattering to Britain.

---

[1] Robertson, W. S., *Life of Miranda*, vol. 1, p. 30.
[2] *Political Herald and Review*, 1785, p. 29.

2. THE LEADER EMERGES

In London Miranda founded the *Gran Reunión Americana*, a society which over the course of years gathered together many of the most distinguished of dissident Creoles, including the future liberator of Chile, Bernardo O'Higgins; the precursor of Colombian independence, Antonio Nariño, who had made a clandestine Spanish translation of the *Declaration of the Rights of Man*; Francisco Montúfar who later became aide-de-camp to Bolívar's great General Sucre; the ubiquitous Vicente Rocafuerte from Guayaquil, who represented his native province in the Cortes of Cádiz in 1812 but had to flee Spain and who later contested the imperial ambitions of the Mexican Iturbide and became Mexican chargé d'affaires in London; and Carlos María de Alvear, opponent of the Uruguayan Artigas and one of San Martín's famous *Caballeros Nacionales*, a body formed specifically to fight for Argentine freedom.

To some extent it is possible to divide Hispano-American liberators into three types: those like Artigas who believed sincerely, stubbornly, and a little simple-mindedly in the innate goodness of mankind and who therefore saw no obstacles to a utopian form of democracy; those who realized that democracy would not come overnight to a people without education or tradition, and who were therefore anxious to work out a form of government that would combine enlightened oligarchy with the new concept of the rights of man; and the unscrupulous such as the Carrera brothers in Chile, Iturbide in Mexico, or Boves in Venezuela who exploited either tendency for their own private ends. The members of the society founded by Miranda formed as it were the intellectual aristocracy of the liberation movement. They were sophisticated enough to want to incorporate into their ideal society safeguards against human weakness.

Miranda had, however, many sides to his nature that contradicted the scientifically-minded intellectual. Napoleon said of him

64

that he was a Don Quixote only that he was not mad. Calling himself Count—a flourish that later liberators would have frowned on—he wandered about Europe in seeming euphoric dalliance, but all the time beneath his mask of foppishness assimilating facts and gaining useful experience. In 1787 he reached Russia where he was presented to the Empress Catherine. She found the good-looking and well-mannered young Latin much to her liking. He in turn found her full of goodness, humanity, intelligence, and noble sentiments. In her questions Catherine showed considerable knowledge of Spain and Spanish America. Miranda, 'travelling in search of knowledge, and improved by it, appeared to her in the light of a phenomenon'.[1] Her chief adviser, Potemkin, seems to have been no less impressed. She therefore gave Miranda funds and issued him with a circular letter to Russian ministers throughout Europe. In case of need he was to count on imperial protection and even asylum. Miranda, however, made his usual mistake of pressing for more money though he had been given a generous letter of credit on Catherine's English bankers. Perhaps it was his unabashed greed, together with his unfortunate entanglement in the French revolution, that caused Catherine eventually to withdraw support.

The storming of the Bastille in 1789 encouraged Spanish Americans, including Miranda, to think that a new age of liberty was at hand; and there was indignation throughout the New World when the Inquisition began to prohibit books that might encourage new ideas—books such as Tom Paine's *Rights of Man* with its 'seditious doctrines', and one called *El Desengaño del Hombre* which created such a stir in Mexico that steps had to be taken to prevent its being smuggled into the capital. In 1790 an edict was passed against works of this kind, including a history of the French revolution which made 'scandalous, heretical, and blasphemous attacks on the Deity himself and was injurious to the Pope, the clergy, and the Holy Office'. Books later placed on the Index included Condorcet's *Esquisses d'un tableau historique de progrès de l'esprit humain*; Gabriel Bonnot de Mably's *Des droits et*

[1] *Edinburgh Review*, January 1809, p. 287.

devoirs du citoyen; Lord Chesterfield's letters to his son; Locke's *Essay concerning Human Understanding*; and Count Volney's *Les Ruines ou Meditations sur les révolutions des Empires*, which was said to be 'a summary of all the evil systems which the libertines of all times had invented', surpassing in maliciousness 'the writings of Hobbes, Spinoza, Rousseau, Voltaire, and others' because it was founded on 'atheism, fatalism, naturalism, and materialism'.

What a time the Inquisition would have had with the 'isms of our century! In the eighteenth, liberals fled from its repressive clutches, from Rome and Spain to France and to England. Miranda, already an Anglophile, now returned to Britain and in 1790 was able to meet Pitt, who 'found his practical local knowledge and experience in the interests, business, and state of the Spanish Provinces in South America . . . coincided with the opinion I had been able to form'.[1]

The intermediary at this meeting was Thomas Pownall, a firm supporter of the pretensions of colonies to more enlightened rule. He believed that in return for helping to liberate Spanish America, Britain might receive part of the revenue the colonies had been accustomed to pay to Spain. The rebels were to reimburse Britain for any expenses incurred in the struggle and were to open ports for at least several years to trade both with Britain and the United States, from whom Pownall thought that help might also be forthcoming. As an afterthought he uttered a caution against injudicious advertising of British commercial ambitions, which he felt sure could be cloaked under the more laudable aim of freeing an oppressed people!

Just at this moment Britain became involved in a controversy with Spain over Nootka Sound on the Pacific coast of what is now British Columbia, which Captain Cook had reached in 1778 but which Spain now claimed. Miranda expected war and presented Pitt with a plan for attacking the Spanish colonies. He handed over certain papers which described conditions in South America, criticized Spain's policy of excluding Creoles from office, denounced censorship and the Inquisition, and declared that—being

[1] Miranda, *Archivos del General*, vol. 15, p. 106.

wealthier and more populated than Spain—South America might with perfect ease have been able to carry out its own revolution without foreign help if only there had not been such a sorry lack of communications. This paucity made concerted action difficult, the more so since the Americans had no navies to match Spain's powerful armadas. Britain, Miranda flatteringly assured Pitt, was the nation best suited to help:

'In view of the similarity that exists in the character of these two nations, and the effects that must naturally flow from liberty and the fact that a good government can instruct the general mass of men, progressively doing away with the religious prejudices that cloud its people's minds . . . these being otherwise honest, hospitable, and generous—we must expect soon to see a respectable and illustrious nation emerging worthy of being the ally of the wisest and most famed power on earth.'[1]

To this eulogy Miranda appended an analysis of the population and resources of South America, her European imports, and a comparison of the situation with that of Spain. Military needs he would go into later, together with the possibility of driving a canal through the Isthmus of Panama in order to help trade to and from the Far East, thus bringing advantages both to America and to Britain.

Miranda estimated the population of the Spanish Indies at about eleven million, consisting on the one hand of peninsular Spaniards, Creoles, Negroes, and *mestizos*; and on the other of an almost equal number of Indians either nominally subject to Spanish rule or not yet conquered. He calculated that the value of the gold, silver, cochineal, indigo, cacao, sugar, hides, and tobacco produced yearly came to 55 million pesos and that this amount was offset by imports from Spain of 22 million and by an approximately equal value of contraband. There were, he estimated, about 13,000 regular troops in the Spanish Indies plus 20,000 colonial militia—but the total forces available to Spain were 36,000. All told, Spain had 123 ships and 44,000 sailors.

Miranda also gave Pitt a project in French for the government

[1] Miranda, *Archivos del General*, vol. 15, p. 113.

of the Spanish colonies once they had been freed. One single nation would be created stretching from the Atlantic and the lands east of the Mississippi to the Pacific Ocean (barring only Brazil and Guiana). The northern boundary would be Parallel 45, from the source of the Mississippi to the Pacific. Cuba would be part of this nation, since it was 'the key to the Gulf of Mexico'.

Memories of Condorcanqui's abortive rebellion led Miranda to hope that executive authority might be vested in a descendant of the Incas on a hereditary basis, with legislative power given to a two-chamber congress: the upper house to be elected for life, the lower by popular vote from time to time. The Inquisition would be abolished but the clergy would be allowed to own property and to try ecclesiastical cases. Government monopolies and the poll tax would be suspended, but other taxes would be collected by the new government and would become the property of the nation. When necessary the government would be able to recruit men into its land and naval forces by suitable contracts with foreign powers. Commercial treaties might be negotiated with Britain or any other nation prepared to acknowledge Spanish American independence. No laws contrary to the spirit of the constitution would be valid, but the constitution itself could be amended if there were a two-thirds majority in both Houses and a three-quarters majority among the members of a council composed of the emperor and his high-court judges. The pattern for this constitution was Britain's limited monarchy but there were some features borrowed from the United States, from ancient Roman law, and from the Incas.

All this was satisfactory to Britain, but it had to be made clear to Miranda that the latter country could collaborate in his scheme only in the event of war with Spain. On the evening of May 6, Pitt's secretary called on Miranda and suggested that he should visit the Prime Minister at some moment when it could be done without rousing too much notice. In his record of the meeting Miranda said he thought that the Prime Minister wanted only to be assured that, as soon as English soldiers appeared on the coast of the selected sectors of Spanish America, the inhabitants would march at once to initiate the revolution.

Unfortunately for Miranda's plans, however, the Nootka Sound controversy was amicably settled in October 1790, war between Spain and Britain was avoided, and plans for liberating Spanish America remained in abeyance. Pownall now regretted that Miranda had left papers in Pitt's hands, for he began to fear that the information contained in them might not after all be used to further the Spanish American cause. Pitt, he concluded regretfully in retrospect, was less interested in the remote western hemisphere than in the European diplomatic chessboard. One of the few people in Europe who did in fact understand the full importance of Spanish America was Montesquieu, who noted:

'The Indies and Spain are two powers under one master, but the Indies are the more important. . . . Politics seek in vain to subordinate the more important to the less. The Indies continue to pull Spain toward themselves.'[1]

3. ACTIVITIES IN FRANCE

Miranda, who was not receiving as much financial backing from Pitt as he had hoped, demanded the return of the papers he had left with the Prime Minister. His relations with British authorities at this time were far from happy, and in the spring of 1792 he embarked once more for France. He served with the rank of Major-General in the French armies under Charles Dumouriez, who was attracted by what he called the sublimity of the Venezuelan's philosophy. Miranda had been strongly recommended to Dumouriez by the Girondist J. P. Brissot, who in November wrote to the General that Spain was ripe for freedom and that a revolution must be waged concurrently in European Spain and in Spanish America. He saw the fate of the latter area as being dependent upon one man, Miranda, who, he suggested,

---

[1] Montesquieu, *Esprit des Lois*, book 21, chap. 22, quoted in the *Edinburgh Review*, January 1809, p. 288.

should be sent in an official capacity to Santo Domingo. Of all the people available, Miranda, he felt, was surely the most capable of putting an end to the 'silly quarrels' of the colonists, of bringing the 'unruly whites' to heel, and of becoming the idol of the coloured people. An invasion by Miranda of the Spanish colonies at the head of more than 12,000 infantry then garrisoned in Santo Domingo, and of 10,000 or 15,000 mulattoes supplied from the colonies, looked feasible and even simple. If in addition a fleet could be mustered, the Spaniards would be impotent to oppose Miranda, whose very name would be worth an army. His talents, courage, and genius would ensure success. To all this, Brissot added a scathing comment on Pitt's 'paltry policies of procrastination', which he felt sure would prevent Britain from doing anything in the matter.[1]

Susceptible to flattery as Miranda often was, he was not entirely favourable to Brissot's plans. He was aware that he knew little about the French Caribbean; and, what was more important, he was beginning to dislike the anarchy he seemed to see spreading in France. This is clear from a letter to Alexander Hamilton in the U.S.A., to whom he outlined his own schemes but added, 'The only danger I foresee is the introduction of French principles which would poison freedom in its cradle and destroy it for us.'

Besides, he got into serious trouble when commanding the right wing of the republican army at the disastrous battle of Neerwinden. His patron, General Dumouriez, was badly defeated and defected; and Miranda, in spite of having fought with distinction, and in spite of having at once denounced his superior officer, was suspected of being implicated. He was tried, and pleaded his case well, but was nevertheless jailed. An English poetess, Helen Maria Williams, who spoke to him in his cell, described his fortitude under the shadow of the guillotine and how by applying himself to a study of history and science he was able to forget his personal troubles. Those who were inclined throughout his life to accuse Miranda of cowardice might not have found it easy to emulate his detachment in the face of physical adversity. He seems

[1] *Edinburgh Review*, January 1809, p. 291.

to have been one of those men whose characters are revealed at their best under the greatest stress.

On several other occasions Miranda was jailed in Paris, having unluckily incurred the enmity of Robespierre who believed him to be a Girondist—with good reason for he was becoming daily more sympathetic to the moderates. Spanish American liberators were not political extremists but nationalists who wanted their people to be allowed common human decencies. It was not easy for French revolutionaries to understand this, though Miranda's whole attitude should have made it clear enough. In 1791, for instance, the same year that Toussaint L'Ouverture rose to prominence as the leader of the Haitian Negroes, Miranda had published a letter to the Americans in which he attacked the Spanish colonial system with what amounted, by comparison with the behaviour of the Haitian radicals, to sweet reasonableness.

4. LIBERATION PLANS PROLIFERATE

In 1790 an anonymous plan had been drawn up in French for liberating Spanish America without the help of the United States but from a base in New Orleans. In 1796 there was a fairly serious uprising of republican Spaniards in La Guaira, Venezuela, and the following year the capture of Trinidad from Spain by a British squadron under Sir Ralph Abercromby gave hope that the island might become a base for operations against the royalists on the Venezuelan mainland. Britain was also threatening Spain through a dissident group known as the *Caballeros Republicanos de México*, centred in Tampico.

Abercromby undoubtedly had an eye on the benefits that might accrue to British trade in the Caribbean although he felt there 'should be no idea of conquest nor of exclusive commerce'. At the time it seemed as if a revolution in Spanish America would be of greater advantage to Britain than to the United States. It was likely, therefore, that the first uprisings would be encouraged in Venezuela (via Trinidad) rather than in Mexico, which even in those days was considered to be more immediately the concern of the U.S.A.

With Britain holding Trinidad, Miranda's obvious course was to try once more to seek British help. In 1797 he received additional encouragement when Lord Melville drew up a circular, which the Governor of Trinidad was to disseminate along the Spanish American coast, asking the inhabitants 'to resist the oppressive authority of the Spanish government'.[1] The plan was that a British naval force should support the rebels and supply them with arms, but 'without any desire on the part of the King of England to acquire any right of sovereignty over them, or to interfere with their civil, political, or religious rights; unless they themselves should in any degree solicit his protection'.

About this time a deputation of Spanish Americans, including Miranda, were working out a proposal to submit to the British government.[2] Its first article slyly drew attention to the help Spain had given the British colonies in America, and suggested that Britain could scarcely refuse to return the compliment by helping the Spanish colonies against Spain. Britain, the U.S.A., and Latin America had such a common regard for freedom that they were natural allies and should therefore join in a defensive pact. The reward to the United States would be Florida, but Britain's would be even more handsome: thirty million pounds; free trade; free access to an ocean-to-ocean canal to be built by way of Lake Nicaragua; and control of the market in precious metals. A small Anglo-American force would help the movement. The aim should be to free the whole area except the Caribbean islands, which could be allowed (those that were already Spanish colonies) to remain as they were. Of these only Cuba, because of its strategic position, should be made independent.

In January 1799 this document was submitted to Pitt who, because Britain was now at war with Spain, had a freer hand in dealing with the Creole rebels and could receive Miranda warmly. He merely hinted that it would be as well if the ubiquitous

---

[1] Quoted in the *Edinburgh Review*, January 1809, p. 296.
[2] *Edinburgh Review*, January 1809, p. 290.

emissary of the Latin American underground movement were to regularize his credentials. At the time Miranda was describing himself as 'chief agent of the Spanish colonies', and claimed he had been appointed by a Junta of Deputies of Mexico, Peru, Chile, La Plata, Venezuela, and New Granada; but he had no document to prove this.

Trying to put moral and political pressure on Pitt, Miranda wrote to him in March 1799 asking him to consider what the consequences would be if Britain failed to honour her promises of aid. Despair and dejection would certainly invade the Creoles. Worse, the future and safety of the United States would be compromised and British commercial interests damaged. France might seize the opportunity of wreaking vengeance upon the Anglo-Saxon world and of imposing revolutionary doctrines—a possibility which Miranda believed to be too terrible for the human race to contemplate.

Soon afterwards two private British subjects proposed to Miranda that Britain should provide him with arms and a small naval force with which he should embark for South America. When this proposal became officially known it was not unnaturally frowned on by British officialdom, especially since at this time Miranda was openly conspiring with other Spanish Americans in London and was meeting Bernardo O'Higgins to whom he gave detailed advice upon how to proceed on returning to Chile. Miranda's fatherly advice offered to a twenty-year-old boy from the store of his European experience was shrewd:

'My young friend:

'The warm interest I take in your happiness leads me to offer you a few words of advice upon entering into this great world whose waves have buffeted me these many years. You know the story of my life and can judge whether or not my counsel is worth hearing.

'In trusting you, which I have done fully up to now, I have proved that I rate your honour and discretion high; and in sending you these reflections I show the trust I have in your good sense, for nothing can be more stupid and at times more dangerous than to give advice to a fool.

'When you leave England do not for a moment forget that outside this country there is in all the world only one other nation where you can breathe a word of politics except to a true friend, and that country is the United States.

'Select a friend then, but select him with the greatest care for if you make a mistake you are lost. I have several times suggested to you the names of some South Americans in whom you could place your trust should they happen to cross your path, though I doubt this since they live in a different area.

'Having but a very imperfect idea of the land you live in, I cannot give you my views about the education, knowledge, and character of your fellow countrymen; but to judge from their greater distance from the Old World I would suppose them to be most ignorant and distraught. In my long connection with South America you are the only Chilean I have dealt with, and so I know no more of that country than what its history tells me, which, though so little has been written, presents it in a favourable light.

'From the facts of that history I hope much from your countrymen, especially in the south where, if I am not mistaken, you intend to live. Their wars and their neighbours should make them skilled in arms, and the proximity of a free country should familiarize their spirits with the idea of liberty and independence.

'Returning to the question of your future confidants, trust no man over the age of forty unless you can be sure he is fond of reading. The views of the others are too deep-rooted for any hope of change, and any remedy might be dangerous.

'Youth is the age of ardent and generous sentiments. Among your contemporaries you will surely meet many who are eager to listen and are easily persuaded. But youth is also the age of indiscretion and rash actions; you should therefore be as wary of these failings in the young as of timidity and prejudice in the old.

'It is also a mistake to think that a man with a tonsure or who has a comfy canonical seat must be an intolerant fanatic and a confirmed enemy of the rights of man. I know from experience that among them are to be found some of the most illustrious and liberal people in South America, but the difficulty is to find them.

'The pride and fanaticism of Spaniards is incorrigible. They will despise you because you are American-born and hate you because you were educated in England. Keep away from them always.

'Spanish Americans, being impatient and communicative, will be eager to hear about your travels and adventures, and by the kind of questions they ask you will be able to form an idea of their character. Making all due allowances for their ignorance you will be able to assess their character by the degree of attention they give you and the amount of intelligence they show in understanding you and thus in giving or withholding their confidence.

'Never let disgust or despair dominate your mind, because if you once allow such feelings you will not be able to serve your country. . . .

'In my conversations I have always tried to stick to this principle, and it is one that I would have you remember every day and hour.

'Love your country! Cherish this feeling always; strengthen it in every possible way, for only if it endures and prospers will you act rightly.

'I would add that the obstacles impeding your service to your country are so many, so formidable, and so insuperable, that only the most ardent love for your homeland can sustain you in your striving toward happiness. . . .

'Read this letter each day on your journey, and then at once destroy it.

FRANCISCO MIRANDA'[1]

Evidently, since it has survived, the young man could not bear to destroy a document of such charm and so revealing of its author's character.

Miranda's hopes were now high; but a treaty between the U.S.A. and France and the coalition formed between Britain,

[1] Vicuña Mackenna, Benjamín, *La Corona del Héroe, a summary of data and documents perpetuating the memory of General Don Bernardo O'Higgins*, Santiago, 1872, p. 240 *et seq.*

Austria, Naples, Russia, and Turkey against France foiled his plans. A letter written by Miranda in October 1799 to an old friend, Manuel Gual, shows that he was disillusioned both by the French revolutionaries and by foreign powers in general. The influence of no foreign power whatever, he told Gual, should be allowed to interfere in the management of the country. If this happened, Spanish America would become a desirable prize and would be despoiled by maritime powers, who might join together for this purpose. Citing the two great examples of revolutionary movements—the French, and that of the British colonies in America—he advised that the latter should be discreetly imitated, the former shunned because of its 'fatal effects'.

It would be difficult to say whether at this period the French or the British were annoying Miranda more. In 1800, furious with *perfide Albión* since his passport to the British West Indies had been refused, he returned to France but was at once arrested for espionage and communication with enemies of the State. A little later he was ordered to leave the country. By the time he returned to England, Addington had replaced Pitt as Prime Minister, and Miranda obtained an interview with Addington's confidant, Nicholas Vansittart. In his journal Miranda describes how Vansittart read and liked the plans which at various times he had placed before Pitt. He also saw Brissot's proposals. He was needled by Miranda's wanting to enlist the help of the United States, and finally returned the ball to the Creole. It still remained to be discovered, he said, just what type of government Spanish Americans wanted to establish. Very properly Miranda said that he could not dictate what his country's government would be but that a system similar to that of the United States might be both popular and expedient. Vansittart agreed but warned against the influence of foreign immigrants, advised that only property-owners should be allowed to vote, and suggested that a project be put in writing for submission to the Prime Minister. 'Where will you put the capital?' he fired at Miranda as they parted; to which the latter—anticipating Bolívar—replied, 'On the Isthmus.'

Though it was nothing more than a truce, the Treaty of Amiens which was signed on March 25, 1802, between Britain, France, Spain, and Holland, once more dashed Miranda's hopes that he might receive British aid. But the treaty had another result that was more sinister. It gave Napoleon the illusion that he might become the ruler of a great American empire. To further his ambitions he needed a base in Santo Domingo. Toussaint L'Ouverture stood in his way, so the Haitian liberator was captured and packed off to jail in France in 1802. A year later he died of the cold in prison. 'The first of the Negroes', as Toussaint termed himself, had been summarily liquidated by 'the first of the whites'. But Haiti's independence had been won and was declared in 1804. Napoleon's victory was hollow.

In 1803 the Treaty of Amiens had been abandoned and there was open rupture between Britain and France. The American Rufus King thought that if war broke out Britain would immediately try to emancipate Spanish America. Haiti's independence had brought new vigour to the cause of the revolutionaries but in Paris Napoleon was being crowned and young Simón Bolívar was expressing his disapproval of the event. Next year the government in England fell, and Miranda in dismay decided to leave Europe.

5. THE 'LEANDER' EXPEDITION

On December 6, 1805, Miranda was in Washington calling on President Jefferson. Private American wellwishers fitted him out with a ship *Leander* which sailed under the newly designed Colombian flag—red, blue, and yellow—for the first attempt launched from abroad to wrest Venezuela from the royalists. On the voyage Miranda stopped at Santo Domingo where he also chartered two schooners, *Bee* and *Bacchus*. He had been hoping for British help, but was disappointed to be stopped by a British frigate, *Cleopatra*, whose commander tried to impress some of *Leander*'s sailors on the pretext that they were British. Miranda was, however, able to convince the over-zealous lieutenant that his undertaking might be of great use to Britain, especially since he intended to open Venezuelan ports to British trade.

With two hundred ill-armed men Miranda was expecting to confront the might of Spain. When on the night of April 27, 1806, he tried to disembark near Puerto Cabello, westward along the coast from Caracas, *Bee* and *Bacchus* failed to keep up with *Leander* and were intercepted. It seemed only common sense that Miranda should save the flagship, but his abandoning of sixty recruits on board the schooners was one of the incidents that later caused him to be accused of cowardice. The raw boys surrendered and the Spaniards condemned them to death by hanging. Their heads were placed on public view and Venezuelans were forbidden to have any dealings with Miranda, for whose capture dead or alive a reward of 30,000 pesos was offered.

Leander took refuge in Barbados, whence in June she sailed for Trinidad accompanied by the *Lily*, the British brig *Express*, and a merchant schooner, *Trimmer*. At Trinidad Governor Hislop received the rebels well, allowing volunteers to be recruited from the island's militia, the troops to serve under Colonel de Rouvray and two other British officers. Miranda's old friends Turnbull and Sons also offered to collaborate in return for economic concessions.

Judging that he had now received all the help he was likely to get from Britain, and finding that the French squadron was bound for Europe from Martinique, Miranda decided to risk another attack with seven British ships. On August 1 the expedition—consisting of fifteen small vessels and five hundred volunteers—reached Coro bay, but for two days heavy seas prevented an attack. The vanguard under Colonels de Rouvray and Downie and Lieutenant Beddingfield then drove the Spaniards from the beach and stormed a battery. With the flourish of a crusader who glimpses the holy land at last, Miranda entered the town of Coro and posted there a proclamation addressed to all South Americans. It ordered Spnaish government officials to cease functioning so that local courts might take over. Those who helped Spain would be treated as traitors; those who left Spanish service would be

rewarded. Public funds were to be transferred to the new administration, and men between sixteen and fifty-five were summoned
to the Colombian colours. The standard of national independence
was to be displayed and Colombian citizens were to wear cockades
in their hats. An assembly was to be formed to act as caretaker
until a permanent government could be created. The public good
was to be the supreme law.

This was to be the great moment, the culmination of years of
scheming; but something had gone wrong. Miranda had been
abroad too long and was out of touch with important sectors of
Venezuelan opinion. The younger generation scarcely knew of his
existence, and the invasion on which he had pinned such hopes
fizzled out like a raggedly organized protest march. In dejected
anti-climax he had to evacuate Coro. British authorities in the
West Indies had received no clear instructions from home and
could do little to help. On the contrary, on October 21, when
Miranda reached Grenada in *Leander*, he was welcomed with an
immediate request for repayment of debts he had incurred on the
expedition. It was almost more than he could stand.

In other parts of America things were not so black. In June of
that year Admiral Sir Home Riggs Popham and Brigadier-General
William Carr Beresford had taken Buenos Aires in a private
attempt to secure a British foothold in South America. Riggs
Popham wrote warmly to Miranda whom he supposed to be still
in England. Miranda's friend Turnbull forwarded him the letter,
which must have provided welcome solace, for it was now clear
that throughout the length of South America things were in
turmoil. Britain's sympathy with Creole ideals, and her mercantile
interests which for so long had been controlled by diplomatic
caution, might at last tip the scales in Miranda's favour.

6. NAPOLEON AND THE BRITISH

In 1807 Napoleon's armies marched into Portugal and on November 29 they were just in time to see, from the hills above Lisbon,

the British navy sail for Brazil carrying away the mad queen María and her court. The Portuguese empire was therefore safe even though a month earlier, by the treaty of Fontainebleau, France and Spain had divided its land (including its colonies) between them. Six thousand Spanish troops now invaded Portugal, and among them—such were the haphazard fortunes of young soldiers in those days—was José de San Martín, soon to become the liberator of Argentina.

Miranda sailed in a British warship from Trinidad to England where he was well received by Canning and Lord Melville. At this time William Burke published a booklet[1] in which he argued that, Spain being now merely a province of France, Miranda should at once be given at least 6,000 men to free Venezuela, the movement to be the spearhead of a war of liberation throughout the whole of Spanish America.

In January 1808 Miranda met Sir Arthur Wellesley; and the future Duke of Wellington, though cautious, was sufficiently interested to prepare a memorandum detailing the arms and munitions that would be needed for attacks on the Mexican Gulf and La Plata areas. It did seem that the British were actually on the point of actively helping Miranda, who had Wellesley's full support. Castlereagh chose Wellesley to command an expedition against the Spanish colonies—preferably against Venezuela where Miranda's influence (in spite of his failed attempt at invasion) was still believed to be strong. Wellesley planned to sail from Falmouth or Cork on July 1, 1808. South Americans were to be invited to establish their own independence under the protection of Great Britain, and Britain's reward was to be a ten per cent relief on duties normally applying to foreign ships.

After studying the plans Wellesley decided it would be best to enter Spanish America by way of Veracruz and Mexico. West-Indian Negroes would be able to join up with British forces returning from La Plata (where things had not gone well); and

[1] Burke, W., *Additional Reasons for our Immediately Emancipating Spanish America, deduced from the New and Extraordinary Circumstances of the Present Crisis, etc.* Second edition, J. Ridgway, London, 1808.

Jamaica could serve as a base for the expedition which could be reinforced later with native troops from India.

Two things worried Miranda. The failure of the *Leander* expedition had shaken his confidence in the determination of his own countrymen to see the enterprise through; and he was wondering what reward he himself would receive if Wellesley's expedition succeeded. While he was sorting out these delicate points the whole situation in Europe altered.

For years Napoleon had been playing a game of cat-and-mouse with Spain through the mediation of the Queen's favourite, Manuel Godoy, who because of the weakness of Charles IV was the real ruler of the country. Godoy's fortunes had however fluctuated between an exalted status as when, in 1793, he had replaced the able Count Aranda as Prime Minister, and disgrace two years later when he was forced to sign the Treaty of Basilea which ceded to France the Spanish half of the island of Santo Domingo. Though called with a certain irony the Prince of Peace, he was removed from office; but his liaison with Queen María Luisa ensured his return to favour even after the disaster of Trafalgar. At Fontainebleau in 1807 he had signed the treaty with Napoleon whereby the two countries declared joint war on Portugal, on which pretext Napoleon was able to march 100,000 men into Spain. A rumour that Charles IV and his wife thought of fleeing to America provoked the tumult of Aranjuez (March 1808). The Prince of Peace was dismissed from office under pressure from the mob. Two days later the same rabble compelled Charles to abdicate, and his son, the Prince of Asturias, became Ferdinand VII.

In April Napoleon summoned Charles and Ferdinand to Bayonne, but before leaving his own country the new king gave the provisional Spanish Junta, known as the Court of the Regency, powers to govern in his absence. On May 5 he and his father were forced to resign the Crown in favour of Napoleon, who proclaimed his brother Joseph King of Spain and of the Indies. Spain was split into a number of small city-states, and on July 21 the army of the Seville Junta defeated the French at Bailén. Joseph

Bonaparte was forced to retreat from Madrid where he had established himself, and it looked as if the Spanish patriots, with British help, might be victorious. On July 12, 1808, therefore, Wellesley's fleet—instead of sailing to the New World—went to Lisbon from where it began to reconquer Portugal and Spain from Napoleon. William Burke placed the following 'Advertisement' at the opening of the second edition of his plea for aid to Spanish America:

'Just as the last sheet of this edition was put to press, it was currently reported that the expedition actually preparing to co-operate in the emancipation of South America has its destination changed; and is now to be sent with all speed to the shores of Old Spain. I should be exceedingly sorry to find we thus risked certain and important advantages, for what are extremely dubious gains; and that we hazarded by delay the present opportunity—rendered so peculiarly favourable, by the events taking place in Spain, for successfully offering emancipation to Spanish America—events which, it is not improbable, the people of that country will seize for asserting their independence themselves.'[1]

The British intervention in Spain did not prevent Napoleon from entering Madrid in December 1808. In Venezuela a copy of *The Times* containing the news of his invasion fell into the hands of Andrés Bello. He translated it for the governor, who exclaimed that the news must be false and due to 'the notorious perfidy of English newspapers'. But an officer in the British navy confirmed it. A few days later Napoleon's special envoys disembarked and the whole population rose in spontaneous loyalty to Ferdinand. French people in Caracas were insulted in a public café, and the Governor sent Bello to warn the envoys that he could not answer for their lives. They assumed an air of bravado and asked for half a dozen soldiers with whom to quell any riots that might break out, but that very afternoon seized the chance of escaping in a British ship that happened to be sailing from La Guaira. In this way, said Beaver, the French captain escaped with his life. Three hundred men were after his blood and the populace was

[1] Burke, W., Advertisement on title page *b*.

clamouring to Casas to surrender him to them. 'Though the governor received me coldly,' added Beaver, 'the most respected of the citizens of the city surrounded me and acclaimed their liberator. They . . . burst into shouts of gratitude to England';[1] for England, they were convinced, was the one power capable of putting an end to the audacities of the little Corsican.

They were right of course. Charles and his wife had gone from Bayonne to Fontainebleau and thence to Rome, where Charles died in 1819; and Ferdinand was kept in confinement in Valençay. There was no hope of action from the Spanish royal house. Wellington's big offensive against Spain, however, did not begin until 1812 when, heavily engaged in Russia, Napoleon was forced onto the defensive in the Peninsula. June 1813 saw the rout of Joseph Bonaparte by British and Spanish forces at Vitoria, and the following year Ferdinand was able to return to his country and his throne; but he did so only to reverse the liberal tendencies of his own Cortes and to rescind the 1812 Constitution which had given such heart to the Creoles. But by that time, in any case, the war across the Atlantic was being bitterly waged.

From 1808 until 1814 there had always existed the possibility, remote though it might have been, that Britain could so far encourage liberal tendencies in Spain that the hatred the Creoles felt for the peninsular Spaniards might be modified. Britain was strongly placed to help both the progressives in Spain and the Creoles. It was in vain, therefore, that in 1808 the Spanish Junta (which, though liberal in composition, included some conservatives) instructed its Minister in London to protest to the British government against intrigues directed from that city by 'a revolutionary who was notorious only for treason against king and country'. The Spanish Minister was to do all in his power to have Miranda arrested or even handed over to Spain, but the British government would not have its hand forced and merely cautioned Miranda against corresponding with friends in Caracas. Miranda almost openly ignored this warning and remained in touch with his colleague Saturnino Rodríguez Peña in BuenosAires (who was

[1] Páez, J. A., vol. I, p. 19.

himself in the pay of the British and whose activities must therefore have been well known in London) and with other dissident
Creoles throughout the Americas and in the West Indies.

7. FIRST STEPS TO INDEPENDENCE

Many people were convinced that Spanish America was ready for
revolt if only the cards could be played correctly. An anonymous
British naval officer testified in writing to this fact; and a 'Letter
to the Spanish Americans' written (as it was later known) by
Pablo Viscardo y Guzmán, an ex-Jesuit and a native of Arequipa
in Peru, gave anonymous expression to the reasoning of the more
restless clergy—the type Miranda had so warmly recommended to
O'Higgins:

'It would be a blasphemy to imagine that the Supreme Benefactor of man had permitted the discovery of the new world
merely in order that a number of imbecile knaves might always be
free to wreck it, and that they should constantly have the odious
pleasure of stripping millions of men, who had given no cause
for complaint, of essential rights received from His divine hand;
to imagine that His eternal wisdom wished to deprive the
remainder of mankind of the immense advantages which, in the
order of nature, so great an event ought to procure for them, and
to condemn them to wish with a groan that the new world had
remained for ever unknown. . . . We are bound, as far as lies in
our power, to fulfil the hopes of which hitherto they [the
Spaniards] had frustrated mankind. Let us again throw America
open to all our fellow inhabitants of the globe, from whence
ingratitude, injustice, and the most senseless avarice have exiled
us. The recompense will not be less to us than to them.'[1]

Now indeed Utopia was to be built in the New World, and all
men were to have access to it! At the time when Lord Castlereagh
was Secretary of State for War, Miranda did all he could to
persuade both him and Wellington that his dream was possible of

[1] Printed in Burke, W., *ibid.*, p. 120.

fulfilment. It was perhaps unwise of him, however, to have given Wellington copies of his letters to Spanish Americans, for the British government was still a little nervous of his activities and it would have been as well not to brandish evidence of them in high places. It must have gone to his head that so many influential intellectuals, including Jeremy Bentham, Wilberforce, and Lady Hester Stanhope, were lionizing him.

He was at this time publishing *El Colombiano*, a journal which the Spanish authorities tried in vain to have suppressed. It bore on its title page the motto: *Nec magis vituperandus est proditor patriae, quam communis utilitatis, ac salutis desertor, propter suam utilitatem, aut salutem* (No traitor to his country is more to blame than he who betrays the general good for his own individual benefit or safety).[1] The choice of the text was the Mexicans', and it was perfectly deliberate. Miranda and the other editors must have been well aware of the philosophical context in which Cicero had placed the words. The universe, of which both men and gods are members—he had said—is governed by divine will. Each of us is part of this universe; therefore a wise and law-abiding man will study the advantage of all and will not act selfishly. It was a sentiment worthy of the descendants of Quetzalcoatl.

As it turned out, the independence movement was to split the sheep from the goats in precisely the sense in which Cicero had divided patriots from traitors. Miranda predicted what was to come when, after hearing the news that a governing Junta had been established in Buenos Aires, he wrote to Saturnino Rodríguez Peña pointing out what a remarkable thing it was that two cities (Buenos Aires and Caracas), without the slightest communication between them, had simultaneously adopted political measures for carrying out the revolution. 'Freedom', added Miranda, defining the situation with a stroke of genius, 'is no more than justice wisely administered; and where dreadful crimes are committed with impunity, genuine freedom cannot live!'

On April 19, 1810, the Captain-General of Venezuela was

[1] Cicero, *De Finibus*.

deposed and an independent Junta was set up favouring Ferdinand. Diverse threads were now intertwined, not least among them being Simón Bolívar's arrival in London together with his mentor Andrés Bello, to confer with British authorities on behalf of the Venezuelan patriots. It was natural that the deputation should meet Miranda, who wrote to the Duke of Gloucester informing him of the mission's arrival and explaining that he and his colleagues considered themselves the true representatives of those Spanish Americans who remained loyal to their king. Their attitude, he was trying to imply, was strictly legal. (He also took the opportunity for some self-eulogy.)

In August Britain promised the Venezuelans naval protection against France; but it was recommended that a reconciliation should be sought with the Spanish government so that loyalty to Ferdinand and trade with the mother country should not be prejudiced.

Miranda, who must already have suspected that the fiery young envoy Bolívar was a serious rival to himself as leader of the revolution, would have liked to return to Venezuela in the latter's company. This was not possible, and Bolívar sailed without him on September 20 in the brig *Sapphire*. Miranda followed on October 10, bearing—incidentally—laws drafted by Jeremy Bentham for the freedom of the Press. In Venezuela the precursor was received with mixed feelings. Many were joyful. Others suspected him of wanting to restore an Inca throne for the sole purpose of putting himself upon it. They were suspicious, too, of his friends including Bentham, Wilberforce, and Turnbull. British officials continued cautious.

In spite of his vanity and his querulousness about money matters, Miranda never wavered in his revolutionary aim; and the Regency in Spain could not fail, therefore, to feel nervous of his arrival in Venezuela. In 1810 it decided to blockade Caracas and call upon all citizens to pledge allegiance to the Crown. In October the Cádiz Cortes declared that all Spanish dominions were one nation and that their citizens had equal rights with those of Spain. Rebellious Venezuelans were asked to disarm, but they

had no intention of doing any such thing and were actually planning to establish a government on the U.S. pattern. Even nominal
support for Ferdinand was waning.

Realizing that some conciliatory gesture would have to be made
if unity were to be preserved, early in 1811 the Cortes declared
that the Spanish Indies were to be equally represented upon it
with Spain,[1] and that restrictions on agriculture and industry
would be lifted. But it was too late. On March 2 the first
Venezuelan congress had met. The opening included a church
ceremony and an oath sworn on the Bible that the rights of
Ferdinand and the Roman Catholic religion would be defended.
Thus, in spite of a frank attitude of rebellion in some quarters,
the first step toward a full independent Venezuela, formally
ratified on July 5, was a loyal one.

Miranda's proposal to issue metal and paper money was
adopted; but the paper currency fell steadily in value, there being
no funds to back it. The new country was in economic straits and
royalist uprisings had to be suppressed. Nevertheless plans went
ahead for a constitution, which was signed on December 21. It
converted the Captaincy-General of Venezuela into a federal
republic, each of its provinces to be broadly independent but with
overall jurisdiction from the centre. There were to be liberty,
equality (with no caste distinctions), guarantees of property and

[1] For a detailed analysis of Mexico's representation in the Cortes, and a criticism of
the view that representation from the colonies was scant, see Benson, Nettie Lee
(Ed.), *Mexico and the Spanish Cortes 1810–1822*, University of Texas Press, Austin
and London, 1966. In spite of the opening of the Cortes to representatives from the
colonies, however, it is doubtful just how far the principle of equality was intended
to be carried. H. G. Ward, for one, was extremely sceptical at the time; see his vol. 1,
pp. 136–9, and especially his footnote on the latter page:
'I do not wish to animadvert upon the conduct of the Cortes with unnecessary
severity.... But in considering the feelings of the Americans towards this assembly,
it must not be forgotten that the Cortes were the first to sanction the barbarous
principle that "with rebels and Insurgents no engagements are binding." They
approved the violation of the capitulation of Caracas by Monteverde in 1812, the
first of a long series of similar breaches of the public faith; and with such facts as
this before them, it was hardly to be expected that the Americans should place much
confidence in their professions of amity, equality, and brotherly love.'
Even in 1811 Americans were not overdisposed to trust the word of the Cortes.
This at least was the view of His Majesty's Chargé d'Affaires in Mexico from 1825
to 1827, and Ward was no mean observer.

other securities, and freedom of thought and the Press so long as public order, private honour, and Christian morals were not endangered. These freedoms were to be extended to foreigners provided (naturally) that they abided by the country's laws. There would be a House of Representatives on the U.S. pattern, and Congress would have the right to declare war or to make peace, to call provincial militia into the service of the nation, and to protect the official religion. Under certain conditions the republic of Venezuela could be extended to include other areas of Spanish America.

In spite of religious guarantees the priests, an important section of the community, opposed this Constitution because it abolished many of their privileges. Miranda also criticized it on the grounds that the powers of government were badly balanced. He alleged that it was ill-adapted to the customs of the country and its people, and that it would in the long run separate rather than unite. Although later events proved him right, at the time the sincerity of Miranda's objections seemed questionable and his popularity was not enhanced.

8. Unpopularity, Betrayal, and Death

The new republic soon had a more terrible problem to contend with than a liberator suspected of cherishing unworthy ambitions; for on March 26, 1812—which happened to be the Thursday of Holy Week and the anniversary of the day on which the Captain-General had been deposed—an earthquake killed about 20,000 people in Caracas and its environs, precisely in the region where the patriots were strongest. By a trick of fate it scarcely touched Coro, the centre of royalist power. Judgment, said the archbishop, the priests, and the superstitious, had fallen from heaven upon the heads of the revolutionaries. So many soldiers deserted, in terror of hell fire, that it became necessary for Congress to proclaim martial law. During this calamity the young Bolívar was seen to leap dramatically onto a heap of rubble, crying, 'If nature thwarts us and our plans, we will fight her and force her to obey us.'[1]

The earthquake left the rebels in such dire straits that they had no recourse but to give Miranda—the only man strong and experienced enough to lead them—dictatorial powers. The measures he adopted to ensure safety were unpopular and he was once again suspected of being over-anxious to obtain foreign aid, even though, in view of continued pressure from the royalists, the country badly needed help from abroad.

Popular support for the peninsular Spaniards was not lacking, and the royalists were so successful that Miranda was soon forced to move his military headquarters from Maracay to La Victoria. Scarcely had he done so, however, when the Spaniards threatened the strategic point of Puerto Cabello where Simón Bolívar was in command. On July 1, 1812, Bolívar sent a message to Miranda that he must immediately attack the royalists or all would be lost. By the time Miranda received it, Bolívar's small force had been so reduced, not only through the usual hazards of battle but also through desertion, that he was forced to surrender.

Though Bolívar was hurt in his pride and made much of the drama, his youthful spirit soon recovered. Miranda's did not. His capitulation to the royalists took place on July 25; and his surrender can be explained partly by the fact that his confidence had been utterly broken. He had also reason to be unsure how far the Spanish colonies actually wanted to be liberated. During some of the later phases of the wars in Venezuela, Argentina, Chile, and Peru, it became clear that Britain's doubts on this score were well grounded, and that many of the liberators themselves had formed too sanguine an opinion about the support they were likely to receive. It seems certain that, had he known the amount of royalist sympathy that still existed in Venezuela at the time of the first uprisings there, Miranda would not have wished to force himself upon his compatriots; and his final capitulation—supposed by many of his younger followers to have been treachery—can be explained by his honest adherence to a policy that united his views with those of the British. In the last resort he was forced to admit

[1] Lecuna, V., *Proclamas*, Document 2.

that his desire for freedom from Spain was leading to bloodshed that might have been avoided.

He hurried to La Guaira where the British brig *Sapphire* was standing by to rescue him, but then made the disastrous decision to spend one last night on Venezuelan soil. Disillusioned by what seemed to them gross betrayal by their leader, the patriots seized him and handed him over to the Spaniards. Foremost among those who treated him so summarily was Bolívar, and this—to Miranda —was the unkindest cut of all.

The Spaniards instituted a reign of terror and persecuted especially the more important patriots. In the meantime Miranda languished in jail, first in La Guaira and later in Puerto Cabello, from where, in the most abject circumstances, he wrote his apologia:

'. . . Caracas having recognized the imminent danger to her safety, I was by general agreement of all her authorities appointed commander-in-chief of her troops and was invested with supreme authority. . . . I believe I fulfilled this exacting duty as honourably and zealously as I was able, exercising all my resources to bring things to a happy end. But though our forces scored continued successes at the port of Guayaca and the town of La Victoria, I saw the disastrous condition to which the capital and the port of La Guaira had been reduced through lack of food supplies and the sudden invasion at that time by slaves from the valleys and coastlands of the north. Egged on by promises of liberty from our enemies, they had already begun to commit the most dreadful murders at Guatire and elsewhere. I was driven to the conclusion that it was absolutely essential to . . . avert the terrible evils that fell upon those who perpetrated them. It was essential to restore peace and calm to these towns, to repair to some extent the disasters of the earthquake; and, in fact, to bring about a reconciliation between Americans and Europeans so that in future they might form one society, one family, and one interest. Caracas would thus give the rest of the continent an example of her political aims and would show that she preferred an honourable reconciliation to the hazards of a devastating civil war.'[1]

[1] O'Leary, D. F., vol. 13, p. 178.

Explaining his capitulation to the *Real Audiencia*, he said:

'I assure you that I never thought I had done my duty so satis-factorily as when . . . I ratified a treaty so beneficial and so favourable to the general good . . . a treaty which Great Britain would also welcome because it would help her ally; and one which would give Spaniards overseas a secure and permanent asylum, no matter how the struggle with France might end. . . .'

The statement is ambiguous. It suggests either that Miranda had given up all hope of success so long as Britain remained an ally of Spain, or that he actually believed his movement superfluous so long as Britain, with her tradition of liberalism, was prepared to support both Spain and her colonies against France. France had become the real enemy; and some form of *Habeas Corpus*, which could perhaps be instituted with Britain's backing, seemed preferable to a locally-based, will-o'-the-wisp freedom which it would be impossible to maintain.

News of Miranda's capitulation and arrest did not reach England until October, when a special appeal was made to Lord Castlereagh to protect Venezuela from the vengeance of Spain. Britain was still pressing for Spain to open Spanish America to free trade and was particularly interested in the fate of Miranda. On certain conditions, notably that force should not be used, Castlereagh was prepared to mediate between Spain and her colonies. But for the time being it seemed his hands were tied. In 1814 Spain agreed to treat Britain commercially on the same terms as any other power, but Britain had of course in return to promise strict neutrality in the independence struggle.

In 1813 Miranda had been sent in chains to Cádiz from where he continued to appeal to his English friends and even to plan his escape. Since Britain's role at this juncture marked the culmination of the long years of treating with Miranda and of apparent vacillation, it seems appropriate before we end the story of the 'Precursor' to examine in more detail the reasoning that moved Castlereagh to adopt policies of suasion both towards Spain and her colonies. On April 1, 1812, he had written to the commission appointed to mediate:

'The conviction of the British Government is, whatever may be the commercial prejudices of the Spanish Government and whatever may be their jealousy of us, that, if they cannot bring themselves to place the inhabitants of America upon a commercial footing of corresponding advantage with the inhabitants of European Spain, and that without loss of time, their separation from the parent state is inevitable and at hand. . . . In pressing this view of the situation upon the Spanish Government it may be desirable to suggest for their consideration the commercial system which we find it not only necessary but advantageous to apply to our East India possessions. . . . Where we have an Empire to govern, as in India, we govern it as far as related to commerce upon a national and not a colonial principle. Whether the trade to Great Britain be carried on as heretofore by an exclusive company, or as it is now proposed, it be thrown open . . . the commerce of India is open to all neutral nations, and as sovereigns we claim nothing but a commercial preference. If this system be, as it has been found to be, no less advantageous than just, even as applied to a country where our political power is exercised without control, how much more necessary is its application to provinces whose rights have been acknowledged to be equal to European Spain and which have been admitted to a share in the natural representation. . . . You may point out to the Spanish Government . . . that Great Britain has derived more real commercial advantage from North America since the separation than she did when the country was subjected to her dominion and part of her colonial system.'[1]

On the same day Castlereagh had written to Sir Henry Wellesley in Madrid:

'. . . It would be both unwise and unjust to presuppose that the subjects of the Crown of Spain in that quarter of the globe are deliberately prepared to throw off their allegiance. If such should unfortunately prove to be the case in any portion of the great Continent, if they should reject the liberal and benevolent offers of the Parent State, it will be time enough for Spain, when this fact is

[1] Quoted by Webster, C. K., *The Foreign Policy of Castlereagh 1812–1815*, p. 70.

established, to consider what ulterior measures are due to herself. The treaties which unite the two Crowns prescribe to Great Britain, as a fundamental duty, to preserve by all means in her power the integrity of the Spanish monarchy. Under the existing relations with Spain, the British Government could not but witness with the deepest regret and displeasure any indications of a purpose so unnatural and unbecoming in any of the Spanish Provinces. It will be their sincere desire to counteract such a disposition by every suitable means. But they cannot, for reasons in which Old Spain has a common interest with Great Britain be bound to make a refusal on their part the cause of war; because in doing so, the consequence might be, not to replace those Provinces in connexion and under the authority of Spain, but to drive them into a connexion with the common enemy. The Spanish Government must, therefore, at once desist from such an expectation if it wishes the Mediation to proceed. . . .'[1]

It was of course impossible for Britain to agree to Spain's request that, should mediation fail, war against the colonies should be declared. The other question upon which Britain has often been accused of insincerity is related to her eagerness to seize every opportunity to enter into trading partnership with the Spanish colonies. As Castlereagh candidly admitted in the same letter to Sir Henry Wellesley:

'. . . Our commercial habits as a nation, and our reluctance to break off intercourse with the Provinces in revolt, have created, not unnaturally, perhaps, doubts of our sincerity, and we may be considered as not unwilling to witness the separation of these Dependencies from the Mother Country. To this view of the question it may fairly be replied that, if the future system of Spain for South America is to be commercial exclusion as heretofore, such might secretly be our wish and our interest, however our conduct as a Government might be regulated by the engagements we have with Spain. But if Spain can be induced to adopt the only

[1] Viscount Castlereagh to Sir Henry Wellesley, April 1, 1812, Foreign Office document 72/127, quoted by Webster, *Britain and the Independence of Latin America*, vol. 2, p. 310.

system by which she can save those dominions to herself, what interest can we have in wishing to see them separated from her? Have we not on the contrary the strongest imaginable interest in their continued connexion? The means of carrying on the war in Europe against France depend on their fidelity. If separated, the wealth of America is withdrawn from the cause in Europe; if united and tranquillized, its treasures may again be poured forth in our support.'[1]

Castlereagh's answer to the accusations against Britain were subtle but they failed to shift Spain from her rigid attitude. His instructions to Sir Henry Wellesley show that, in spite of the apparent ruthlessness with which Britain pressed for material gains in Spanish America, her foreign policy was a mixture of shrewdness and idealism which turned out to be empirically correct. It was Britain's fundamental integrity that Miranda must have been aware of through all the years of vacillation, when he must often have felt like abandoning all hope of gaining the help he needed.

But Miranda was never to see the fruits of his endeavours or of British side by side with Creoles and Indians in the important battles that finally won his people's independence. Still in jail, in Cádiz, on July 14, 1816, the anniversary of the French revolution he had come to detest, he died miserably of typhus.

For many years his vanities, over-anxious cherishing of his financial interests, and (it was thought) over-reliance on foreign aid, had put him out of favour with his fellow Venezuelans. Long years of residence abroad had left him insensible to their shifts of mood. Only time could place his achievements in their true perspective. Only time could show that his final surrender and apparent weakness were dictated precisely by the principles that ruled the all but equally disastrous vacillations of San Martín; a desire to cause the minimum of bloodshed compatible with securing national freedom, and the refusal to impose upon a people any liberties they had not elected for themselves.

He did not live to see the great campaigns between the Penin-

[1] *Ibid.*, p. 312.

sular Spaniards and the Americans, nor how valiantly his compatriots proved the truth of his own statement: '*Cities* are not made of hard stones, strong beams, and skilfully built walls; but wherever there are *MEN* who are able to defend themselves— there are the fortifications, there the great Cities!'[1]

[1] *No las piedras duras, robustos leños, ni artificiosos muros, forman las* Ciudades; *mas donde quiera que hai* HOMBRES *que sepan defenderse por si mismos*—allí *están las fortificaciones,* allí *las ínclitas Ciudades!* Printed in facsimile in each volume of the *Archivo del General Miranda.*

3. Area showing San Martín's campaigns in the South

PART TWO

The Fighting Phase

4. Area showing Bolívar's campaigns

CHAPTER I

THE UNITED PROVINCES, CHILE AND PERU

1. The Early Stages of the Rebellion in Río de la Plata

Unrest was not confined to Venezuela. It had spread by now to Buenos Aires, capital of the viceroyalty of La Plata, and to Montevideo over a hundred miles away on the other side of the estuary. These were important centres that might be expected in time to influence the whole area from Cape Horn to Lake Titicaca.

The Viceroyalty had been created in 1776, two years before José de San Martín, the Argentine liberator, was born. As an administrative unit it was comparatively new, and it could scarcely be expected that an area so widely flung across the pampas, so broken by the Cordillera, could possess much natural cohesion. Nevertheless Buenos Aires was the focal centre for its heterogeneous population of peninsular Spaniards, sophisticated Creoles, Indians beyond the pale of civilization, and British merchants living largely off scarcely veiled contraband.

Suddenly, virtually as an act of piracy since the attack had no official sanction, the city was captured on June 27, 1806, by Sir Home Riggs Popham and Brigadier-General William Carr Beresford, who of their sixteen hundred men lost only one killed and twelve wounded. Caught unprepared at a theatrical entertainment, Rafael Sobremonte, the Spanish Viceroy, fled ingloriously to Córdoba, and Beresford proclaimed British sovereignty, named himself governor, and demanded the allegiance of the people of

99

Buenos Aires to George III, of whom probably few had heard. Beresford did, however, concede a point to local susceptibilities by promising that the Roman Catholic faith would be respected together with the sanctity of private property, justice, and free trade. He also borrowed a million pesos from the viceregal coffers and sent them to England with a request for reinforcements. In the meantime Popham was writing to Miranda in London and inviting him to make Buenos Aires the base for his attacks on the rest of Spanish America. He need not have given himself the trouble, for by August 12 he had been forced to surrender, he was himself interned, and most of his men were taken prisoner.

The attitude of the Whig government which by now had replaced Pitt's had done nothing to allay fears that Britain had come to colonize and not to free. The British being unable or unwilling to make their intentions clear, it was left to Santiago Liniers, a French officer serving in the Spanish navy, to invade Buenos Aires from Montevideo, to join forces with the Argentine Juan Martín de Pueyrredón (who was to play a large part in the independence movement), and to recapture the capital. The Creoles, aided by a Frenchman, succeeded where the Spanish Viceroy had failed, and this in itself was a boost to morale. In a *cabildo abierto* the Porteños, as the inhabitants of Buenos Aires are called, appointed Liniers their supreme military commander. So it came about that the Popham-Beresford combination actually precipitated the Argentine freedom movement, though in a manner the British had scarcely expected.

The British government refused all responsibility for Popham's act and reprimanded him. Popham retaliated that Britain had been planning such an act at least since 1775. His case was strengthened the following year when under a new cabinet Britain followed up the Popham-Beresford private enterprise with a fully authorized naval expedition under Sir Samuel Auchmuty, who in February of 1807 stormed Montevideo and prepared the way for a second but equally abortive assault upon Buenos Aires, this time under the command of Major-General John Whitelocke who held the city for only two days. Whitelocke's attempt to depose Liniers only gave the latter fresh glory. The Spanish Crown appointed him acting viceroy.

At the time of the first attack even Miranda, though he had worked so hard to secure British aid, was inclined to have nothing to do with it; and he called Sir Home Riggs Popham to task for entering the country aggressively and not as a co-ally, which would better have fitted his own and British government policy. The people of Buenos Aires showed themselves hostile to the British in their manifest role of conquerors when they might have been happy to receive them as liberators. Justifying his actions, Sir Home wrote from Río de la Plata on August 25:

'The object of this expedition was considered by the natives to apply principally to their independence; by the blacks, to their total liberation; *and if General Beresford had felt himself authorized, or justified, in confirming either of these propositions, no exertions whatever would have been made to dispossess him of his conquest.*'[1]

The distinction between 'natives' and 'blacks' is uninformed, and the use of the word 'conquest' unfortunate. Sir Home did nevertheless at least realize that the Creoles would have sided with the British had the former felt that in doing so they would have been taking the least step toward freedom. It is tempting to wonder what difference a more sympathetic attitude by the British at that moment would have made to the future course of Spanish American history. The instructions given to Lieut.-General John Whitelocke, who commanded the second and official expedition, were something of a corrective to Sir Home's imperialistic attitude but were nevertheless ambiguous:

'. . . you will proceed to execute the service entrusted to you, by the reduction of the province of Buenos Aires under the authority of His Majesty . . . [you are] not to introduce into the government any other change than that which must necessarily arise from the substitution of His Majesty's authority for that of the King of Spain.'[2]

[1] Burke, W., p. xix. (Italics as printed.) This paragraph was suppressed when the letter was officially made public.
[2] Quoted in the *Edinburgh Review*, January 1809, p. 297.

Whitelocke himself was well disposed to the Creoles whose point of view he seems to have understood:

'It has been repeatedly told to me . . . that had General Beresford and the Admiral, on their first arrival, and before any blood was shed or property confiscated, declared South America an independent state, we should now have her as an ally without her witnessing any of the horrors attendant on revolutions. Indeed it is, I believe, true that such proposals were made by the chiefs of the people to our commanders; but they, feeling themselves authorized to act only as conquerors, the reconquest of the place was planned by Pueyrredón, Liniers, and the leading men of the country. The result might have been expected and foreseen.'[1]

A chance had been lost; for, describing the enmity with which he was received, Sir Samuel Auchmuty (one of the few British officers not brought to task by his government for the whole affair) wrote to England from Montevideo on March 6, 1807:

'The seizure of the Viceroy by the inhabitants of Buenos Aires, an event certainly very important in itself, first gave me an insight into the views of many of the leading men, and convinced me that however inimical they were to us, *they were still more so to their present government. . . .'*[2]

After announcing that the royal court of the *Audiencia* had been abolished, the Spanish King's authority set aside, and the Spanish flag could no longer be hoisted, Auchmuty continued:

'These reports were circulated with avidity, and I soon found that they were acceptable to the principal part of the inhabitants. The persons who before appeared hostile and inveterate, now pressed me to advance a corps to Buenos Aires; *and assured me, if I would acknowledge their independence, and promise them the protection of the English government, the place would submit to me. . . .* The party now in power are mostly natives of Spain. . . . It has been their policy to inflame the minds of the lower order against the English, by every species of exaggeration and falsehood, and to lead them to such acts of atrocity as may preclude the possibility of any

[1] Burke, W., p. xxv.
[2] Quoted in the *Edinburgh Review*, January 1809, p. 301.

communication with us. The second party consists of natives of the country, with some Spaniards that are settled in it. . . . They aim at following the steps of the North Americans and erecting an independent state. If we would promise them independence, they would instantly revolt against the government, and join us with the great mass of the inhabitants. But though nothing less than independence will perfectly satisfy them, they would prefer our government, either to their present anarchy or to the Spanish yoke, provided we would promise not to give up the country to Spain at a peace. But until such a promise is made, we must expect to find them open or secret enemies.'

No assurance that independence would be respected was given, however. By an error of psychology and by lack of consideration for the wishes of a potentially friendly population, Spanish America was deterred from entering into some form of loose alliance with the British community of nations. When, toward the end of the century, Domingo Faustino Sarmiento analysed the events, he was more sympathetic to the British than to the Argentine man-in-the-street, about whom he had no illusions:

'Everyone asks today, and the heroes themselves were asking the same thing ten years after the event, how it came about that we fought against England which brought us free trade, a free Press, *Habeas Corpus*, and a civilization that embraced all branches of human culture, in order to uphold the most despicable of rules that existed at that time, that of Charles IV and Ferdinand VII, the Prince of Peace and the Inquisition.'[1]

Sarmiento deduced that the antagonism was due largely to two factors: ignorance, and Roman Catholic bigotry.

According to Sarmiento, Beresford used his leisure as a prisoner on parole in trying to make English institutions better loved. For the time being the only signs of British influence being accepted, however, were the publication of a bilingual newspaper, *The Southern Star*, and an abundance of British goods on sale. Popham had sent loads of silver back to England, which caused an influx

[1] Sarmiento, D. F., *Conflicto y Armonías de las Razas en América*, Vol. 37 of *Obras*, p. 50.

of British merchants into the La Plata region, all of them eager to profit from the new market but few of them conversant with it. The skates, stays, warming pans, and coffins that were being imported became a laughing stock. Nevertheless the very success of the occupation of Montevideo was giving the Creoles a glimpse of the kind of life they might establish for themselves if only they would have more self-confidence instead of relying on foreigners, whether Spanish or British. With the help of a protégé of Liniers, Francisco Xavier de Elío, Montevideo threw off dependence upon the more important Buenos Aires and the city flourished both on free trade and contraband.

Antagonism began to grow between Elío and Liniers and between the two cities, which to this day remain traditional rivals with little love lost between them. In 1808 the only thing that united them was a threatened invasion from Brazil, which since Napoleon's invasion of the motherland had become the seat of the Portuguese Court, ruled over by Dom João the Prince Regent and his wife Carlota Joaquina, daughter of Charles IV of Spain. Miranda's friend Saturnino Rodríguez Peña was proposing to establish a constitutional monarchy in La Plata under Princess Carlota Joaquina; and an Englishman, Nicholas Paroissien, who was in Brazil, was given secret letters on the matter addressed to Saturnino's more famous brother Nicolás in Argentina.

On September 21 the Montevideo town council repudiated viceregal authority and established a Junta in the name of Ferdinand VII, with Governor Elío at its head; but the arrival of a new Viceroy, Baltásar Hidalgo de Cisneros, to replace Liniers, caused so much rejoicing that the Junta had to be dissolved. From Montevideo Cisneros entered his capital of Buenos Aires on July 29. Montevideo had won a moral victory by imposing her own viceregal preference upon Buenos Aires. The supporters of Liniers were mortified, the more so because Montevideo—capital of what was known as the Banda Oriental—was a small garrison town with not even a gunboat to its name. It was also a centre of reaction and a Spanish base. The Porteños were rebellious now not against Spain but against their neighbour city, and on the first day of the year 1809 the Buenos Aires Creoles tried vainly to depose Cisneros and to form a Junta of their own.

All this would have been uninteresting local politics had it not been a dire warning that Spanish America would never unite as Bolívar hoped until her rulers ceased to think in terms of petty provincialism. They have scarcely been able to do so even yet; but now in the twentieth century it is the economists and not the soldiers or politicians who are pressing for unity. Even in 1809 there were those who understood that in a hard-headed world political and social freedoms depend upon a sound economy. In September of that year Mariano Moreno—who has been called the Argentine Adam Smith—put forward a proposition upon which the Alliance for Progress has so much later been based: that a prosperous people will be disinclined to revolt. As the British goods entering Buenos Aires were a source of income, Moreno thought they might well be legalized and that free trade should be given at least a two-year trial. These arguments received enthusiastic support from the very Creoles who had driven the British from Buenos Aires two years before; and even the Spaniards were inclined to agree that free trade would avert an economic crisis.

In order better to understand the general antagonism against the British, which continued in spite of the many advantages that were to be gained from trading with them and entering into political friendship, it may be interesting to digress in order to examine an emotional religious scene that took place in Córdoba, which was under the special protection of a brown Virgin something analogous to Mexico's patron saint, the Virgin of Guadalupe. Taking it for granted, as they so frequently do, that heaven is on the side of the Establishment, the rich hoped that Córdoba's Virgin could be enlisted to prop up their private interests. To do this it was necessary to devise some type of propaganda showing that those who were attempting to undermine viceregal power were in effect withholding the protection of this bountiful and beatific lady from the poor. Cunningly Liniers placed in her hands the Viceroy's mace which his enemies were threatening to wrest from him. A similar scene occurred later when General Manuel

Belgrano, head of the patriot armies, was to offer his own mace of office to the Virgin of Mercy in Tucumán. Both men understood the power not merely of the Roman Catholic Church, but of the blend that had by now taken place between Rome and the beliefs of ancient America. It was the kind of Spanish American mystery which the British could scarcely be expected to fathom.

It was as well for the Creoles that they did not at this juncture join up with the British, who were again at peace with Spain in 1809, a year which saw open manifestations of rebellion all over South America. On May 25 the *Audiencia* of Chuquisaca protested loyalty to Ferdinand and refused to recognize either the loyalist Creole General José Manuel Goyeneche as the agent of the Junta of Seville, or the Junta itself as representing Ferdinand. In July the local governor and the Bishop of La Paz were overthrown and a Junta was established in that city under a *mestizo*, Pedro Domingo Murillo. The Chuquisaca and La Paz revolutions were stifled, the former by Goyeneche and the latter by General Vicente Nieto, and Murillo was executed.

Chuquisaca was a university town where many Argentine Creoles, including Mariano Moreno, had been educated; and the alumni were filled with anger at the brutal handling of the rebels, particularly since locally-born conspirators were treated far worse than Spaniards. In 1809 Saturnino Rodríguez Peña and the English Paroissien were thrown into jail for their involvement in the dubious plot to establish Princess Carlota Joaquina on the throne; and Juan José Castelli, a lawyer friend of Rodríguez Peña and also a graduate of Chuquisaca, used their trial as a platform for arguing the Creole cause. Castelli called in question the legitimacy of the Junta of Seville and argued that it had much less right than the people of America to represent Ferdinand, who was captive to the French and whose government did not exist. According to Castelli, therefore, he was acting legally when on May 24, 1810, he demanded an open meeting of the chief citizens of Buenos Aires; for he could be considered the rightful spokesman of the Spanish Crown. This argument ignored the fact that Ferdinand had bestowed powers of regence upon the Junta, but reluctantly the Viceroy was forced to agree to it. He was appointed president of a Junta of four, of which Castelli was also a member; but this compromise between Spain and the Creoles did not fit the prevailing mood, and the following day a new Junta replaced it which, although swearing loyalty to Ferdinand, in effect declared Argentine independence. Rodríguez Peña and Paroissien were released from jail knowing that their detention had served a useful purpose.

The leaders of the Creole junta included the lawyer Castelli; Manuel Belgrano, who was more suited by nature to bureaucracy than to soldiering though San Martín esteemed him highly; Bernardino Rivadavia who was to have a distinguished diplomatic career and to become a friend of Jeremy Bentham; and the pompous Cornelio Saavedra who was well to the right of his colleagues. The leader was Mariano Moreno who was responsible for easing trade restrictions, reshaping the army, and editing *La Gaceta de Buenos Aires*. However sincere the others may have been in professing loyalty to Ferdinand, Moreno acted from the beginning tongue-in-cheek, realizing that lip service at this stage would be the best means of securing independence in the long run. He was, however, too radical for most, and little by little opposition to him gained ground. Saavedra infiltrated the Junta with reactionary provincials; and there began a struggle between the *unitarios* who wanted centralized power, and the federalists who preferred a form of government such as had been adopted in the U.S.A. After seven months in office Moreno was forced to resign.

On July 24, 1810, little Asunción, capital of the unimportant province of Paraguay, decided to recognize Ferdinand and to maintain good relations with the Buenos Aires Junta; but relations with the latter soon deteriorated to such an extent that a military expedition under the command of Belgrano was organized to put the rebels in their place. Asunción, with its Guaraní Indian tradition of fierce fighting, emerged victorious and Paraguay fell into the hands of a dictator, Dr. José Gaspar Rodríguez de Francia, who secured his country's independence on October 12,

1811, and who encouraged the development of industry and agriculture but who also suppressed many freedoms and maintained Paraguay in a state of isolation from its neighbours. Francia can be taken as a type of South American dictator who inspired both disgust and admiration even in objective onlookers. A certain Captain Richard F. Burton, who travelled in Paraguay at the time, saw him as a bulwark of order against anarchy. He was a rigorously disciplined soldier who drilled his own army, hated the Church, and established what Burton calls a 'stratocracy' in which the military took precedence above the civil authorities. He abolished the Inquisition, did away with tithes, converted monasteries into barracks, and seized the gold and silver plate, doubloons and other property which belonged to the religious houses. For all that, Burton considered him 'high-minded and self-reliant, disinterested and far-seeing, sombre, austere and ascetic', although he would become 'intolerably fierce when the east wind blew'. 'Evidently,' added Burton inconsequentially, 'the Republic of the Dictator was a reproduction, in somewhat sterner mould, of the Jesuit Reduction System, and it throve because the popular mind was prepared for it.' But it throve also at the cost of fear, for as time went on Francia was compelled for his own safety to order everyone off the streets when his cortège passed by. He survived, but with an iron hand, and died in 1840.[1]

It was through the friendliness of Francia that a British merchant, John Parish Robertson, began to deal in Paraguayan tea, sugar, tobacco, and cloth. Francia entrusted specimens of these products to him with a view to interesting British buyers, but suddenly fell out with Robertson who, luckily for his future, was expelled from the country. Being related to the powerful House of Baring, he succeeded in establishing one of the most lucrative of British mercantile businesses in an area reaching from Buenos Aires to Santiago and Lima, where he eventually became a director of the Pasco-Peruvian Mining Company. But he fell upon bad times, and an idealistic colonization scheme by which he had hoped to settle Scottish immigrants (skilled in agriculture and of

---

[1] Burton, R. F., pp. 45 *et seq.*

moral and religious integrity) proved too costly. He was forced into liquidation and returned to England in 1829.[1] The story of Robertson and his brother William who joined him in his enterprises is illustrative of the enthusiasm of the British to enter untried markets, of the immense profits that were within reach of bold spirits, but also of the risks that foreign capital ran in a revolutionary area with politics and society unstable.

Throughout Francia's dictatorship, with Paraguay actively hostile to the Buenos Aires liberals, there was no possibility of extending the revolution toward the north-east into the Banda Oriental, and the only line of advance seemed to be in the direction of Upper Peru. This situation continued even after 1812, when, with the British Minister acting as mediator, the Portuguese were persuaded to retire to the borders of their legitimate domain.

In July 1810 New Granada joined the rebel movement and formed the by now well-known type of pro-Ferdinand Junta with the Viceroy at its head. Cartagena refused to accept the authority of the capital, the Viceroy was deposed, and anarchy ensued.

In August Argentina's liberating army, which had marched west to Córdoba, forced Liniers to flee; and both he and the Governor were shot under orders from the Junta and in the presence of Castelli who was showing a bloodthirsty streak. By the end of the year Francisco Xavier Elío was Viceroy of La Plata, and the Junta had lost the valuable leadership of Moreno. He was appointed Minister Plenipotentiary in London but died on the voyage in 1811.

On November 7 the liberating army under General Antonio González Balcarce gained its first great victory at Suipacha, and this opened the way to Upper Peru. Throughout all the Spanish territories east of the Cordillera the battle had now been joined in earnest, and the patriots were finding stronger resistance and less enthusiasm for their cause than they had hoped. In June 1811 Goyeneche surprised and defeated Castelli at Hauquí on the Río Desaguadero which formed part of the boundary between La

[1] See Humphreys, R. A., *British Merchants and South American Independence*, in Proceedings of the British Academy, vol. 51, 1965, p. 151.

Plata and Peru; and in August the patriots were routed at Sipe-Sipe. In spite of the setbacks, Martín de Pueyrredón was able to march upon the important mining centre of Potosí where he seized the public treasure and then retired to Jujuy and thence to Tucumán. The defeats caused consternation in Buenos Aires. A conservative triumvirate was set up, and Castelli was arrested and tried, and died the following year, poor and in disgrace.

2. JOSÉ DE SAN MARTÍN

The first generation of Argentine revolutionaries had met only frustration, and many had been liquidated. In 1812, however, José de San Martín—who had been in Europe since a child and had received a sound military training there—returned to his native land and almost at once became a central figure in the freedom movement.

He was born in 1778 in Yapeyu, a Jesuit village on the northern frontier of Argentina. His father was a Spanish officer of a serious and scientific turn of mind, and the boy was sent to a military academy in Spain. Service in infantry and cavalry regiments and in the navy—during which time he had occasion to fight the British —gave him all-round experience of war; and at the age of 33 he was already a Lieutenant-Colonel. When Ferdinand fell there was a popular outbreak in Madrid and people flocked to the palace to demand an immediate attack on the French squadron lying in Cádiz bay. In the confusion some shots were fired. San Martín, who happened to be the officer of the guard, shepherded his troops into a house where a cannon shot blew in the door. The Captain-General of Andalucia fled across the roofs but was caught and butchered. San Martín could never blot this scene from his memory and it gave him a hatred of unnecessary killing even in war. Even more, he had a horror of mob emotion and of governments that encouraged them.

After this the young officer resigned his commission, and the year 1811 found him united with the rebel conspirators in London.

Next year in the frigate *George Canning* he sailed for Buenos Aires together with Carlos María de Alvear and Matías Zapiola, both of whom became members of the first group of cavalry officers trained by San Martín for the independence struggle.

It was shortly after he had returned to his native land that he founded the famous regiment of mounted grenadiers which was to fight in most of the battles of the Army of Liberation. He demanded 'only lions in the regiment', and imposed such a standard upon it that in any country it would have been outstanding for its corporate spirit. In order to train his men he founded a military school whose cadets he chose himself according to rigorous criteria. All of them were tall and were drilled in duty, courage, and tactics. Each had a war name to which he answered, and to it alone. Officers were encouraged to write on a blank sheet of paper an account of any misconduct they had observed among their fellows. Serious accusations were discussed in the absence of the person concerned, and it was decided by general vote whether he should remain with the regiment or not. If he were exonerated, a full and public apology was made. Transgressions worthy of punishment ranged from striking a woman even if insulted by her, to evasion of danger and serious personal misconduct.

San Martín's own private life was blameless. He married happily, his wife being a woman of high family, Doña María de los Remedios Escalada. He was sober in dress and habits and detested theatrical gestures and social life although he was capable of great courtesy and even of conviviality if occasion required. He was above medium height, thick-set, with skin darkened by exposure to the sun and with thick black hair worn short. His large black eyes were fringed by long lashes, and his eyebrows nettled when he frowned. His nose was long and aquiline, his small lips firm and red. A portrait of him in old age shows him soberly but neatly dressed, slightly gaunt beneath the well-formed cheekbones, with the clear, broad forehead of a thinker, the direct gaze of integrity, and the firm courage of a soldier. He read much in French, understood English, and wrote in a characteristic laconic style.

As time wore on he suffered from ill health but forced upon himself a stoical disregard for pain and a devotion to duty, in spite of which he could be tolerant and kind to others in their afflictions. As his career unfolded and he acquired or assumed supreme powers there were English observers such as Maria Graham and a certain Farquhar Mathison who—taking perhaps a superficial view, for they were mere tourists upon the scene—accused him of arbitrary repressions, cruelties, vanity, and excessive pride. Maria Graham especially was critical, but she was a great admirer—not to say a hero-worshipper—of Lord Cochrane who was openly at enmity with San Martín at the time. In contrast to the views of these visitors, Chile's historian Benjamín Vicuña Mackenna (and Chileans were far from being prejudiced in his favour, his temperament being too austere for this more open nation) called him 'the greatest of Creoles of the New World'.

San Martín had returned to Buenos Aires at precisely the right moment to save the independence movement from the burden of its early failures. He immediately became a member of the local branch of Miranda's *Logia Lautaro* which was pledged to bring 'independence and happiness' to Spanish America and which was to have a profound influence on the early years of Argentine and Chilean independence. Membership was open only to Americans by birth. By the rules of its constitution, if any member were elected to the supreme rulership of the State he could take no important step nor make appointments to high office without consultation. All members were pledged to help one another and, at the risk of their lives, to uphold the rules of the Lodge and to keep it informed of anything that might influence public opinion or affect public security. To reveal the secret of the Lodge's existence 'by word or by sign' was punishable by death, so it can never be known how far it influenced San Martín's policies. Once when General Miller questioned him on this point he replied that these were entirely private matters. While admitting that Freemasonry had great influence upon the revolution both in Buenos Aires and also in Peru, where lodges had multiplied in an extraordinary way, he made it clear that it would be a gross failure on his part to abide by sacred pledges if he were to enter into details as to the kind of influence they exerted.[1]

These Masonic lodges were the binding force between Creoles in all parts of Spanish America, and through them they were able to achieve remarkable cohesion in spite of local jealousies and the extreme difficulties of communication. The lodges must have played a vital part in ensuring that the principles which were at stake were not lost sight of. They explain the resilience of the movement, its ability to recover after the most shattering blows and to snatch victory out of defeats as apparently irrevocable, in their way, as any Dunkirk.

In July 1812 a vast conspiracy of European Spaniards, aided by the garrison in Montevideo and the Spanish squadron in the roadstead, was to have broken out; but the Triumvirate acted quickly and punished the conspirators. In the north Belgrano—who had been in retreat—boldly disobeyed orders, turned on an army double the size of his own, and on September 24 completely routed it near Tucumán.

The Triumvirate, however, soon lost popular support, and the victory at Tucumán precipitated a revolt against it which resulted in a genuinely national government headed by Nicolás Rodríguez Peña and others. Free elections were called and the famous 'Assembly of 1813' was elected. It abolished the Inquisition, tithes, forced labour, judicial torture, royal symbols, and the nobility and initiated a movement against slavery; but it could come to no agreement about a constitution though it drew up a blueprint for one. Nor would it accede to the demands of the Uruguayan guerrilla leader, José Gervasio Artigas, for a formal declaration of independence and the acceptance of deputies from rural areas of the Banda Oriental.

Militarily the Assembly decided upon a two-pronged campaign. To begin with, Montevideo must be seized at all costs. The royalists were sacking towns along the west bank of the Paraná; and in order to draw the patriot army off from attacking Monte-

[1] Letter from San Martín to General William Miller, Brussels, April 19, 1827, quoted in Gutiérrez, J. M., p. 241.

video itself, a flotilla was concentrated below the Paraná delta and would have to be dealt with. San Martín took part in this campaign and, disguised in a *sombrero* and *poncho*, kept watch on the Spanish ships. Taking tactical advantage of a bluff commanding the river he was able to rout the enemy and ensure that communications were maintained with Entre Ríos.

But even more important than Montevideo, the Assembly felt it essential that Belgrano should continue his campaign with the object of driving the royalists from Salta where they were now resting, heavily reinforced. In those early days there seemed only one possible route by which to drive the royalists from the continent, and that was northward along the path traditionally taken by the traders whose mule trains had run a shuttle service between Lima and Buenos Aires, taking in as they went the mining districts of Upper Peru. Any coastal campaign on the Atlantic north of Montevideo was precluded by virtue of Portuguese possession of the area; and to the west the main spine of the Cordillera presented what had always appeared an impenetrable wall between the Argentine pampas and the Pacific. The central valley of Chile, enclosed by two parallel Andean ranges which unite further north but separate again where the valley of Popayán formed the extreme south of New Granada, was isolated and would have to solve its own problems as best it might. In any case there was no navy.

At the outbreak of the revolution New Granada had 1,400,000 inhabitants, Venezuela 900,000, and the *Audiencia* of Quito 600,000. Of these, 1,234,000 were Europeans or Creoles, 913,000 were pure Indians, 615,000 *mestizos*, and 138,000 Negroes. Peru had a population of about a million and a half, with another half-million in Upper Peru. Of these the Indians formed about half, *mestizos* a fifth, Negroes about a tenth; so Europeans and Creoles were in the minority. These lived mainly in the coastal cities or in fertile mountain valleys, the Indians being confined to the hills. *Mestizos* and Negroes provided city labour, and farms were cultivated by Negro slaves. The military Spaniards and Creoles ruled this broken terrain with an iron hand, and the area was one of the most reactionary in Spanish America. Clearly, therefore, it would be far more difficult to free the Peruvian area than La Plata, especially because in the high Peruvian Andes the Inca tradition had mingled with the Spanish to reinforce all that was most conservative in both traditions. The rich silver-mining areas about Potosí were particularly firmly rooted in their old ways, for here even the lesser clergy were hand-in-glove with vested interests; whereas in Mexico—the other centre of a once ancient culture—village curates were strongly liberal and had much influence on their parishioners. (It was awareness of Peru's innate conservatism that led San Martín later to hesitate before entering Lima, lest he impose upon the land a freedom for which it had no inclination.)

Belgrano, therefore, had not only a difficult, broken terrain in which to campaign; he had also as he went along to inculcate into the inhabitants a taste for the liberty to which he and his fellow-radicals in the La Plata area were dedicated and which they were convinced was the only way out from colonial stagnation—whether the ordinary people knew it or not.

The year 1813 began well for him. He had soon defeated the royalists at Salta and had freed 3,000 prisoners taken in combat on condition that they never again bore arms against the patriots. But the Spaniards broke their word, and in October Belgrano was defeated at Vilcapugio. This disaster was followed by a worse one when Joaquín de la Pezuela almost totally annihilated the patriot forces in November at Ayohuma. The inhabitants were still far from convinced that the royalists were their enemies, and Pezuela could still draw freely on local manpower.

His confidence broken, Belgrano asked to be relieved, and early in 1814 San Martín agreed to take command of the Army of the North. Nevertheless he wrote to his government imploring it not to dispense with the services of so fine a general, saying that he knew of no other officer as good as Belgrano, and protesting that he himself had no knowledge of the people, customs, and topography of the battle area. Professional jealousy seems to have been unknown to San Martín and he was entirely sincere in believing that only his predecessor could teach him what was necessary if fighting were to continue in Upper Peru.

The Army of the North now numbered scarcely 2,000 men, mostly raw, ill-clad recruits, and desertions were frequent; whereas the royalists under Pezuela had levied at least 2,000 men in the highlands and had about 4,000 regulars plus a vanguard of 2,000 more. San Martín's first act was to insist upon regular payment for his men, whose morale was disintegrating in a strange land far from home. The highland royalist troops had the advantage of being accustomed to mountain warfare; but the gain this brought began at last to be vitiated by their cruelties, which slowly but inevitably alienated the sympathies of the local people. Heads of rebels were exposed on the highways, properties were confiscated, towns sacked, and prisoners of war sold as slaves to the owners of vineyards and plantations. Under this treatment the Indians fought back with such ferocity that they would surely have triumphed if they had had more effective weapons than clubs and slings. The peasants often helped the rebels by concealing their movements.

San Martín entrenched himself defensively at Tucumán, where with the aid of his devoted grenadiers he established a military school. His irregulars, known as the '*Gauchos* of Salta', harried the royalists who could make no inroads into the patriot defences; but there could be no illusions about the long-term prospects. In spite of royalist blunders the way north through Upper Peru was still blocked, and a plan began to form in the commander-in-chief's mind for an invasion across the Andes into Chile and thence by sea to Peru.

He communicated this apparently lunatic idea with the utmost secrecy to his closest confidant, Nicolás Rodríguez Peña. Then, pleading ill health, he left his command and retired to Mendoza in the shadow of the Andes, where he had leisure to elaborate his plans. In September 1814 he was appointed governor of the province of Cuyo whose chief towns—Mendoza, San Juan, and San Luis—had been populated both from Chile and Argentina and formed a kind of junction between the two countries. Here, in a sparsely inhabited province of scarcely 40,000 people, thrifty, industrious, and amenable to discipline, San Martín found just the kind of spirit he was looking for; and here began the slow, methodical build-up toward one of the most remarkable military exploits in history. But before that story can be told the situation on both sides of the Andes must be known.

While San Martín was plotting quietly in Mendoza the Argentine government had equipped a small naval force which, under an Irishman called William Brown, almost destroyed the Spanish squadron at Montevideo and the city was obliged soon afterwards to surrender to the Argentines under Carlos María de Alvear, whose ambitions and those of his family were causing San Martín much distress. In February 1815 the city came under the rule of the tough, forthright, controversial Artigas who hated Alvear and waged constant war upon him. Artigas represented the more plebeian type of South American liberator. He has been regarded on the one hand as a bandit, the type of half sincere, half ruthless reformer who led in direct line to men like Pancho Villa in Mexico; and on the other as a man of complete integrity. He was certainly effective, and even General Miller, who called him a 'public criminal', admitted that he applied the whole powers of his mind and body to the task of exterminating the numerous bands of vagabonds, robbers, and smugglers by whom the country was overrun; so that in a short time the authority of the government was respected and private property was safer than it had ever been in ostensibly more peaceful periods.[1]

The extremely complex situation in Argentina was made more so by the missions of Belgrano, Rivadavia, Manuel García, and Manuel de Sarratea to Europe to obtain recognition for the independence of the United Provinces and to ask for help in founding a constitutional monarchy. In Rome Sarratea tried to persuade the exiled Charles IV to crown the infante Francisco de Paula Antonio of Bourbon (brother of Ferdinand VII); but the

[1] Miller, J., vol. 1, p. 55. There is no space here to examine the character of Artigas as it deserves, but John Street's *Artigas and the Emancipation of Uruguay* provides a complete study of this fascinating leader.

deposed Emperor, fearing the wrath of the Spanish Government, refused. Alvear thought there would be anarchy if the United Provinces attempted self-government; and he wrote to the British Foreign Minister hinting at a better solution. These provinces, he said, 'wished to belong to Great Britain, to receive her laws, to obey her government, and to live under her powerful influence. They will abandon themselves unconditionally to the generosity and good faith of the English people. . . .'[1] In April 1815 Alvear was deposed, and no more was heard of the United Provinces coming under British protection. The new government was more favourable to Artigas, but Alvear's sentiments seem to demonstrate that the odium engendered by the invasion of Buenos Aires had evaporated and British institutions were again respected.

The Congress of Tucumán, which sat during 1816 in Tucumán itself and for the next three years in Buenos Aires, began by naming Juan Martín de Pueyrredón Supreme Director of the United Provinces and was guided throughout its deliberations by this loyal friend of San Martín and Belgrano—which put the liberating armies in a strong position politically. The Congress also had the side effect of uniting the army and the state owners—the two most powerful sectors of the community. On July 9, 1816, after an invocation to 'the Eternal ruler of the Universe', it drew up a Declaration of Independence. The document embodied most of the contradictions inherent in the liberation wars. Whatever achievements it could claim were more the work of its two moving spirits, Belgrano and Pueyrredón, than of any formulation it was able to achieve or any legal effectiveness it possessed; for at that time Argentina was too unsettled to apply any of its precepts. These took the form of didactic and moral aphorisms rather than clear laws, and the sentiments expressed are typically Spanish American: impeccable, but so sweeping as to make practical deductions impossible. Ignorance 'is the cause of that immorality which stifles all virtues and produces all the crimes that afflict society'. (Hence an over-emphasis on booklearning by rote.) 'Because of man's very nature . . . no nation can for long

---

[1] Quoted by Levene, Ricardo, vol. 2, p. 111.

be either free or happy unless it legislates for itself.'[1] (Foreigners, therefore, are automatically suspect until they prove by some unequivocally altruistic act that their intentions are friendly.)

In Mitre's eyes Tucumán was a product of the weariness of the Argentine people, a Congress elected in the midst of public indifference; federal in composition but centralist by force of circumstance; revolutionary in origin and reactionary in ideas; incapable of dictating a single positive law in the whole course of its sessions; proclaiming a monarchy while founding the Argentine republic. For all that, he had to admit, it saved the revolution at a critical moment and thus ensured the country's independence on a politico-legal level.

Militarily, in Upper Peru since San Martín's departure, things had been going badly. On November 29, 1815, the patriots under General Rondeau were defeated by Pezuela at Sipe-Sipe, for which victory he was created Marquis of Viluna. In the same year a royalist expedition under Pablo Morillo was triumphant in Colombia, and Spaniards on both sides of the Atlantic sang a *Te Deum*. But San Martín, who had temporarily resigned the governorship of Cuyo because of ill health but had been forced by popular demand to return to his post, remained undaunted. He invited his officers to a banquet and proposed a toast 'to the first shot fired beyond the Andes against Chile's oppressors'. This remark committed him to his strategy of attacking over the Cordillera and along the Pacific instead of through Upper Peru. From now on it was to be Argentine-Chilean determination pitted against the granite wall of the Cordillera. San Martín was gambling his reputation and—more important—the very existence of the two republics. There could be no half-measures. But he had faith. When it was suggested to him that to consolidate independence was not an easy matter like 'blowing and making bottles', he replied that independence seemed to him a thousand times easier than that one single American should make one single bottle.[2]

---

[1] *Constitución de las Provincias Unidas en Sud-América. Sancionada y Mandada Publicar por el Soberano Congreso General Constituyente en 22 de Abril de 1817*. Imprenta de la Independencia, Buenos Aires.

[2] Barcía Trelles, A., vol. 1, p. 416.

He knew the idealistic nature of his countrymen and he knew that they were brave. To make them industrious was another matter.

3. CHILE

San Martín's plans were, of course, dependent upon affairs west of the Andes. 'Never', said Mitre, 'were two peoples more analogous and less alike than those of Chile and the United Provinces.' Geopoliticians might draw a moral from the fact that one was shut in between mountains and sea, the other spread over vast plains. Chile possessed a landed aristocracy ruling over the *mestizos* in grandeur; but whereas the other two Spanish American feudally-structured societies, Mexico and Peru, were based on a European pattern, those of Chile and Argentina were built loosely by the colonists themselves and were therefore infused from the outset with a democratic spirit. Throughout their history it has been this blending of cavalier proudness and plebeian ease, together with the toughness necessary to a people living precipitously between mountain and sea, that has given Chileans their special charm.

Again unlike the situation in Mexico and Peru, the indigenous peoples of the southern part of the continent had had no high civilizations of their own and were more easily assimilated culturally. Because they had not been demoralized by the kind of superstitious belief in gods who would return from over the sea (which was Moctezuma's undoing), they were also more effective fighters.

In Chile the first uprising against the Peninsulars had taken place on June 22, 1810, when the Captain-General called a meeting to demand obedience to the French Regency in Spain. The government was dismissed and a new Captain-General appointed on condition that he remain loyal to Ferdinand. But a desire for complete independence had been roused; and, as Simon Collier says in his microscopic analysis of this period, 'it soon became abundantly clear that Creole agitation for a national government would continue.'[1] On September 18 the office of Captain-General was abolished and a Junta was appointed which acknowledged the rights of Ferdinand but resisted all foreign dominion over Chile. The immensely rich Brigadier-General Mateo de Toro Zambrano, Conde de la Conquista and ex-Captain-General, was named President with a casting vote. Other members of the Junta included the Marquis de la Plata, richer if anything than Zambrano; Juan Martínez de Rozas, a strong federalist and probably the most able of the early Chilean nationalists, who was later banished by the Carreras to Mendoza; and Ignacio Carrera whose son José Miguel was to play one of the leading if malevolent roles in subsequent events.

The bloodlessness of this first Chilean uprising is in marked contrast to the civil strife that was to follow when the Carrera family opposed both Rozas and O'Higgins. It contrasts also with the uprisings in other areas, including Peru, Argentina, and Mexico, in the unanimity of opinion that pervaded all classes. As usual the sovereignty of Ferdinand was acknowledged by the Junta and communications with the Viceroy in Lima were maintained. Perhaps because there were fewer peninsular Spaniards in Chile than elsewhere, no Spaniard was removed from office; and there was little to disturb the peace except, in its rambunctious journalistic way, *La Aurora de Chile*, a political newspaper whose first appearance aroused such enthusiasm that, according to a contemporary, men ran through the streets with the paper in their hands, stopped any friend they happened to meet, read and reread its contents and congratulated themselves on their good fortune, convinced that the ignorance and blindness in which they had lived would vanish and be followed by an age of enlightenment and culture that would transform Chile into a country of wise men. There was much of Wordsworth's mood in the Andean countries just then. 'Bliss was it in that dawn to be alive.' Not in Utopia, nor in any secret island, but in the very world where *La Aurora* was printed, they would find happiness and wisdom. Chile was not

[1] Collier, Simon, p. 48.

without dissenters, however. For example, on April 1, 1811, a Spanish Colonel named Tomás Figueroa tried to overthrow the new government, and fifty-six lives were lost before the ringleader was summarily shot.

In July the first Chilean congress assembled and became the first legislative body in Spanish America to abolish slavery. Children born of slaves were declared free and all slaves brought into the country were to be released from bondage after a specified period. Congress also established freedom of the Press and proclaimed almost unrestricted trade. The previously hereditary or purchasable office of *Regidor* was henceforth to be by election, the clergy were to be paid by the treasury and could not take fees from parishioners, and an arsenal and artillery school were established. It was a promising beginning but there are conflicting opinions as to whether the early establishment of a parliamentary system helped or hindered Chile. Paradoxically, Mitre believed it was the natural outcome of the feudal character of Chilean society. 'In the parliamentary drama,' he said, 'the people played the part of the Greek chorus, which repeated the words of the chief actor.'[1] Parliament, in other words, was no more than a stage prop. Vicuña Mackenna thought it premature and said that 'the dictatorship of a Caesar rather than a Cicero' would have been preferable for a people still constitutionally uneducated. Others thought on the contrary that in due time it brought Chile the tranquillity that was noticeably lacking in other parts of South America; but it certainly took a long time to come! Demetrio Lastarria felt that the establishment of the doctrine of popular sovereignty even in a restricted form was the only way to weaken colonial systems and to promote the dignity of man. He was advocating a hard way, as many newer countries than Chile had discovered.

At the time the relatively quiet change from colonialism to democracy was upset by the ambition of the Carreras, of whom José Miguel was the leader. He was a dashing young officer of quick intelligence and great ambition, but he was undisciplined and unscrupulous. With the active support of his brothers Luis

[1] Pilling, W., p. 89.

and Juan José, of his beautiful, scheming sister Xaviera, and above all of the American Joel Poinsett who boasted that he had been able to induce the autocratically-minded young officer to espouse republican ideas, he had soon made himself head of the patriot armies. Far too proud to remain for long under the thumb of Congress, he staged a coup, established a new Junta, and declared himself President. He proceeded to give key posts to his family, and this nepotism so outraged the upright Martínez Rozas that he marched against José Miguel but managed to persuade him, without bloodshed, to return to the seat of government in a mood that was at least temporarily chastened. Poinsett, who had been suspected of playing a double game and of encouraging royalist resistance in the south (though this is unproved), gave Carrera a suggestion for a draft constitution based on that of the U.S.A.; but this was unsuited to the new country and José Miguel compromised with a rather feeble document that did the patriot cause little good.

Meanwhile the Viceroy of Peru, José Fernando Abascal, ordered his admiral, Antonio Pareja, who was a competent sailor and had distinguished himself at St. Vincent and Trafalgar and who at this time was commanding the fort of Chiloé, to restore royal government at the first opportunity. Pareja found support from Chilean royalists in Concepción and Valdivia, but in spite of this he was unable to gain ground. The patriots decided to make the deep and rapid Río Maule the line of defence, but José Miguel's military acumen proved less than his courage and it was Bernardo O'Higgins who finally drove the enemy south to Chillán and freed the whole country between the Maule and the Itata.

This was the first decisive success of the son of an ex-Captain-General of Chile, an Irish soldier of fortune, Ambrosio O'Higgins, Marquis of Osorno, who had himself maintained order against the still unconquered Araucanian Indians and who had built roads and made other improvements that opened up wild areas of the country. With the rise of Bernardo O'Higgins, who now took command of the army, the Carrera brothers' star was temporarily eclipsed. The Carreras paid lip service to the new commander but were making things so difficult for him behind the scenes that there was danger of civil war. A royalist attack under General Gavino Gaínza, who landed at Arauco on January 31, 1814, drew the patriots together once more; but José Miguel and Luis Carrera were captured by the royalists at Penco as they were on their way to Santiago. The situation was critical. O'Higgins was in Concepción with only 2,000 men and without money, arms, uniforms, or horses. Gaínza was fast advancing upon another Irishman, Juan Mackenna, who was north of the Itata with a force of 1,500; and a third small section of the patriot army, under Manuel Blanco Encalada, was beyond the Itata on the road to Santiago. Fortunately for the patriots, Gaínza could not make up his mind on strategy, crossed and re-crossed the Itata, and finally blundered upon a strong-point of Mackenna's and was defeated. O'Higgins then joined Mackenna and their combined forces marched north toward Santiago. Against instructions from O'Higgins, Blanco Encalada advanced on Talca, but he met royalist resistance and had to retreat to the plains of Cancha Rayada where on March 28 he was routed. O'Higgins was able to repair the damage by gaining control of the Maule and placing himself directly between Gaínza and Santiago.

There was now something of a stalemate and it became possible in May of 1814 to negotiate an armistice under a guarantee from a British naval captain. Under the resulting Treaty of Lircay Chile was to acknowledge the sovereignty of Ferdinand and the royalist troops were to retire to Chiloé, Valdivia, and Peru. General Gaínza promised to hand over the Carreras for trial and to evacuate his own army from Chile; but he had never any real intention of abiding by these conditions. He allowed the Carreras to escape from prison, and O'Higgins rashly let them reach Santiago where on July 23 José Miguel once more seized power and established a new Junta.

Even worse news for O'Higgins was that the Viceroy of Peru, repudiating the Lircay treaty, sent Colonel Mariano Osorio to replace Gaínza and finish off the war. Frustrated by quarrels with José Miguel who was insisting upon taking command of the armies, O'Higgins marched to Rancagua where Juan José Carrera was to have joined him. But the latter never arrived. On October 1 he found himself surrounded by royalists and fighting from house to house through the streets of the town. Even so he refused to surrender. Forcing his way through the defences he succeeded in reaching the capital where he hoped that he and José Miguel could put up an adequate defence. But panic seized the government. Carrera ordered the powder magazines to be demolished. All public papers and acts of the new government were burned, and José Miguel retreated to Mendoza. Osorio entered Santiago on October 5, re-established the *Real Audiencia*, appointed himself Captain-General, and exiled many of the leading patriots. Six hundred troops followed Carrera across the Andes together with about 2,000 private citizens many of whom died of cold and hunger crossing the mountains. San Martín disapproved of the swashbuckling José Miguel and packed him off to Buenos Aires. Here he and his brother Luis made more trouble, Luis being responsible for the death of the able Juan Mackenna in a duel. The patriots must have breathed many sighs of relief when Carrera decided to go off to the United States in search of support for the war and his own private cause.

The royalist government in Chile was supported by certain Creoles who preferred colonialism to anarchy and were tired of war. A moderate policy might therefore have kept the Spaniards in power; and Osorio, understanding this, was inclined to be tolerant. Not so Marcó del Pont, officially the Captain-General, who was determined upon a reign of terror. Spaniards occupied all public posts and they alone were allowed to carry arms and to give evidence in court. Native Chileans had to be in their homes by nine at night and could not travel without permits. Fights between royalist soldiers and the tough Chilean *rotos* or rough labourers occurred constantly. Inevitably there were retaliations and a number of Spanish soldiers were murdered.

At the beginning of 1815 Osorio and Pezuela were ordered to cross the Andes into Cuyo; they were, in other words, to undertake the corollary of the invasion planned by San Martín, but of course they did not know this and to them the enterprise seemed impossible. They were defenders, not attackers, and the empire they were protecting was without an effective head. It was hardly surprising that they did nothing.

4. THE CROSSING OF THE ANDES

Nobody who baulked at the prospect of crossing the Andes with a large army could be accused of either cowardice or lack of enterprise. Even to San Martín, in the face of the physical obstacle, the royalist armies came to appear a mere bagatelle. 'It is not the strength of the enemy that spoils my sleep,' he is supposed to have said, 'but how to cross those huge mountains.'

At 35° south latitude the main range of the Andes divides into two parallel ridges. Between them a central valley is traversed by oblique spurs that continue into the Pacific, there to form island clusters. The lower or coastal range is a succession of granite hills with rounded summits and gentle slopes. The other, which can be seen from Mendoza, is craggy with peaks rising to upwards of 20,000 feet. Its lakes are fed by torrents of melting snow, its defiles are narrow and fissured by volcanic action. Condors soar high above cacti, thorn, and scree strewn across the trails. Man is an intruder in the landscape and if he ventures into it he must endure whatever Nature chooses to put in his way. Here, where he must feel himself more than usually a plaything of the elements, his fate cannot be easy.

In those days the mountains could be crossed only through a few passes and only in summer, since in winter—at heights between nine and twelve thousand feet—they are blocked by snow. Until San Martín's day they had never been attempted except by lonely bullock carts or by muleteers who travelled in single file carrying their merchandise of wine, dried fruits, and flour. The passage of a large army with its guns and equipment was to all appearances out of the question, but San Martín believed that Los Patos and Uspallata (the passes closest to Mendoza and

San Juan) were not impregnable, especially when he considered the quality of the men with whom he had the good fortune to work. The local cattle and sheep farmers were renowned horsemen, the Indians fierce fighters. As Mitre put it, 'Without knowledge of the character of these people it is impossible to understand how San Martín could in this one province have raised an invincible army which . . . freed two republics and spread the principles of the Argentine revolution over an entire continent.' San Martín's great vision transformed Cuyo into a corporate State with its own militia and even its regiment of young people. He invited foreign residents to enlist, and many British responded. Men with names like Lynch, MacGregor, Ferguson, Martin, Holmes, were so impressed by the General that they told him they could not view the situation with indifference and were 'prepared to shed their last drop of blood', if necessary, in defence of Argentine independence.[1] Many people became so enthusiastic that they contributed voluntarily to the public service, lending mules, horses, and harness. Carters and muleteers carried ammunition and supplies, and landowners pastured the troop horses free of charge. Fines collected as punishment for minor offences were paid into the public coffers. When money was scarce the ladies of Mendoza threw their jewels into the public chest, and they made cloth and dyed it blue for uniforms.

San Martín had no need for an iron rule because, as so exceptionally happens, everyone from the proudest aristocrat to the poorest peasant was giving time, labour, goods and chattels unstintingly to the cause; and nobody had the slightest reservation about the General's capacity to lead or his trustworthiness. His own interests came last, and his followers could do no less than emulate him. It is vouched for by John Miers, a London botanist, who went to Chile to set up a copper-refining plant, that he had a miniature likeness of himself hung between prints of Napoleon and Wellington, all three being in identical frames.[2] The detail in no way tallies with the picture we have of him in Cuyo, of a very simple military commander with no wish for self-aggrandizement.

[1] See Arciniegas, G., p. 274. [2] Miers, John, vol. 1, p. 159.

He achieved cooperation by caring for the health and welfare of his people, improving education, introducing vaccination, and irrigating farmlands. Soon, as Mitre says, the people began to regard him as a father whom they loved. Very much alone—for though he was surrounded by friends he had no close confidant—he looked after everything himself with the help of one secretary and two clerks. He was an austere figure, symbolizing a kind of paternal despotism which was wholly acceptable under the pressure of war but which as we shall see was a handicap once the mood of corporate sacrifice to an ideal had passed.

In these Mendoza days San Martín always wore the plain uniform of the mounted grenadiers with the Argentine cockade in his hat. He was an early riser and usually spent the morning at his desk. At midday he would eat a quick meal, not even bothering to sit down. This was washed down with wine and coffee, the latter prepared by himself. In the winter he would then take a short walk and smoke a cigarette of black tobacco. In summer, when it was too hot for exercise, he would sleep for two hours on a pelt stretched on the verandah. Then after more desk work he would make a tour of inspection. The visitors who frequented his house of an evening were forbidden to talk politics but would be challenged instead to a game of chess, which their host played well. At ten o'clock he would retire to bed but because of sleeplessness caused by chronic ill health he would often return to his desk for long spells during the night.

In spite of his loneliness he had a number of invaluable associates. One was a self-taught, robust mendicant friar named Luis Beltrán, a native of Mendoza who became chaplain to the new army. He was a jack-of-all-trades, a mathematician, a chemist, a maker of watches and fireworks, a carpenter, an architect, a blacksmith, a draughtsman, a cobbler, and a physician. There seemed no end to his manual dexterity. He made limbers for guns, saddles for the cavalry, knapsacks and shoes for the infantry; forged horse-shoes and bayonets, repaired damaged equipment, and drew designs for carriages especially adapted to take war equipment over the steep passes. Another aide, Major Juan

Antonio Alvarez Condarco, established a laboratory for saltpetre and a factory for producing gunpowder. And the Englishman Paroissien, who was much respected, organized the medical staff.

One of San Martín's greatest strengths was an efficient system of espionage. He sent secret agents into Chile to spread false intelligence about his preparations. Using the pretext that they were fleeing from the tyranny of the patriots, these men were easily able to cross the border; and the subterfuge so deceived the royalist government that it actually used them for counter-espionage. As the spies, mainly Chileans, passed freely to and fro, it was possible to discover which of the Spaniards in Mendoza were holding secret communication with the enemy. San Martín arrested these men and made them send letters dictated by himself, which persuaded the royalists that he was planning to attack Chile in the south.

Another of San Martín's ruses concerned the Declaration of Independence of the Congress of Tucumán. He sent Alvarez Condarco with a copy of it to be delivered personally to the Governor of Chile, Marcó del Pont—who in December 1815 had replaced Osorio in the royalist command—but this messenger's real task was to reconnoitre the passes of Uspallata and Los Patos. As San Martín had foreseen, Marcó del Pont took the Declaration and burned it, but allowed Alvarez Condarco to return un-molested to Mendoza, which he did with accurate maps of the passes stored safely in his head.

O'Higgins had by now been given command of two Negro regiments and was collaborating with San Martín. Also on the Chilean side of the border, the intrepid guerrilla fighter Manuel Rodríguez had organized bands of volunteers, and these so harried Marcó del Pont that he was forced to adopt repressive measures against them. In September 1816, impulsively and without orders, Rodríguez began an insurrection in the south. His ragtaggle troops were no match for the Spaniards; but San Martín, far from castigating his subordinate, managed to take advantage of the situation by writing Rodríguez a despatch perpetuating the myth that the invasion from Argentina was to be in the south, and then allowing it to fall into royalist hands. (Rodríguez, who had begun his career as secretary to José Miguel Carrera, rendered invaluable service organizing the resistance of Santiago after the disaster at Cancha Rayada, and—at the head of his 'Hussars of Death'—played an important part in the victory of Maipú; but fell foul of O'Higgins and was assassinated by his guards when he was under arrest.)

As the invasion date drew near, San Martín summoned the Pehuenche Indians who lived further south at the point where two other trails, the Planchón and the Portillo, cross the Cordillera. They gathered at the fort of San Carlos, south of Mendoza, where gifts of wine, sweets, cloth, glass beads (in the tradition of the *conquistadores*) and harness were lavished upon them. Would they, San Martín asked, grant him permission to march his army through their lands? They replied that they would, but with a duplicity that the General had foreseen they at once informed Marcó of the plan. This news put the Spanish commander into a flurry. Ignoring advice that he should concentrate his strength in the capital, he split his forces, sending some to the ports in case of an invasion by sea, others to the southern passes, others to Uspallata.

Final preparations were now being made. *Charquicán* (beef dried in the sun, roasted, ground to powder, and mixed with fat and chilli) was to provide a compact but nourishing diet for the men. Eight days' supply could be stored in a knapsack. The soldiers made their own rawhide sandals, water-bottles from animal horns, and slings out of the waste cloth used for their uniforms. Cables and anchors formed a portable bridge for crossing mountain torrents. Argentine horses and mules usually went unshod, but thirty thousand shoes were made to help the cavalry over the stony passes. In spite of having to repress a rebellion that had broken out in Córdoba, Pueyrredón helped San Martín with clothing, saddles, tents, and arms; but he wrote:

'Don't ask me for anything else unless you want to hear that I have hanged myself from a beam in the fort! . . . You may well say that among us there has never been an army so well equipped, but neither has there been a Director who had such confidence in a General, and—it should be added—never a General who so well deserved that confidence. My mind would be easier if you had another thousand soldiers.'[1]

Within the limits of the means available, all was now ready. On a hot afternoon in January 1817 an itinerant vendor arrived at the house of a patriot officer in Santiago. He had, he said, 'fat hens to sell'. He was one of San Martín's spies, and his hen was the fatter for containing a coded note from the commander-in-chief. It was the signal that the Andes crossing was about to begin.[2]

This was an occasion without precedent. True, Bolívar had made his early west-to-east crossing from Ocaña to Mérida in 1813, but this had been an impromptu affair involving only small detachments of men recruited on the journey. San Martín's enterprise was on a totally different scale. Months of meticulous preparation were now to be put to the test, and every protagonist knew that the only alternative to success was total annihilation.

San Martín's final instructions from his government are evidence that the aims had been carefully formulated and that no irresponsibility would be tolerated. 'The consolidation of the independence of America from the Kings of Spain and their successors, and the glory of the United Provinces of the South' were to be the sole purposes of the campaign. San Martín was to announce the fact in his proclamations, through his agents in the cities, and by all possible means. The army was to have this principle made so clear to it that it could entertain no thought of plunder, oppression, or conquest.[3]

The strategy had been planned to the last detail. The Uspallata pass goes by the valley of Aconcagua, dominated by the great peak of that name, and leads to the frontier town of Santa Rosa. The Los Patos road is longer and skirts the north of Aconcagua to emerge west of Santa Rosa. Any force caught between two detachments advancing by these passes would have to retreat

---

[1] Quoted by Pilling, W., p. 136.   [2] Arciniegas, G., p. 284.
[3] Quoted by Pilling, W., p. 137.

southward to the Sierra of Chacabuco; and it was here that the royalists would probably be engaged.

One detachment left San Juan on January 12, 1817, and was through the northern passes by February 8. The whole province of Coquimbo welcomed it and northern Chile was won with remarkable ease. In the south, Talca was occupied on February 12 so that communication between Santiago and the south was cut and Chilean guerrilla fighters were able to join the invading troops. On January 12 Juan Gregorio de las Heras led a flying column through Uspallata, his instructions being to entrench at Chacabuco but to retreat if attacked by superior forces. His troops, mounted on mules, travelled in single file through intense cold, many sickening in the rarefied air. In spite of the extreme difficulties, at three in the morning of February 2 they had crossed the summit of the Cordillera. The heavy artillery followed two days behind. On February 4 at sundown a royalist advance post was attacked and taken at the point of the bayonet. Then, obeying orders from San Martín, Las Heras feinted a withdrawal. Thinking him to have repented of his rash advance and to be in full retreat, the enemy now left the Uspallata pass undefended and this allowed the patriots to debouch upon the plain and occupy Santa Rosa.

The main body of the army marched by Los Patos, the vanguard commanded by Miguel Soler (a veteran from the early wars in the Banda Oriental), and the rear by O'Higgins. Soler had been told to enter the valley of Putaendo, seize the bridge over the river Aconcagua near the town of San Felipe, contact Las Heras, and attack the enemy in the rear of Santa Rosa. He too, once he had made contact with the royalists on February 7, feinted a retreat. Then he charged, breaking the enemy completely. As the royalists fell back they destroyed the bridge over the Chacabuco; but by the 12th the patriots had repaired it and crossed the river. At this moment O'Higgins nearly upset the plan by attacking impulsively and too soon; but the cavalry made a concerted attack on the enemy's right flank, which gave O'Higgins time to rally and make a bayonet charge straight at the centre of the enemy line. The shock was so great that the royalists broke and fled, completely routed. They lost five hundred dead and six hundred prisoners out of a total force of 1,600, whereas the patriots had only 150 casualties.

San Martín's crossing of the Cordillera had succeeded beyond all expectation. It must rank with those other famous marches across the mountains by Hannibal and Napoleon. But the Alpine passes are much lower, the cold less intense. Besides, as Mitre proudly pointed out, the crossings of the Alps resulted only in the 'sterile victories of Trebia and Marengo'; Chacabuco altered the face of a continent. And yet in general history books of the west neither it nor the march that led to it receive much attention. The Andes are too remote. They belong, somehow, not to history but to romance.

5. Chile's Independence Consolidated

The liberation war in Chile could have ended there; but San Martín, instead of pursuing the enemy or ensuring that the royalists did not entrench in the south which was their area of greatest influence, marched upon the capital. This was a bad mistake although it was not at first apparent, for the success of the Andean crossing had produced a sense of euphoria among the patriots. If there had been panic when they were driven from Santiago, there was even greater panic among the royalist sympathizers now. Up to that moment things had gone the way of the peninsular Spaniards. Now they were thrown into confusion, though once the more terrified had fled to Peru the population abandoned itself to rejoicing in spite of the fact that 2,000 ounces of gold and silver had been stolen from the treasury and prisoners had broken loose.

San Martín refused the supreme directorship of Chile and recommended O'Higgins for the appointment, he himself to remain at the head of the army. This was in accordance with his principles, but he knew, too, that he was out of sympathy with the light-hearted character of the Chilean people. He was also suffering from neuralgia and rheumatism and thought his life was drawing to a close. Though General Antonio González Balcarce, hero of Suipacha, was sent from Buenos Aires to join him as second-in-command, he did not allow ill health to impede his activities. He became friendly with the commodore of the British Pacific squadron and through his good offices sent letters to the Viceroy of Peru proposing an exchange of prisoners. He regarded this as an act of humanity, but it would also procure official recognition of Chile as a belligerent power and—still more important—would give a chance for his confidential agent to meet prominent people in Lima and to sound out their views about the liberation movement.

In Chile the royalists, reinforced from Peru by a fresh army of over 3,000 men under Mariano Osorio, assembled at the port of Talcahuano (called by O'Higgins the Chilean Gibraltar). Here the patriots were kept at bay, though in May O'Higgins did succeed in recapturing a great part of the province of Concepción. But by January 1818, on orders from San Martín, he began a retreat to Talca in Chile's central valley, where on February 12—the anniversary of Chacabuco—he proclaimed the independence of Chile as already decreed by general vote the year before. In view of the royalist successes this was a somewhat quixotic moment to do so; but San Martín and O'Higgins were hoping to entice Osorio beyond the river Maule and then to converge upon him and destroy him. However, on the evening of March 19 at Cancha Rayada the royalists fell upon San Martín. In the confusion pack mules stampeded, and O'Higgins was isolated in the darkness with only one division that was soon hopelessly outflanked, O'Higgins himself being wounded. If only he had been able to see what was going on, he could have turned the royalist line. As it was the victory went to a royalist colonel—Ordoñez—Osorio having retired to a church in Talca to pray for success!

O'Higgins evacuated Talca and retreated northward, and on April 5, at the battle of Maipú, on the plain south of Santiago, a decisive action was fought at which at least 1,000 (perhaps as

many as double that number) of Osorio's men were left dead on
the field, over 2,000 were taken prisoner, and artillery, medical
equipment, and the army coffers all fell into patriot hands. The
patriots also suffered very heavy losses, more than 1,000 killed
and wounded, the greatest sufferers being the freed Negroes of
Cuyo. Osorio escaped with two hundred horse. Ordoñez and all
but one of his officers surrendered their swords to Las Heras and
victory was complete. At this battle the Englishman Paroissien
distinguished himself by rigging up a hospital where he performed
amputations. He was rewarded with a gold medal and a generous
parcel of land.

This was the last serious effort of the Spaniards to retain their
hold on Chile; but the patriot government had still to contend
with the brothers Juan José and Luis Carrera who tried to re-
enter Chile in disguise. They were seized near Mendoza, where
they were sentenced to death by San Martín's secretary, Bernardo
Monteagudo, and executed (San Martín, with O'Higgins's agreement, had actually dictated a pardon but it arrived too late).
Shocked by this event, since she had met some of the Carrera
family and had a certain sympathy for their spirit and good looks,
Maria Graham, widow of a British naval officer who had died
rounding Cape Horn, wrote in her journal:

'Their death excited pity for them, and fear of the party that so
wantonly used its power: that fear has been deepened into horror
against some of the individuals. It must be confessed that severity
was *useless*; and useless severity in governments is always criminal.
Their authority is that they may increase and guard the happiness
of the community with the smallest possible abridgment of
freedom or happiness to individuals. But even while the struggle
for independence was going on, the new governors became so
intoxicated with power that, with the name of freedom on their
lips, they oppressed and murdered, and while they gratified their
own base passions, they called it public duty. The Carreras were
neither good nor useful citizens, but the two who had now
suffered were, at least, harmless, and might surely with their
families have been permitted to breathe in some climate where

they could not have interfered with the soldiers or the governors of Chile.'[1]

Such events were shocking to a nice British lady no doubt; but the Carreras were far from harmless and had shown extraordinary powers of rebound, so that banishment would not in their case have been a safe procedure. Maria Graham does, however, put her finger on the dilemma of the independence fighters—how to secure peace without repression; for their was still a dangerous minority favouring the royalist cause, and a number of leading Santiago citizens were not above betraying the patriots for the sake of private profit. After Maipú a portfolio containing Osorio's secret correspondence was captured and handed to San Martín. It contained, as he suspected it would, letters from certain people who after the defeat of the patriots at Cancha Rayada had thought it expedient to be on the winning side. Carefully, one by one, he burned the letters, and no one but himself—who so often in his life was suspected of harshness—ever knew who the writers were.

In February 1819 an alliance was formally signed between the governments of Argentina and Chile, who vowed 'to put an end to Spanish domination in Peru by an expedition financed by both nations . . . in order with the free will of the Peruvian people to set up whatever government is best adapted to its physical and moral constitution. . . .'[2] This alliance, the first in the New World between independent nations, was essential for patriot success. It sealed a friendship formed during the years of the patriots' early frustrated efforts between 1811 and 1814, when it became obvious that each country needed the other. Chile alone was too weak to throw off the Spanish yoke, whereas Argentina alone could never have invaded Peru.

6. THE EXPEDITION TO PERU

A delicate situation now forced San Martín to return to his own country at a moment when his absence exposed the army to mass

[1] Graham, Maria, p. 35.   [2] Quoted by Levene, R., vol. 2, p. 163.

desertions. In Buenos Aires political chaos had caused Pueyrredón to resign, and a Spanish invasion was feared. The new Supreme Director, José Rondeau, ordered San Martín to concentrate his forces in Buenos Aires. Unless the commander-in-chief was prepared to commit a flagrant act of disobedience, the liberation campaign would have to be abandoned. It was a hard decision; for if he were to undertake the enterprise and fail he would undoubtedly be accused of treason. But the whole future of South America was at stake. San Martín knew that the security even of Buenos Aires, let alone the continent, could be firmly based only if independence were extended to the north. He might hesitate after battles; he was not going to let the fear of personal disgrace stand in the way of an ideal. Moreover, he was able to take the risk with his officers unanimously behind him.

Chile having been freed, he therefore turned his attention to the formation of a navy with which he might invade Peru, a country that had of late been showing signs of breaking free from its traditional conservatism. Partly as a result of Belgrano's and San Martín's campaigns in Upper Peru, an independence movement had erupted in Cuzco in 1814 with the brothers José and Vicente Angulo as its intellectual leaders and a *mestizo*, Mateo García Pumacahua, its military strong man. Vidaurre, who had been a staunch supporter of García Pumacahua, turned against him at a critical moment, but the old warrior (he was already in his sixties) continued to fight in the hope of joining forces with Buenos Aires patriots. One of his aides, a priest called Ildefonso Muñecas, actually occupied La Paz for a short time; and García Pumacahua and the Angulo brothers captured Arequipa where they recruited important intellectuals into their ranks. Arce and others issued a decree dated December 4, 1814, 'the first year of Peruvian independence', stating that it was the will of God that the revolution be carried out. But the rebel armies were uncouth and equipped only with farm implements such as pitchforks. They were soon defeated. García Pumacahua was executed on March 12, 1815; and the poet Mariano Melgar, who had been one of the intellectual rebels, suffered a similar fate on the day following.

These events were an added incentive to San Martín to press on to the conquest of the north. After the battle of Chacabuco the Spanish flag had been kept flying in Valparaiso harbour. As expected, the ruse deceived the enemy and a brig, *Aguila*, was lured in, captured, renamed the *Pueyrredón*, and given to a mercenary called Morris to command. Morris had at once set out for the island of Juan Fernández and rescued patriot prisoners there. A few months later the *Wyndham*, a frigate of the East India Company which had been put up for sale in Valparaiso, was bought with a loan from local merchants and a guarantee from the Argentine government. Renamed the *Lautaro*, she was commanded by George O'Brien, and her marines were under Captain —later General—William Miller. With the *Pueyrredón* she put out to sea in search of the Spanish fleet and sighted the *Esmeralda* and the *Pezuela*. O'Brien was killed, but the combat was won and the Chileans redoubled their efforts to form a squadron. Alvarez de Condarco was sent to London to buy the *Cumberland*, which was renamed *San Martín*. An American privateer was acquired and renamed *Chacabuco*; also a brig, the *Araucano*. The fleet was placed under the command of Manuel Blanco Encalada.

On the Atlantic, nine Spanish transports escorted by a fifty-gun frigate were seized and brought to Buenos Aires where their whole complement of crew and infantry joined the patriots to whom they gave information about forces being sent from Spain to the south of Chile. A courier hurried across the Andes with the news, and a small patriot fleet put out to sea. 'Four ships gave the western continent to Spain,' said O'Higgins, 'and four will now wrest it from her.'[1]

Neither he nor San Martín wanted more bloodshed, and San Martín's proclamation to the Peruvian people shows that he did his utmost to avert it. He made it known that after the battle of Maipú he had written to the Viceroy suggesting that he should consider the extent of the combined resources of Argentina and Chile and the inequality of the struggle which threatened. He had suggested that the Viceroy would have to consider himself

[1] Quoted by Pilling, W., p. 189.

responsible for the devastation that war might cause; had entreated him to call a meeting in which the complaints of the patriots could be laid before him; and had suggested that the people should then be allowed to adopt whatever form of government they wished. He promised to bow to the will of such an assembly.[1]

This liberal proposal was answered, said San Martín, by 'insults and threats'. Preparations for the invasion of Peru, and particularly the formation of a navy, had therefore to continue. On October 28, 1818, the Chilean squadron sailed into Talcahuano bay and discovered the *María Isabel* lying there with royalist transports. They were in such poor condition, a third of the crews and soldiers having died on the voyage because of overcrowding and insanitary conditions, that the patriots had little difficulty in overpowering them. Thus of the nine Spanish vessels that had left Cádiz together, one went to Buenos Aires, seven were captured by the Chileans, and one disappeared without trace.

By another piece of good fortune Chile was at this moment offered the services of Lord Cochrane who became one of the most controversial personalities in the whole freedom movement. He had been cashiered from the British navy and dismissed from Parliament for a dubious stock exchange deal, but his popularity had been such that his fine had been paid by subscription and he was allowed to re-enter politics. His naval skill was beyond question, and Alvarez Condarco's offer that he might care to throw in his lot with Chile appealed to his adventurous temperament and liberal views. To command a navy in the making was more to his taste than to be disciplined by the Admiralty. At a farewell banquet in London he made a fiery plea for the freedom fighters; then, sailing in the *Rose*, he arrived in Valparaiso in November 1818 together with his wife and two children.

So it turned out that when the Chilean fleet sailed from Valparaiso on January 15, 1819, Lord Cochrane was in command. It comprised the *O'Higgins*, *San Martín*, *Lautaro*, *Chacabuco*, the smaller *Galvarino*, and a former British sloop *Hecate*. General

[1] See appendix to Graham, Maria, p. 481.

Miller described the crews of these vessels: mostly *cholos*, or *mestizo* peasants, who had never before set eyes upon the ocean. The officers were nearly all English or North American and spoke Spanish imperfectly if at all. With a few exceptions they affected that British superiority which scoffs at anything differing from its own tradition, and were at first too full of preconceived ideas to appreciate the special qualities of the physically tough but emotionally sensitive ratings. Luckily, however, the commodore was a young man who, in spite of a manner which Miller found unattractive on first acquaintance, was able to instil into his men the team spirit necessary for maintaining order. During a long passage the crews were brought into something like a state of efficiency. The marines and native *cholos* turned out to be excellent raw material, obedient and brave, eager and quick to learn. They were not on the whole used to very humane treatment and were grateful for any little attention to their comforts. Even so, a small mutiny broke out on the *Chacabuco* which had to put in to Coquimbo while the leaders were tried and punished.

Incidents such as this made Lord Cochrane less enthusiastic than Miller about the *cholos*, who, however, on reaching Peruvian waters soon had a chance to prove their mettle. The *O'Higgins* captured a gunboat. Then, running into Callao harbour in a heavy mist which gradually cleared, Cochrane attacked. With no wind to help them the *Lautaro*, *Chacabuco*, and *San Martín* could not come within range of the shore batteries, which concentrated the fire of three hundred guns on the *O'Higgins* alone. The crew caught the Admiral's enthusiasm and replied to such effect that from that moment Lord Cochrane's name became a legend. *El Diablo*, as he was called, declared a blockade of the Peruvian coast and harried the Spaniards throughout the whole of the summer and autumn of 1819. He even invented a system of shooting off rockets, but this was unsuccessful and the devices backfired alarmingly, apparently because of sabotage. Spanish prisoners in Valparaiso had been employed to charge them and had apparently packed them with sand, lime, and manure!

Not wanting to return to Valparaiso unless he could do so in triumph, Cochrane asked Miller impulsively one day, 'What would you say if with this one ship [the *O'Higgins*] I took Valdivia?' And he answered his own rhetorical question, 'They would think me a lunatic.' Lunacy had always been a quality much to his liking and he exploited it now with his usual panache. On February 3, 1820, he arrived off Valdivia flying the Spanish flag and signalled for a pilot. The Spaniards were suspicious and opened fire from every battery in the bay. Nevertheless a landing of three hundred men was effected and by next day the city had been captured and the Spaniards had lost their last base in the south together with the islands of Chiloé.

Cochrane's victories at sea had prepared the way for San Martín's invasion of Peru, but when the two men met in Santiago there were already signs of temperamental antipathy. The Admiral was primarily a fighting man, the General a liberator who would have preferred peace. Cochrane, proud of his exploits in Valdivia, wanted to be placed in command of the Peruvian expedition and was so piqued at not being appointed that he would have resigned if San Martín had not prevented it. On the eve of sailing the latter made a simple declaration that, whatever his lot in the Peruvian campaign, he was determined to prove that since returning to his native land his only endeavour had been to achieve independence. He had, he said, no ambition but 'to deserve the hatred of the ungrateful and the esteem of the virtuous'. He wrote to the *Cabildo* of Buenos Aires that as soon as a central authority could be established he would consider himself bound by its orders.

The 'Liberating Army of Peru' was composed of the original Army of the Andes plus nearly as many men again: a total of over 4,000. On August 20, 1820, the expedition sailed from Valparaiso, Cochrane leading in the *O'Higgins*, San Martín and his staff bringing up the rear in the vessel that was his namesake. On September 8 San Martín feinted a landing at Pisco, whereas he was actually hoping to establish a base further north in the Province of Trujillo. He reminded his men as they landed that they had come not to conquer but to liberate. He penalized those found plundering or maltreating the inhabitants, and he freed six hundred slaves whom he recruited into his forces. He also established a Peruvian cavalry.

Surprised by the landing, the Viceroy proposed peace on condition that Chile and the United Provinces should send representatives to the Spanish Cortes to settle outstanding differences with the mother country. Chile insisted that Peru must be declared independent first, and refused to accept the new Spanish constitution or to send deputies to the Cortes. In October, with negotiations foundering and with the Viceroy placing the blame on San Martín, the latter sent a flying column under José Antonio Alvarez de Arenales marching toward Lima. This was a feint allowing himself to re-embark and sail north. Cochrane failed to understand San Martín's purpose, which Mitre described graphically:

'The commander-in-chief . . . had two campaigns before him: one military whose plans he carried in his own head; the other political. . . . The first described a circle, one half of which was drawn along the coast by the keels of Cochrane's ships; the other half through the highlands of Peru by the feet of the flying column under Arenales. These two halves separated at Pisco to reunite in the north, enclosing Lima between them. The second was more complicated. The idea was to foment the moral force of public opinion, stirring up a spirit of insurrection among the Peruvian people. . . . From Pisco he flooded the country with proclamations and organized secret agencies in Lima and the interior.'[1]

On the night of November 4, with fourteen small boats rowing with muffled oars, Cochrane entered Callao harbour and captured the Spanish frigate *Esmeralda* lying there. (Afterwards, under the impression that the Americans had helped him to do so, Spanish soldiers massacred the crew of a U.S. frigate's market boat.) The whole convoy then sailed on to Huacho where San Martín established his quarters for the next six months. Soon he had driven the royalists out of Huaylas where the population swore to achieve Peru's independence; the northern provinces being so wholeheartedly in favour of the revolution that they became known as the *Departamento de la Libertad*. Alvarez de Arenales, who had been one of Belgrano's most promising young officers, was also victorious over the royalists at Pasco and San Martín's success seemed assured.

But things never seemed well in all theatres at once. In February 1820 the Buenos Aires army had been defeated in civil strife between federalists and centralists and the government had collapsed—the provinces becoming autonomous. Order was restored only after a Junta had been established under Martín Rodríguez, who was a veteran of the Paraguayan campaigns and of Sipe-Sipe.

In Chile a turncoat who had joined the royalists, one Vicente Benavides, was waging war in the south, and José Miguel Carrera was at the head of a small but determined army that had fought its way from Buenos Aires to the eastern slopes of the Andes, making alliance with the Indians, keeping up a correspondence with Chilean malcontents, and generally making himself a nuisance until he was delivered up by his own men to the Buenos Aires government. (He was shot in the market place of Mendoza on September 4, 1821, at the age of 35. Benavides was hanged in Santiago in the same year, and O'Higgins and San Martín were thus at last rid of their most obstructive fellow patriot and of their remaining royalist gadfly in Chile.)

In Peru the year 1821 opened with a withdrawal by the royalist General José de la Serna. To avoid disturbances, the Viceroy Pezuela was forced to resign his power into the hands of the Spanish constitutionalists. In May the royalists, still hoping for an armistice, referred to San Martín's suggestion that a monarchy be set up but rejected it on the grounds that the Spanish constitution would provide the best basis for a liberal régime in Peru. The patriots continued to insist on prior recognition of Peruvian independence but agreed to suspend hostilities for the time being if the fortifications at Callao could be handed over to them as a guarantee. 'If Don José de San Martín is determined to achieve the independence of America by arms or by negotiation,' ended the note proposing this temporary solution, 'he is no less desirous of uniting this part of the New World to the mother country by those bonds of friendship and commerce which would redound to the prosperity of both.'[1]

The Viceroy agreed to hand over Callao provided twelve heavy guns were dismantled from the fort; and a twenty-day armistice was arranged which neither side trusted and which each used as a cover to reorganize its forces. De la Serna redeployed his troops in the highlands; while on his part, in a confidential letter to O'Higgins, San Martín admitted that he was grateful for the pause so that he might rest his men and rehabilitate the sick.

In June San Martín and de la Serna met at Punchauca; and the former, admitting that Spanish America was not yet mature enough for a republican government, reverted to his idea of a regency until a prince of the royal house of Spain could be installed. At this time Captain Basil Hall secured an interview with San Martín on board a schooner in Callao roads, and he has left us a description of the General:

'There was little at first sight in his appearance to engage attention; but when he rose up and began to speak his superiority was apparent. He received us in very homely style, on the deck of his vessel, dressed in a loose surtout coat and a large fur cap and seated at a table made of a few loose planks laid along the top of some empty casks. He is a tall, erect, well-proportioned, handsome man with a large aquiline nose, thick black hair, and immense bushy dark whiskers extending from ear to ear under the chin; his complexion is deep olive, and his eye, which is large, prominent, and piercing, is jet black. . . . He is thoroughly well-bred and unaffectedly simple in his manners; exceedingly cordial and engaging and possessed evidently of great kindliness of disposition; in short, I have never seen any person the enchantment of whose address was more irresistible. In conversation he went at once to the strong points of the topic, disdaining as it were to trifle with its minor points; he listened earnestly, and replied with

[1] For this quotation and a more complete account of the armistice negotiations, see Pilling, W., p. 252 *et seq.*

distinctness and fairness, showing wonderful resources in argument and a most happy fertility of illustration. . . . I saw nothing
in his conduct afterwards to cast doubt upon the sincerity with
which he spoke. The contest in Peru, he said, was not of an
ordinary description—not a war of conquest and glory but entirely
of opinion; it was a war of new and liberal principles against
prejudice, bigotry, and tyranny. People ask, said San Martín, why
I don't march to Lima at once; so I might, and instantly would,
were it suitable to my views—which it is not. I do not want
military renown—I have no ambition to be the conqueror of
Peru; I want solely to liberate the country from oppression. Of
what use would Lima be to me, if the inhabitants were hostile in
political sentiment? How could the cause of independence be
advanced by my holding Lima, or even the whole country, in
military possession? Far different are my views. I wish to have all
men thinking with me, and do not choose to advance a step
beyond the march of public opinion. . . . I have been gaining . . .
day by day, fresh allies in the hearts of the people. . . . Public
opinion is an engine newly introduced into this country; the
Spaniards, incapable of directing it, have prohibited its use; but
they shall now experience its strength and importance.'[1]

About this time San Martín published an address to the
Peruvian people in which he succinctly described the dilemma of
South America from his day to our own:

'All civilized peoples are in a condition to be free; but the degree
of freedom that a country can enjoy ought to be in exact proportion to the measure of its civilization. If the first exceed the last,
no power can save them from anarchy; but if the reverse happens,
namely, that the degree of civilization goes beyond the amount of
freedom which people possess, oppression is the consequence.'[2]

On July 6, 1821, with the armistice broken, the patriots finally
entered Lima; and on the 28th Peru's independence was proclaimed. Soon afterwards San Martín was named Protector; and
his decree for the occasion, published in Lima on August 3, 1821,

[1] Hall, Basil, vol. 1, p. 210 *et seq.*
[2] Quoted by Hall, Basil, vol. 1, p. 253. He also gives the original Spanish, p. 370.

shows his characteristic dignity. Once again he protested that his sole desire was to advance 'the sacred cause of America and to promote the happiness of the Peruvian people'. Though he had been in great part successful, he said, the work would remain incomplete, and his wishes imperfectly accomplished, if he were not to ensure the security and prosperity of the inhabitants. From the moment of his landing at Pisco, therefore, he had made it clear that the 'imperious necessity of circumstances' had obliged him to assume the supreme authority, and he held himself responsible to the country for its due exercise. So long as a foreign force remained in Peru, the circumstances that had made his absolute power necessary still held, and the political and military authority must therefore continue to be united in his person. He pleaded that throughout the course of his public life he had kept his word with religious scrupulousness, and this gave him the right to be believed. Solemnly he pledged that the very moment Peru was free he would resign.[1]

On the following day he proclaimed fair and just terms to the Spaniards. Those who continued peacefully at their appointed tasks would have their persons and properties respected, but those who did not would be asked to leave the country with all their movable property. One British traveller, Farquhar Mathison, thought that the peninsular Spaniards were treated with less than the promised consideration. He described how after the fall of Callao about six hundred were deported, 'dragged from their beds at a moment's warning', the old and infirm strapped to the backs of mounted soldiers to be embarked on a dilapidated merchantman, the *Monteagudo*, where 'the decks above and below were so thickly crowded with the unfortunate wretches that they could hardly move; and the stench and heat occasioned by such a multitude . . . was literally unsupportable.' Many were ready to expire with thirst.[2]

San Martín's answer to such accusations was that most of the peninsular Spaniards had been and would continue to remain dangerous to the patriot cause. The British tourist could only

[1] Quoted by Hall, Basil, vol. 1, pp. 266 *et seq.*   [2] Mathison, G. Farquhar, p. 288 *et seq.*

remark that the poor people, whichever side they espoused, were subjected to 'anarchy, tyranny, and military rapine'. But San Martín wrote to O'Higgins:

'At last, by patience, we have compelled the enemy to abandon the capital of the Pizarros; at last our labours are crowned by seeing the independence of America secure—Peru is free—I now see before me the end of my public life, and I am looking for a way of leaving this heavy charge in safe hands in order that I may retire into some quiet corner and live as a man should.'[1]

The royalists still held Callao which they surrendered only on September 21. Cochrane, angry with San Martín for his procrastination in taking both the port and the capital (a delay which was typical and which allowed General José Canterac to escape into the interior where he continued to harry the patriots), and also for the fact that his sailors had not been paid, called him a sanguinary tyrant, an incompetent general, a hypocrite, a thief, a drunkard, and other more or less slanderous epithets. The admiral, people thought, had gone too far, though he had certainly been provoked when all mention of the fleet had been omitted from the medals struck to celebrate independence. Pay to the sailors was in arrears; and 50,000 dollars promised to the captors of *Esmeralda* had been overlooked. San Martín denied that he was responsible for paying crews in the service of Chile and, as a precaution against the Admiral's hotheadedness, placed the treasury bullion on board a ship at anchor in Ancón harbour. Incensed, Cochrane seized the treasure on the pretext that it was contraband, and with this he paid his men. San Martín thereupon ordered Cochrane to return to Chile and report to his government, and Cochrane weighed anchor in a fury. San Martín wrote to O'Higgins proposing to declare Cochrane an outlaw; but O'Higgins, realizing that an open rupture would do the patriots no good, admitted Chile's partial guilt in the matter and made public recognition of Cochrane's inestimable services. These in any case could now be ended since the Admiral's appointed task had been concluded, and soon afterwards he left the area for good.

[1] Pilling, W., p. 272.

He had served the Chilean and Peruvian cause loyally and had given it help without which the land fighting could have come to little. In the north it could not even have begun.

It is not easy to set in its right perspective the foreign aid at this time available both to San Martín and to Bolívar. A passage from the unbiased General Miller is relevant:

'There have been some attempts to inculcate an opinion that the ex-colonies of Spain, particularly Chile, mainly owe their independence and the formation of their naval forces to the assistance of European merchants. The fact is that the latter often assumed rather more credit than they were entitled to, from the circumstance of their happening to be the consignees of a few old ships, and of second-hand slops and stores. As men of business, indeed, these gentlemen were fighting to make the most of the market and their commodities; but then their claims to ardent patriotism, unmixed with views of profit, must be disallowed. It is true that many of them displayed the liberality of feeling which is generally found to exist in the commercial world; but in this case their sympathies and their interests went hand in hand. When these became unhappily at variance, poor Sympathy often went to the wall, and the royalists were supplied with the munitions of war whenever they could give a favourable price. The North Americans were not behind-hand in this sort of traffic. Commodore Stewart was accused of affording them a degree of support inconsistent with his instructions and the laws of neutrality. The commodore was brought to a court-martial on his return to the United States, but the charges were not proved and he was acquitted.

'Foreign merchants did occasionally make advances to the new governments; but it was always upon terms of profit proportionate to the risk. Thus, speaking of the merchants as a body, and within the sphere of their counting-houses, their pretensions to disinterested liberalism fall to the ground. But speaking of them individually, a very great many may be instanced as having given unequivocal proofs of their zeal and adherence to the cause of independence. When the destiny of Chile depended upon the uncertain chances of a battle, some English merchants armed themselves, joined the patriot cavalry as volunteers, and participated in the brilliant charges which, at Maipú, decided the fate of the country. To such feats of gallantry might be added some splendid acts of philanthropy and benevolence which reflect particular honour on the parties concerned. It was such conduct, and not assistance bestowed in the way of business, which caused the British to be looked up to with distinguished consideration. Another powerful reason for their preponderating influence was the strict observance of the laws of neutrality by the English naval commanders, and the honourable, straightforward, courteous, and manly frankness with which their officers conducted themselves. Hence also became established a feeling of gratitude in the Chileno people towards England as a nation. They persuade themselves that she is the friend of liberal institutions, and consider her their well-wisher. But it is well known that Spanish America owes nothing to the *British government* [italics Miller's] but the foreign enlistment bill of 1819, which Mr. Canning stated in Parliament in 1827 was passed at the express request of the King of Spain.'[1]

For his own part in the liberation of Peru, General Miller was rewarded with the command of a regiment of infantry. His views were at one with those of the Protector, who went about abolishing many of the repressive practices to which the Indians were subjected and who declared that all slaves who joined the army, and all future children of slave parents, were now free. Torture and other excessive forms of punishment were abolished. The political organization of Peru was, however, deliberately left to be thought out by the Peruvians themselves at a later date.

San Martín also instituted an 'Order of the Sun' in imitation of Napoleon's Legion of Honour and equivalent to the Chilean Legion of Merit which he had previously created there. He voted himself a yearly salary of 30,000 dollars which he used almost entirely in the interests of Peru, but it gave rise to much criticism

---

[1] Miller, J., vol. 2, p. 221. The enlistment bill referred to made it illegal to recruit men for service in Spanish America.

and aggravated the recurrent fears that he would crown himself king. He had no such intention, and had sent Juan García del Rio and Paroissien to Europe to secure recognition of Peru's independence and to offer a crown to a European prince: either to the Prince of Saxe-Coburg, a member of the British royal family, a German or Austrian prince (provided they had British support), or even a Frenchman or the Duke of Lucca. These were bizarre choices, for the monarch would have to swear allegiance to the Roman Catholic faith, to uphold a liberal constitution, and to be loyal to a country on which he had never set eyes.

These measures were not popular with people who were by now determined to live under a republican form of government; and San Martín, in his eagerness to get on with constructive policies and to have done with war, had also made his usual mistake of not destroying or rendering ineffective the royalist forces. With all the cards in his hands he once again let total victory slip away. In April 1822 the patriots were defeated at Pisco, but the following month Sucre defeated the royalists on the slopes of Mount Pichincha, a battle that secured the emancipation of Ecuador.

On the intellectual front forty of the most influential Peruvians were banded into the *Sociedad Patriótica*, formed by the Argentine Monteagudo to be representative both of extremist liberals and of those rebels who favoured a monarchy—but carefully balanced toward the latter since Monteagudo believed with San Martín that only an aristocratic government could keep control. He had not, however, reckoned with the withering pen of José Faustino Sánchez Carrión who, under the pseudonym 'The Recluse of Sayán', wrote two satirical letters which effectively put a stop to the schemes to import a king from Europe.

This was dispiriting for San Martín; the more so since things were not going well in Chile either. A provisional plan of government had been drawn up by O'Higgins in 1818 and adopted though many felt it was too autocratic. A second document, by O'Higgins and a disciple, was approved in October 1823 but was received even less favourably. The following month a serious earthquake shook Valparaiso and a tidal wave twelve feet high

eroded the coastline and toppled buildings. It was not the first
time that Nature had intervened to obstruct the liberators' plans.
The resulting chaos did nothing to bolster O'Higgins's waning
popularity; and now he was being accused of assuming dictatorial
powers when in fact, like San Martín, he was only trying to prevent the disasters of a too early acceptance of republican ideals in a
country that had not yet acquired political maturity. His position,
however, became untenable, and he was forced to resign and to
retire to Peru, where he lived until his death in 1842. The Junta
that ruled after his abdication was ironical and not a little self-
righteous about his régime:

'By a misfortune which often attends the fate of nations, the
government which might have done the most good wanted the
talent to accomplish it . . . Chile never was in a more dangerous
state. Our revolution presents vicissitudes in which almost all the
errors and inadvertencies of which the human mind is capable
have been committed. . . . Prudence, and a generous contempt of
petty interests, which are nothing compared with the general good
of the state, and principles of exact equality and justice, alone will
avert disorders, the divisions, which might lead the people to
curse the day when they shook off their peaceful slavery.'[1]

The fact of the matter was that the liberators had unleashed an
impulse toward democracy which, since the people did not really
know what they wanted, turned out in the event to be premature.
But at the time most intellectuals could not see the situation in
that light. Daniel O'Leary, Bolívar's faithful aide, always regarded
O'Higgins as stupid (*imbécil*),[2] and a nineteenth-century Chilean
sociologist, Francisco Bilbao, wrote that Chile had had two types
of government, the revolutionary and the reactionary; and he
accused O'Higgins—the leader of liberation—of being the first,
also, to assume despotic powers. O'Higgins, he said, did not
work for the total triumph of the revolution in its social, religious,
and political aspects, but sought only political power.[3] This

---

[1] Quoted by Graham, Maria, p. 359 *et seq.*
[2] Lecuna, V., *Relaciones Diplomáticas de Bolívar con Chile y Buenos Aires*, vol. 1, p. 167.
[3] See Lillo, S., p. 209.

judgement was far from just. O'Higgins had had to contend with uprisings against his régime in Concepción, Coquimbo, and Santiago; and when he saw that he was no longer wanted he faced the malcontents courageously and asked them in effect what credentials they had for representing the people. They had none, and the people acclaimed him, but in order to avoid more civil strife he laid down his command. One more South American reformer had fallen to enemies who understood neither the man nor the situation. O'Higgins, if not of the stature of San Martín or Bolívar, had always acted scrupulously according to his principles.

Simón Bolívar had by now made his own crossing of the Andes and had entered Colombia. The famous and controversial meeting between the liberators of north and south was about to take place, but to understand the significance of this encounter we must go back to the year 1812 when Miranda had just been betrayed by Bolívar in Venezuela.

CHAPTER II

SIMÓN BOLÍVAR

1. CHANGING FORTUNES

Simón José Antonio de la Santísima Trinidad Bolívar was born in Caracas on July 24, 1783, into an aristocratic family that had lived in the New World for two centuries. He was a typical product of New World *mestizaje*, a mixture of Basque, German, Negro, and Indian blood. He was exceptionally articulate considering that he was also a man of action; exceptionally one-pointed in aim for a person so given to the storms of passion and the vagaries of sensual love; exceptionally clear-sighted for one so fanatically dedicated. It is in his writings rather than those of San Martín (which are scarce in spite of his long life), O'Higgins, Hidalgo or Morelos, that we find the most complete expression of the Spanish American mind and are able to appreciate the sophistication with which very difficult philosophical, military, and cultural problems were assessed in those early days before the Spanish American nations were created.

We have already heard something of his father, Colonel Juan Vicente de Bolívar y Ponte, one of the group of dissident Creoles who wrote to Miranda asking him to lead their freedom movement. But the boy was left orphaned, his father having died when the future Liberator was two years old, his mother six months later. Simón was looked after by uncles who placed him in the charge of a free-thinker and revolutionary named Simón Rodríguez, the natural son of a priest. From Rodríguez the young Simón learned his first lessons in nonconformism; and though his uncles were probably unaware of the extent of Rodríguez' commitment to radical views, they were certainly themselves no more loyal to Spain than any proud Creole of the time could be expected to be. When Rodríguez became implicated in a conspiracy in Caracas he was caught but managed by burning his papers to convince the authorities of his innocence. He was allowed to leave the country, and Bolívar lost sight of him until years later he discovered him in Vienna where under the name of Robinson he was carrying out experiments in chemistry.

Like most Creole aristocrats, Bolívar went to Europe to complete his education. According to his own assessment he was not very conversant with Aristotle or the criminal code, his reading being mainly of seventeenth and eighteenth century thinkers such as Locke, Condillac, Buffon, d'Alembert, Helvetius, Montesquieu, Mably, Filangieri, Rousseau, and Voltaire. After a time in Madrid, he found himself in Paris during the last phase of the French revolution. On his return to Madrid he fell in love with María Teresa del Toro, married her in 1802, and swept her back with him to Venezuela where he had hoped to spend a leisurely life looking after his large estate. But his wife died of yellow fever the following year, and the heartbroken young man, vowing never again to marry, returned to Europe via the United States. Had he been able to settle down to family life his future might have been different, though one can scarcely imagine the fiery, proud and ambitious Bolívar, the genius of the liberation movement, vegetating on the margins of the battle.

He kept his vow never to take another wife, but a love affair with a cousin, Fanny Dervieu de Villars, was to last for twenty years and to prove its endurance against many more transitory affairs of the heart. Fanny undoubtedly gave Bolívar something of the intellectual stimulus he required, and only two other women in his life ever rivalled her in influence. One, Josefina Machado, died in 1820. The other and more famous, Manuela Sáenz, had married an English doctor named Thorne but fell in love with Bolívar in Quito in 1822 and left her husband for the more adventurous Liberator whom she accompanied on his campaigns though apparently never—as myth has it—in men's clothes and sharing life with the troops. Bolívar needed the stimulus of women and their intellectual as well as emotional encouragement. He stood only five feet six inches in height and was narrow-chested and tubercular with a thin whipcord of a body; but his black eyes, aristocratic nose, curly hair, and small white hands all gave him a distinction which women found hard to resist, especially after he had become the hero of a continent. It has frequently been said that he shared much of Napoleon's despotic nature; but he refused to witness Napoleon's crowning in Notre Dame Cathedral though he expressed delight, during the second coronation in Milan, when the conqueror wore a plain suit ornamented only with epaulettes; surely the most fitting garb for a revolutionary!

It is open to doubt to what extent the Liberator was taken in by his own later apotheosis, or how far he used pomp and finery simply as convenient ways of attracting the multitude to himself and through him to his policies. His own public protestations that he wanted no personal glory, reinforced by statements in private letters, have a sincerity in which—unless we are to assume that the two opposing sides of his nature were more than usually strangers to one another—it is hard to disbelieve. As a young man, climbing the Aventino with Rodríguez, he swore never to rest until he had freed America from her tyrants. In spite of his power and the temptation to do so, he never became one himself. Oaths, for Bolívar, whether these concerned women or patriotic policies, were sacred. So were religious matters. He refused to kiss the Pope's sandals not because he could not find it in himself to honour the representative of Christ on earth, but because the symbolism seemed to him unworthy. The Spanish Ambassador was shocked but the Pope intervened, 'Let the Indian do as he likes'; and the Indian found it well within his conscience to kiss the ring of St. Peter. He was as staunch a Catholic as most.

An influence partly romantic and partly scientific upon the young Bolívar was Alexander von Humboldt, who had brought to Europe a wonderful collection of Latin American geological and botanical specimens together with unbounded enthusiasm for the New World. This latter he transmitted to the young Creole who was astonished and delighted to find a European who, far from looking down upon his own kind, believed that the future possibilities for humanity lay with Latin America.

Bolívar was back in Caracas by 1810; from where in that year, after playing a leading role in an insurrection, he was sent to London together with his mentor and lifelong friend Andrés Bello and with Luís López Méndez who afterwards acted as his recruiting agent in Britain. The trio formed an official deputation sent by the Caracas Junta in the name of King Ferdinand (the latter had naturally not been consulted) to ask Britain for help. In a private room at Apsley House Arthur Wellesley received the Creoles amicably but expressed the hope—which sounded to Bolívar like an overbearing command—that they would remain loyal to their King. A second meeting went more favourably, protection against France being promised should this be required. Bolívar spent three months in England before sailing back to his homeland ahead of Miranda, thus gaining the edge on the older man in a country of scheming and split loyalties.

Events in Venezuela have already been reviewed in our survey of Miranda; how on July 5, 1811, Congress declared the country independent, with Bolívar already giving articulate form to his vague longing for freedom; how the young man gave proof during the earthquake of an unconquerable spirit; how he was repelled at Puerto Cabello, and how he afterwards betrayed the Precursor—an act of which he boasted to the end of his days convinced that Miranda was an untrustworthy ally of freedom.

The peninsular Spaniards, feeling that he had done them a service in delivering Miranda into their hands, spared Bolívar's life and allowed him to take refuge in Curaçao. (They had ample cause thereafter to rue that act of clemency.) Before embarking, Bolívar said that he would like to seek a commission in the British army. It would seem that at this time he despaired of there ever arising within Venezuela sufficient determination or will for the people to secure their liberation. There were too many jealousies between provinces and capital, too many personal vanities. True, the Spanish expeditions sent from Havana and Puerto Rico had been repulsed by the Marquis del Toro and by that very talented soldier, José Antonio de Sucre, a fact that gave heart to the liberals. But these were flashes in the pan. The Church was against the cause of independence, and people as a whole were too fearful of the wrath of God and the world to come, not to be mindful of the priests' admonishments. Bolívar was convinced that to unite only to fall into apathy would be a subtle kind of treason; and undoubtedly people were as a whole apathetic. The Spaniards were reconquering the liberated areas; and the Colombian historian José Manuel Restrepo paints a picture of New Granada and of Quito at that time in which he sees the will to independence undermined by internal dissensions, by people's ignorance of their civic rights, by the fanaticism of priests who taught that kings ruled by divine authority, by weak provincial governments and lack of experience. Throughout the Americas it was much the same story. All the signs suggested that God was on the side of the royalists.

But Bolívar's spirit, though it could despair, was hard to break. In Curaçao he raised an army and by September 1812 was able to return to Cartagena where in a famous Manifesto, written in order 'to persuade America to improve its behaviour', he analysed the cause of Venezuela's failure:

'The most far-reaching error Venezuela committed when it entered politics was without any doubt the disastrous adherence to a system of *tolerance*: a system proved by the whole thinking world to be weak and ineffective, yet tenaciously adhered to with exceptional blindness to the very end.'[1]

Moreover the new laws of his country were, according to Bolívar:

'framed by certain well-meaning visionaries who, building republics in the air, have tried to reach political perfection on the assumption that humanity is perfect. So we have had philosophers

[1] Lecuna, V., *Proclamas* No. 5; see also in English, *Selected Writings of Bolívar*, document 9.

instead of leaders, philanthropy instead of legislation, dialectic instead of tactics, and sophists instead of soldiers.'

After this forthright condemnation of the weaknesses inherent in a sentimental interpretation of democracy—weaknesses which he himself, visionary though he also was, took care to avoid (hence those accumulating suspicions that he was dictatorial)—Bolívar turned the venom of his pen upon federalism. It was, he said, a system which:

'though it may be the most perfect and the most capable of bringing happiness to human society, is nevertheless the most detrimental to the interests of our infant countries. Generally speaking our citizens are not yet able to exercise their rights fully and for themselves, because they lack the political virtues that characterize true republicans. . . . Moreover, what country in the world, however well-behaved and republican it may be, could in the midst of internal strife and foreign wars, be ruled by anything so complex and so weak as a federal government? A government must so to speak identify itself with the kind of circumstances, the times, and the men who surround it. If the latter are prosperous and calm, it should be gentle and protective; but if they are unruly and turbulent, it should be stern and should arm itself with a firmness equal to the dangers, not concerning itself with laws and constitutions until such time as happiness and peace are established. . . .

'Popular elections by country rustics and intriguing city-dwellers are one more obstacle to the practice of federation among us; because the former are so ignorant that they cast their votes mechanically, and the latter so ambitious that they convert everything into factions; therefore in Venezuela there has never been a free and just vote, and the government has been placed in the hands of men who have either betrayed the cause or were inept or immoral. It is our lack of unity, not Spanish arms, that has returned us to slavery.'

The Manifesto sees the chief causes of Venezuela's failure as federalism, weakness of government, the lack of seasoned troops, religious fanaticism, political squabbles, and—to a minor degree—

the earthquake of 1812. It is a lucid and mordant document from the pen of so young a man—realistic to a point of ignoring law if law gets in the way of efficiency, and pervaded throughout with a deep understanding of the dilemma man faces as he stands between the Scylla of despotism and the Charybdis of anarchy. Its firmness so impressed the authorities that Bolívar received a commission to fight Spanish troops on the Magdalena river. Congress, 'seeing the cause of Venezuela and Nueva Granada as one', readily acceded to his request that the former's troops be used to liberate both countries. In the Cartagena forces he served at first under a French mercenary, Pierre Labatut, but becoming impatient of his superior officer he decided to march up the Magdalena valley on his own initiative. His recruitment of peasants and repulsion of the royalists so impressed the Cartagena government that it overruled Labatut's charges of insubordination. Bolívar turned east at Ocaña, crossed the eastern ridge of the Cordillera, and entered Mérida to reinstall a republican government; and it was here that in June 1813 he issued his famous decree of 'war to the death'. The controversy that has raged ever since around this pronouncement tends to ignore the fact that it was an answer to a proclamation made by the royalist commander Toribio Montes six months previously, when he wrote to his officers in Popayán that any patriot prisoners who were pardoned but then took up arms again should be killed forthwith. This led to a document being published in Cartagena by a former neighbour of Bolívar's, Antonio Nicolás Briceño, who proposed to bleed the peninsular Spaniards of money for the benefit of the liberating armies. But the proposal went further and suggested that patriots might earn a commission in their armies by the grizzly method of producing as many Spanish scalps as they could. Bolívar disapproved, but Briceño went ahead with the plan, beheaded two Spaniards, and sent the heads as gifts to Bolívar and one of his colonels. In retaliation the royalists fell upon Briceño and his men. At the moment when Bolívar entered Mérida it looked very much as if Briceño's forces would be massacred, which in fact did not happen though the avenging patriots were court-martialled and eight of them shot. The attitude adopted by Toribo Montes had, however, roused Bolívar's temper and in his 'war to the death' speech[1] he fully believed he was returning savagery for savagery:

'Fugitive and wandering like the enemies of God the saviour, they [the Spaniards] are everywhere cast out and persecuted by all men. Europe expels them, and Americans reject them because in both worlds their vices have heaped upon them the opprobrium of human kind. The whole globe has been stained with innocent blood spilled by the fierce Spaniards, who are all stained with the crimes they have committed for no love of glory but in their search for that infamous metal which is their sovereign god. The hangmen who call themselves our enemies have violated the sacred rights of men and nations. . . . But these victims shall be avenged, these hangmen exterminated. Our vengeance shall rival Spanish ferocity. Our good will is at last exhausted; and, since our oppressors compel us to mortal warfare, they shall disappear from America and our land shall be purged of the monsters that infest it. Our hate shall be inexorable and our war shall be to the death.'

The Mérida speech was followed a few days later by one at Trujillo which should be read in conjunction with it:

'Moved by your misfortunes, we have been unable to look indifferently upon the afflictions the savage Spaniards have caused you to suffer, exterminating you by plunder and destroying you with death; violating the sacred rights of men; breaking the most solemn agreements and treaties; and, in short, committing every kind of crime, reducing the Republic of Venezuela to the most dreadful desolation. Therefore justice demands vengeance, and necessity compels us to exact it. May the monsters that infest our land and have covered it with blood vanish forever from Colombian soil. Let their punishment be equal to the enormity of their betrayal, in order thus to wash out the stain of our disgrace and to show the nations of the world that the sons of America cannot be offended with impunity.'[2]

[1] Lecuna, V., *Proclamas*, No. 10.
[2] Lecuna, V., *Proclamas* No. 11; *Selected Writings* No. 12.

The peninsular Spaniards could not take such words lightly, nor have they been forgiven yet. Bolívar's severest critics forget, however, that the rules by which war was played in those days were not pretty; also that having made his bitter statement he went on to offer a way out. Any Spaniard who did not conspire against tyranny and favour the patriot cause both actively and effectively would be regarded as an enemy and put before the firing squad. Those who came over to Bolívar's army, with or without arms, and those who helped in any civilian activities, would be pardoned. Army officers and civil magistrates who proclaimed the government of Venezuela and joined the patriots would be retained in their posts. In short, those who were not with Bolivar were against him and would be shown no quarter. On the other hand there were those numerous innocent people who had been persuaded by treacherous arguments from the path of justice; those who, blind, ignorant and through no fault of their own, had erred because they were enslaved and must be forgiven their backslidings:

'Fear not the sword that comes to avenge you and to sever the unworthy bonds with which your executioners have bound you to their fates. In all that concerns your honour, life, and property, you may count upon absolute immunity. The very title of Americans will be your guarantee and safeguard. Our arms have come to protect you and shall never be used against a single one of our brothers.'

This amnesty extended even to the traitors who had most recently committed felonies, and Bolívar promised that he would scrupulously fulfil it even if the offenders gave overriding cause for his wrath:

'Spaniards and men of the Canary Islands, if you are lukewarm and do not work actively for America's freedom, you may be certain of death. Americans, even if you have done wrong, you may be certain of life.'

Thus Bolívar created two laws, one for the peninsular Spaniards who by their educational advantages and general upbringing could be held responsible for their actions; and one for Americans whose state of abject servility absolved them from all blame. Nevertheless, though Bolívar was threatened on all sides by the nineteenth-century equivalent of Quislings, he was prepared to be merciful even to the peninsulars provided their actions showed that they had repented. At a later stage of the war General Miller paid tribute to the 'forgiving spirit of the South Americans', which could be observed in the freedom with which Spaniards were allowed to trade and to hold civil offices of trust—and even, in some cases, military commands.

After the controversial proclamation Bolívar's Secretary of State, Antonio Muñoz Tebar, was to sign his letters and manifestoes beneath the date: 'Third [year] of Independence and First of War to the Death'. Bolívar never repented of his strong words and never spared any love for the peninsular Spaniards. Listing his military exploits, he boasted that the enemy bands melted away even before he appeared, 'because they fear the exterminating sword which the justice of heaven has placed in your hands to revenge humanity'. He invited Spaniards to enjoy the happiness of living among the Creole patriots in peace and concord and to abandon 'the treacherous Monteverde who has left you with a desperate choice: of dying either on the field or the scaffold, of losing your families, homes and properties'.[1]

He was having spectacular military success. After a series of victories he reached Victoria, close to Caracas. Thence, in August 1813, he entered his birthplace in triumph and the Spaniards were forced to take refuge in Puerto Cabello. Bolívar gave the world a moving and terrible account[2] of the atrocities and arbitrary behaviour of his enemies during the previous twelve months. In spite of these provocations, in January 1814 he issued a general pardon.[3] He was friendly to foreigners who were friendly to Venezuela, and he offered them government protection if they would settle in that fertile land. Any who served in the country's armed forces would be granted citizenship.[4] Having thus ordered affairs he assembled the public authorities and resigned to them

---

[1] Lecuna, V., *Proclamas* 14. [2] Lecuna, V., *Proclamas* 22 and 23.
[3] Lecuna, V., *Proclamas* 30. [4] Lecuna, V., *Proclamas* 19.

the supreme command. His resignation was not accepted, and instead he was acclaimed 'dictator' (not at that moment a term of abuse) and 'Liberator'.

His successes were brought to an abrupt halt by the activities of José Tomás Boves, a Spaniard born in Asturias, who ruled with an iron hand over the *llanos* or great plains of central Venezuela. With a band of ruffians whom he held together with promises of plunder and glory, Boves was able to destroy the meagre divisions Bolívar could spare against him. The *llaneros* were a perpetual threat to the patriots; so much so that Bolívar, fearing that the very large number of Spanish prisoners in La Guaira and Caracas might rise and join his enemies with disastrous results, ordered all prisoners—even those sick and in hospital—to be killed. In three days eight hundred people, many of whom were innocent of any crime against the revolution, were massacred. Bolívar found no way to justify himself for this, the worst blot upon his record. After it he began to retract, though atrocities did continue on both sides, and British officers who arrived to help the Liberator's cause were appalled to see how prisoners were stripped naked, bound, and stabbed in the back of the neck till they died.

Bolívar's ruthlessness had its effect for Boves, defeated at last, threw himself upon his own sword; and a new leader, José Antonio Páez, disciplined the plainsmen into a formidable force which now took the Liberator's side. At the time of Boves' death Bolívar called him 'heaven's wrath casting thunderbolts against his country'. And with reason; for at this moment, in 1814, it was Boves rather than the Spanish regulars who had finally forced the patriots out of Caracas. Several thousand citizens had fled before this highly effective guerrilla brigand.

In the east all was confusion, the royalists being undisputed masters of Caracas and its environs. This reverse was the more bitter for the patriots because it had been caused by many of the ordinary peasant population supporting the peninsular Spaniards, who were soon reinforced by ten thousand troops from Spain. Bolívar had been compelled to embark from Cumaná with the broken remnants of his army and twenty-four boxes of silver and jewels. Reaching Carúpano he issued a sad and dignified apology for his failure. He realized that, though he had been chosen to break Creole chains, he had also been the instrument used by Providence to pile afflictions upon them. True, he had brought peace and freedom; but in the wake of these inestimable benefits had come war and slavery. He saw it as both a humiliation and a glory to the liberating armies that their conquerors were their blood-brothers—those Creoles in other words who persisted in siding with Spain. The liberating army had wiped out enemy bands but it could not nor should it wipe out those Americans born and bred for whose wellbeing it had fought in hundreds of engagements. It was not right, he said, to destroy men who, however mistakenly, did not wish to be free, nor could freedom be achieved by force of arms and by contending against fanatics 'whose depravity makes them love the chains that fetter society'. The patriots, therefore, should be deeply sorry for those blind slaves among their countrymen who wanted everyone to share their own bondage.

The next part of the apology is in typical Bolivarian style, grandiose and dramatic yet concise in its verbal counterpoint:

'Be noble in your grief, as the cause that produces it is noble. . . . The destruction of a government. . . . the overthrow of established principles, the changing way of life, the remoulding of opinion, and, in a word, the establishment of freedom in a land of slaves is a task beyond all human capacity to carry out quickly. So our excuse for not having achieved what we hoped is inherent in our cause; since even as justice justifies the boldness of having taken it upon us, so does the impossibility of achieving it reflect the inadequacy of the means. It is praiseworthy, it is noble and sublime, to avenge Nature when it has been outraged by tyranny. Nothing can compare with the greatness of such action, and even if desolation and death are the reward of such a glorious endeavour, there is no reason to condemn it, for it is not the easily attainable that should be undertaken, but that which justice demands that we do. . . .

'It is fatally stupid to attribute to public men the changes of fortune which the unfolding of events produces in states, for it is not within the sphere of influence of a general or a magistrate, in a moment of unrest, of clashes, and of divergent views, to stem the torrent of human passions. Agitated by revolutionary movements, these grow in proportion to the force that resists them. And even though serious mistakes or violent passions in the leaders cause frequent harm to the Republic, these very setbacks ought nevertheless to be fairly assessed and their roots sought for in the primary causes of all misfortunes: that is, the frailty of our species and the hazardous nature of all events. Man is the weak toy of fortune, which he may often predict quite well but can never be sure of; for our situation has no contact with it, it being of a much higher order than ours. To imagine that politics and war will proceed according to our plans, unfolding blindly by the mere strength of our desires and encouraged by the limited means at our disposal, is to wish by human means to emulate divine power.'

These are the words of a man essentially humble even at the moment when he seems called upon to lead. Bolívar went on to say that, far from being so stupid as to imagine himself blameless for his country's disaster, he believed himself to be the cause. Nevertheless he felt himself innocent because his conscience, although it might have given bad and imprudent counsel at times, had never been a party to wilful error or malice. He hoped his public life would be carefully examined so that he could be cleared of wrong accusations. Though ready to blame himself, to acknowledge the impotence of a man tossed hither and thither by fate and fortune, he was not prepared to stand meekly by while his fellow men, no whit above him in qualities or actions, condemned him unfairly. He knew that as a leader he stood for noble principles. 'Do not compare your physical strength with the enemy's,' he ended proudly, 'for spirit is not to be compared with matter. You are men, they are beasts, you are free, they are slaves. Fight and you shall win. God grants victory to the steadfast.'[1]

With his back to the wall and much of the country on the side

---

[1] Lecuna, V., *Proclamas*, 40; *Selected Writings*, 81.

of its enemies, Bolívar was acutely aware of the dilemma of every man who wants to bring freedom to those who know neither what they want nor what is good for them. He saw the injustice of giving to men what men themselves do not show that they desire. He was fighting physical battles, but behind them were metaphysical problems that have never been nor are likely to be solved until they are honestly confronted by at least an influential minority of Spanish Americans. Pity and love inform his resounding periods and make them more than hollow rhetoric. He was pleading not for Spanish America alone but for humanity, and his endeavours reached beyond politics to fundamentals. That is why, in spite of some nineteenth-century histrionics, he speaks to us vividly for today.

He now proceeded to Cartagena and offered his services to Nueva Granada, then agitated by internal disputes. A congress assembling at Tunja gave him command of the country's forces, with which he proceeded to march against the separatist Santa Fé de Bogotá which had been the centre of an independence movement in 1811 when a Junta had declared independence and called the new state Cundinamarca. Bolívar now wanted to effect a union between it and Cartagena. In December 1814 he besieged and captured Bogotá. Atrocities were committed during this campaign for which, as commander, Bolívar must be held responsible. Moreover, Santa Fé was obliged to bend to his will in a way that San Martín, for example, was careful to avoid when he had reason to suspect that hearts were not all with him in Lima.

2. Exile

In May 1815, feeling the position in South America to be hopeless, Bolívar resigned his commission and went to Kingston. During his stay in the British island three attempts were made on his life. In the most serious of these he was saved only through having vacated his hammock in order (it has been supposed) to pursue one of his many love affairs; but there is no particular evidence for this and the change of sleeping quarters may have been caused by his having to escape a landlady's wrath; for he was penniless. He had to sell all the silver he had brought with him and was thinking of ending his life to avoid the humiliation of begging from men who were, he said, harder of heart than the gold they coveted.[1] As it was, he outlived his own pessimism and the assassin's dagger, and a member of his guard of honour, who had lucklessly taken over Bolívar's hammock, was stabbed to death in his stead by a Negro servant acting for one of the Liberator's political enemies. Clearly he bore a charmed life.

On May 19 Bolívar had addressed a note to Maxwell Hyslop, a successful British merchant in Jamaica who was exporting rum, timber, coffee, cocoa and other commodities in return for British soap, earthenware, ham and cheese; and who was therefore financially interested in helping the independence movement. Bolívar suggested that the present moment might be the last opportunity England would have to share the fate of the western hemisphere. America, he warned, might collapse if Britain did not protect it from the disruption into which it had been thrown 'by its own people, by vicissitudes in Europe and by the eternal laws of Nature'. A little help in the present crisis might be enough to spare South America cruel devastation and losses. Otherwise, by the time England decided to look to America, there might be no America left.[2]

In much the same sense he wrote to Richard Wellesley. But with the Duke of Manchester, Jamaica's governor, he could not even get an audience though he had promising commercial propositions for handing to Britain the provinces of Paraná and Nicaragua, which last, by the opening of an ocean-to-ocean canal, would become the pivot of world trade.[3]

Bolívar was not of course the first to have thought of this idea, but he was one of the earliest to see its possibilities for modern commerce. His vision and correct forecast of historical events was

---

[1] Lecuna, V., *Cartas del Libertador*, vol. 1, No. 106.
[2] Lecuna, V., *Cartas del Libertador*, vol. 1, No. 93.
[3] See Rivas-Vicuña, F., vol. 2, p. 81.

at this time remarkable, as may be seen from the famous letter he wrote from Kingston to an anonymous Englishman.[1] As usual he attacked Spanish policies bitterly, and then went on to analyse the situation in various parts of Latin America, remarking that in New Spain the population had been much reduced by insurrections since Humboldt's day. In spite of everything, he believed that Mexicans would be free. 'Is Europe deaf to the clamour of her own interests?' he cried, returning to the theme he had touched upon with Hyslop. Europe would do Spain a service by dissuading her from her obstinate rashness, for she would at least be spared expense and bloodshed. Turning her attention to her own lands, Spain would then be able to base her prosperity and power upon more solid foundations than those of 'uncertain conquests, precarious trade, and tributes extorted from remote, powerful, and enemy peoples'. In order to maintain the world's balance of power and—still more important—to acquire overseas trade, it would have been expedient for Europe to aid America's independence, the more so since the rest of Europe was less apt than Spain to be shaken by violent passions of revenge, ambition, and greed. She would seem, therefore, 'by all the rules of justice' to be entitled 'to teach Spain where her best interests lie'.

Once again Bolívar enlarged upon the theme that his people were immature. He longed to see the greatest nation in the world established in America, great not in size and wealth but by virtue of its freedom and glory. Although he wanted the government of his country to be perfect, he dared not believe that the New World could become a great republic yet. The American nations still required the care of more mature governments. Indeed if a single government were to infuse life into the New World, to put into use all the resources for public prosperity, to improve, educate, and advance the peoples of the hemisphere, it would have to possess the authority of a god or at least the knowledge and virtues of all mankind.

He thought it might be useful to establish one central capital

[1] Lecuna, V., *Obras Completas*, vol. 1, Document No. 125; *Selected Writings* No. 103.

and suggested Mexico City as being stronger than the more obviously central point of contact—Panama. Partisan rivalries, he warned, would grow constantly stronger if some kind of central power were not established; but he feared that the leaders in other capitals would not tolerate being ruled by metropolitans whom they would regard as petty tyrants doing their best to imitate the hated Spaniards.

He could see no reason why republicans, who had no imperialistic ambitions, should ever seek to expand their boundaries, for such aggrandizement would over-stretch their own resources. If they sought to conquer for the purpose of bringing other lands to liberalism, the result would be to reduce them to the status of colonies or conquered territories. At best they would be allies but without rights or advantages, as happened to the satellites of Rome. In either case the principles of republican justice would be violated. Bolívar went even further and thought that a state which grew in this way must do so to the detriment of its own citizens, because a state which became too large—taken alone or together with its dependencies—was bound in the end to decay. In such a state, freedom would become merely another tyranny. The principles that ought to preserve it would lapse and the result would be despotism. It seemed to Bolívar that the distinctive feature of small republics was their permanence; that of large ones, a tendency toward empire. Almost all the former, he noted, had lived long; whereas of the latter, only Rome lasted several centuries, but this was because the capital was a republic—the rest of her dominions being governed by other laws and institutions.

According to Bolívar, a king must always and necessarily be wanting to increase his possessions, wealth, and authority, which were the basis of his power. He believed, therefore, that Americans, being anxious for peace, science, art, trade, and agriculture would prefer republics to kingdoms.

Bolívar's argument in the Jamaica letter contradicts his later desire for a large single republic to include the whole of Spanish America. His views on this point changed as he grew older, but his dislike of the monarchical form remained for it was more deep-rooted, instinctive rather than logical, though he could always find logical reasons for opposing it. He knew, moreover, that a limited monarchy is difficult to maintain. 'Only people as patriotic as the English', he said, 'are capable of controlling the authority of a king and of sustaining the spirit of liberty under the rule of a sceptre and crown.'

The Jamaica letter continues with an analysis of the characteristics of the different areas of Spanish America. The people of Chile Bolívar regarded as simple and virtuous, more apt than the others for freedom and a republican form. And indeed Chile today—with the exception possibly of the tiny Costa Rica—is the most democratic of Spanish American countries; whereas Peru, which Bolívar considered had been corrupted by gold and serfdom, has remained feudal as he predicted it would.

Although rejecting the possibility of one large united republic, Bolívar elaborated his dream of a united nations:

'How wonderful it would be if the Isthmus of Panama were for us what the Isthmus of Corinth was to the Greeks! Would to God that some day we may have the good fortune to convene there an august assembly of the representatives of our republics, kingdoms, and empires to deliberate upon the high interests of peace and war with the nations of the other three-quarters of the world.'

Bolívar went on to condemn the federal system as over-perfect ('Do not adopt the best system of government,' he said, 'but the one most likely to succeed.') After this Machiavellian pronouncement—and is not Machiavelli the most misunderstood of political theorists?—we find Bolívar in metaphysical mood, reminding his unknown correspondent how Quetzalcoatl, 'the Hermes or Buddha of South [*sic*] America', gave up his ministry, promising his people that he would return to re-establish his government and bring them back prosperity:

'Does not this tradition lead us to suppose that he will shortly reappear? Can you imagine the effect that would be produced if an individual were to turn up among the people having the characteristics of Quetzalcoatl, their Buddha of the forest . . . ?

Is it not unity alone that is required to enable us to throw out the Spaniards, their troops, and the supporters of corrupt Spain, in order to establish in these lands a powerful empire with a free government and benevolent laws? . . . Is it not that very prophet or god of Anáhuac, Quetzalcoatl, who will be able to bring about the prodigious changes you suggest? This deity is scarcely known to the Mexican people, and even where he is known he is not greatly honoured: such is the fate of the defeated, even when they are gods.'

Bolívar was happy that the Mexicans had at least been wise enough to raise their brown virgin of Guadalupe into a national symbol. How much more so he could be today to know that Quetzalcoatl, the plumed serpent, has come into his own and is now one of Mexico's chief heroes, uncovered from hundreds of archaeological sites, reproduced (albeit in mechanistic cliché) on stalls for tourists, on the walls of university buildings and modern housing estates, studied and written about as the argument still rages whether he was the disciple Thomas, or a Celt wandered accidentally into the ancient Mexican world. To at least one foreign minister of a South American country the plumed serpent became a symbol of the potentialities still unrealized in his homeland: if only the creeping thing could once more learn to fly! A study of the philosophy hidden in his cyphers and legends and poems and philology might give Spanish Americans just that inner thrust without which no outward system of reform has ever for long succeeded. Did Bolívar, in the nineteenth century, know this? If so, he was ahead of all but a handful of perceptive Mexicans—Sor Juana Inés de la Cruz among them—in understanding their country's heritage.

As the Jamaica letter also shows, Bolívar was well aware of the implications of the power struggle between the two world blocks: the reactionary Holy Alliance of Austria, France, Prussia, and Russia; and the liberals represented by Britain and the U.S.A. He had a vision of a transatlantic alliance in which Spanish America would play its part side by side with the two great English-speaking nations. Britain, with command over the seas, must take a prominent part in this alliance, greater than the people of the United States were likely to countenance with a good grace; and Britain was the power that could perhaps bring France back into the liberal fold after the deplorable backsliding that had blocked and bedevilled the latter stages of the revolution. If Britain in particular had shilly-shallied for too long in her desire not to offend Spain, the United States was for different motives equally insensible to the pleadings of the nations to the south that they should be helped to achieve freedom. The war waged by the states of New England against Britain was fresh in memory; and there was also at one time the hope of obtaining very favourable terms from Madrid for the purchase of Florida. Therefore, though some aid came from private citizens, the U.S. government remained even more aloof than Britain's. There was no direct support from the first nation in the new hemisphere to break imperial ties, for those still struggling along the same path. So Bolívar found himself—as Miranda before him—crushed between the Napoleonic and political struggle on the one hand, and commercial greed on the other. However much he tried to persuade Britain that her interests would actually be furthered by a successful freedom movement, and however much he hoped that the United States might become a brother in arms, he must have realized that only expediency would move either power to take part. Expediency from Britain he was prepared to tolerate, because like Miranda he admired British institutions and character. Expediency from the U.S.A. was another matter, for like many Spanish American statesmen who have come after him he could not feel deeply sympathetic—try as he might to conform with the orthodoxy of his age—with the democratic point of view. He was himself too much of an aristocrat. His paradox was to be also a republican.

Both Jamaica and Trinidad were of obvious strategic importance to the Spanish American cause, and Spain knew this as well as Bolívar did. When General Pablo Morillo arrived in Trinidad, bound for the war front in Venezuela, he congratulated the British Governor for refusing to allow 'the traitors of His Catholic Majesty' to remain in the island. The loyalty that England had shown to Spain allowed him to hope that the Governor would not only refuse to admit the fugitives, but would deliver up those listed in an attached note, together with the longboats that were sheltering in the island and also the ex-Marquis of Toro and all his followers including Colonel Sucre. He felt sure that the Governor would not allow arms and munitions to be sent to Spanish America 'merely for commercial speculation'.[1]

The Governor replied (June 11, 1815) that nothing had given him more satisfaction than to observe the friendship and alliance between the two nations and to have tried to avoid the passage of arms and munitions to the insurgents; which he thought he had succeeded in doing in spite of the extent and openness of the coasts. He pointed out, however, that most of those named in Morillo's note had either never been in Trinidad or had already left. As to the few who remained, the Governor regretted that without receiving orders from his Sovereign he had no authority to give them up; but he could nevertheless assure Morillo that he would punish as a traitor any immigrant who should try to cause disturbances in His Catholic Majesty's territory or invade it. Morillo, in short, could be sure that the government of His Britannic Majesty had always sincerely wished for the pacification of the Spanish colonies, and had never lost an opportunity to reunite them with the Motherland.[2]

So many empty words drove Morillo into despair, and he wrote to the Spanish Minister in Washington asking him to help in obtaining a guarantee of neutrality from the U.S.A. A little later the peninsular Spaniards announced to the British fleet that there would be a blockade, and on July 30 the rights of His Catholic Majesty were invoked 'to prevent foreign ships from coming to these possessions'.[3] An order to the British ships in Cartagena, dated August 10, asked that all ships should leave those waters before hostilities began.[4] The British did what they could to obey

[1] Rodríguez Villa, A., document 408, quoted by Rivas-Vicuña.
[2] Rodríguez Villa, A., document 438, quoted by Rivas-Vicuña.
[3] Rodríguez Villa, A., *El teniente General Don Pablo Morillo*, vol. 2, document 408 quoted by Rivas-Vicuña, P., vol. 2, p. 96.
[4] Rodríguez Villa, A., document 439, quoted by Rivas-Vicuña.

Morillo without leaving their own subjects stranded. Even after the fall of Cartagena the blockade was not raised, and this was one of the most important factors contributing to Morillo's success. By the end of 1815 he had everything under his sway and could even spare troops for Peru.

In the meantime Bolívar had gone from Jamaica to Aux Cayes in Haiti, where President Petión gave him a small force and where such capable officers as Manuel Piar, Santiago Mariño, and Carlos Soublette had joined him together with the Scottish Sir Gregor McGregor. This latter adventurer with a suspect knighthood had been a cavalry colonel under Miranda, had married a niece of Bolívar, and had achieved fame for his military exploits until, falling foul of the ambitious General Piar, he was forced to resign from the Venezuelan service although he continued piratical and highly individualistic activities for some time until he eventually suffered an irrecoverable defeat at Río Hacha.

The talent among Bolívar's officers proved an embarrassment, for there were some who did not readily submit to his authority. Their mutinous mood was inflamed by the Liberator's dalliance with Josefina Madrid, Señorita Pepa as she was known, who had first caught his eye during his triumphal entry into Caracas and who now held up the invading fleet for days at Aux Cayes while Bolívar, dressed not very suitably for warfare, waited for his favourite and her mother to join the squadron. Dissension was quelled only when Luis Brión, commander of a small Dutch contingent, declared that he would serve under none but the Liberator. It was Brión who, with the rank of Admiral in the Venezuelan navy, commanded the squadron that sailed from Haiti in March 1816 carrying three hundred men whom Bolívar compared to the three hundred Spartans of Leonidas (just as he compared his reconquest of Venezuela to the redemption of Jerusalem by the Crusaders—he was much given to historical analogies).

Reaching the island of Margarita early in May, Brión boarded and captured two Spanish ships but only after desperate resistance in which—according to Miller—three-fourths of the Spaniards' crews were killed. From her Bolívar proceeded to Carúpano on

174

the mainland, where he made contact with parties of *llaneros* who had been fighting in such isolation that some groups imagined themselves to be carrying on a lonely resistance. Now and then, by sheer accident, one guerrilla band might contact another and their spirits would rise. Now Bolívar was able to encourage them by supplying them with arms; and with their help he occupied Ocumare until heavy enemy concentrations and treachery within his own ranks forced him to retreat and return to Haiti. Much later, in 1830, Bolívar wrote to José Fernández Madrid who was Colombian Minister in London:

'The incident at Ocumare was the most extraordinary event in the world. I was betrayed simultaneously by an aide-de-camp of General Mariño, who was a traitor, and by the foreign sailors who behaved atrociously, abandoning me to my enemies on a deserted beach. I was about to put a pistol to my head when one of them . . . returned from the sea in a boat and took me to safety.'[1]

This is a very different story from that given by H. L. V. Ducoudray Holstein, a French soldier of fortune, who had never a good word to say of Bolívar and who accused him on this occasion of the basest cowardice. Whatever the truth, there had been some extraordinary confusion. Brión, thinking that the army had been landed and his own mission completed, had sailed away. Santiago Mariño and José Francisco Bermúdez (defender of Cartagena) appeared to be pursuing their own private liberation, and Bolívar thought he had been bereft of all support.

3. Recruitment of Legionaries

His fortunes were at their lowest ebb. And it was now that Ducoudray Holstein, collaborating with López Méndez, Bolívar's agent in Britain, suggested that the patriot troops would benefit from training under foreign officers. It was a suitable moment to take advantage of the inevitable economic depression that seems

[1] Lecuna, V., *Cartas del Libertador*, vol. 9, No. 1994.

to follow upon great victories. Waterloo had brought glory to Britain but also low wages and a scarcity of jobs for the heroes. As soon as López Méndez made it known that contracts for service in Spanish America could be signed, enthusiasm therefore spread. The terms were good: a step-up in rank, various allowances including a generous one for equipment, and certain guarantees. Among the first to offer his services had been Colonel Gustavus Hippisley who with a burst of bombastic idealism volunteered to overthrow the despotic tyrant Ferdinand. But like many who went out from England he was less than sincere with himself about his motives. The journal he wrote after his return to England shows him to have been more interested in the uniforms of himself and his hussars, upon which he lavished extraordinary care, and on a 'good table', than upon fighting the freedom war. He was disgusted by scenes of drunkenness, bickered about pay, felt insulted at having to share quarters with the ranks, and seemed totally unable to appreciate that men like Bolívar, who so openly philandered with women and indulged in feasting and display when tensions relaxed, were prepared also for their ideals to endure the living conditions of the most backward and wretched peasants.

The legionaries had a tough time of it from the moment they set out from England, for a ship carrying a whole regiment of lancers foundered on Ushant Rocks. This did nothing to boost the expedition's morale, and those who reached Venezuela were attacked by smallpox, yellow fever, insect bites, and other endemic maladies. Preparation of food was primitive and insanitary. But these were the kind of hazards that men who were fighting for an ideal, or those who were merely running away from personal predicaments, might have expected in foreign parts, and the Venezuelans saw no reason why the legionaries should not be satisfied with conditions that they themselves tolerated more or less uncomplainingly. Besides, the foreigners, not only the British but the Germans and French among them, seemed all clamouring to be generals! They grumbled about the lack of supplies, about insults real or imagined, about the poor quality of the native troops. 'At the present moment', wrote Hippisley, '(with the exception of one man, bred in the British service, who . . . now indeed and most deservedly is a colonel in the independent service) there is no person in command who can claim the appellation of soldier.'[1]

He was not the only grouser. An Irish division had been recruited by one, John D'Evereux, who lingered at home enjoying his profits until he was finally forced to join his men on Margarita island. This legion, having comported itself magnificently at Río Hacha under fire, mutinied because it was not allowed to pursue the defeated enemy and because there was no water and no pay. Among those who remained loyal was Francis Burdett O'Connor who was to be one of Bolívar's most trusted aides thereafter.

A certain Colonel Wilson behaved less than honourably in trying to incite General Páez, the *llanero* leader, to renounce allegiance to Bolívar. Wilson was dismissed from the army and joined the malcontents spreading despondency in Europe about the Creole cause. Bolívar was glad to be rid of such men, but he did not on that account turn chauvinistic. Immediately after the Wilson episode he sent Colonel James T. English back to Britain to recruit more men, and the result was the formation of the British Legion or Albion Battalion, which had for its motto 'Die or conquer'. The new recruits in their turn found conditions on Margarita island far from happy. English himself—now a General —turned out to be so overbearing that a serious mutiny among his men was avoided by a hair's breadth. After a not very successful command he finally died of a fever on Margarita.

Bolívar received in the end full value from those members of foreign legions who understood his aims—from Ferguson, O'Leary, O'Connor, James Rooke, and others who distinguished themselves at the great battles that were to come. They gave an example of discipline to his own troops and brought a military professionalism into the liberating armies. As he pondered his future course of action during his second exile in Haiti, and encouraged López Méndez to recruit for a cause that looked at

[1] Hippisley, G., p. 526.

that moment to most foreigners hopeless, he could scarcely have dreamed either of the troubles Hippisley, Wilson, D'Evereux and English were to bring him, or of the prestige the mere presence of the legionaries would give to his armies—of their steadfastness at Junín and Ayacucho, of the loyalty and friendship of those who were to become his personal aides. All that was for the future; and the present was black enough to preoccupy him wholly just then.

4. TESTING TIME IN ANGOSTURA

A second expedition from Haiti was successful. By January 1817 Bolívar had landed at Barcelona on the Venezuelan mainland. This time he was making no mistakes. He knew that he could not afford to dally along the coast and decided that his campaign could better be waged in the Orinoco valley where transport was easy and horses and cattle abounded in the lush pastures. He was counting on help from Páez and his *llaneros* who were completely at home in that region and knew every trick of the land. Like Boves, Páez was of humble origin, having been raised among his father's herds and having received no formal education. He possessed herculean strength and was always ready to challenge his own soldiers in single combat. He was a master of horse-taming and could perform veterinary operations with skill. Dressed in a coarse blue cloth blouse, a cloak and slouched hat, he was a man of the people, ready to turn to any job however lowly or however hairbrained. Once in Bolívar's presence he and fifty *llaneros* decided to capture enemy skiffs on the far bank of the Apure. In spite of Bolívar's protestations the men plunged into the swift current, their lances between their teeth, and so surprised the Spaniards that they jumped from their ships and swam for shore leaving their craft to be captured by the liberators.

Another personality in Bolívar's armies during this period was Manuel Piar, a brave mulatto adored by his followers. With this magnificent fighter (who afterwards deserted, was court-martialled and shot), with Páez, and with a fleet of gunboats commanded by Brión, Bolívar forced the royalists out of Angostura and established his capital there, only to be defeated by Morillo at La Puerta (where Boves had once inflicted a crushing blow to the patriots) on March 15, 1818. Meantime Cumaná had been lost to the royalists and Mariño, who had defeated Boves in March 1814, had defected for reasons of personal vanity. Things were as black as they had ever been. Bolívar had suffered reverse after reverse—the years 1812, 1814, 1816, and 1818 had all seen disasters each of which would have been sufficient to exhaust the determination of a man less fired by a rare spark of genius or of fate. Brilliant divination seemed to tell him that Angostura was the key. Páez in his autobiography says that Venezuela has three lines of defence after the sea itself: the mountains where 'the European cannot take a step without struggling against great obstacles'; the plains, land of cavalry with raging rivers, rapids, and wild beasts; and the forests. At Angostura, where the river Orinoco suddenly narrows, forests and plains meet. The town, now Ciudad Bolívar, became famous under its original name because a surgeon, J. G. B. Siegert, who served in Bolívar's foreign legions, and who had experimented there with tropical plants in the hope of finding a palliative for the ills caused by the tropical climate, hit upon the formula for Angostura bitters. Between 1820 and 1875, when the Siegert enterprise transferred to Trinidad, Angostura was the centre for distribution of this preparation whose exact formula remains a secret to this day, though it is evidently based on the bark of the Cresparía febrifuga which contains bitter aromatic alkaloids and was once used against dysentery and fever.

In 1819 Angostura became in a sense to the Liberator what Mendoza had been to San Martín: a place to assemble forces and gather strength. The parallel is not exact but there was the same enthusiasm in the midst of apparent failure, albeit with less whole-hearted devotion from some, especially among the legionaries. All the elements of the Spanish American drama were assembled in the little town with its simple architecture, the surrounding tropical jungle laced by the swirling currents of the Orinoco and

Apure rivers. In this environment only the hardy could survive. There was no pampering of the flesh.

Hippisley, who as we have seen was not among the staunchest, does, however, give a good picture of Angostura and its surroundings, of the long street with its line of stone-walled houses, stucco-faced and with balconies along the upper floors, of the natural basin formed by a circle of rocks that served as a dock for the *flecheras* or river skiffs, of men and women reclining in hammocks amid lemon and fig trees as they smoked cigars together, the women free with their favours and provocatively attractive. Maliciously Hippisley tells how Bolívar made General Soublette's sister his favourite for a season, then cast her off onto a merchant who was pleased enough to marry the former mistress of the supreme chief, the more so since he received as a marriage gift the finest house in town and what was most likely the only four-poster bed, with gilded cupids twining garlands among the drapery.

Hippisley sets the life of the town against its forest background with the trees growing improbably tall and circled by carrion crows, noisy with chattering ring-tail monkeys, slithering with serpents, its river infested with alligators and swept by the scarlet wings of flamingoes and other colourful water birds.[1] He admires the Indian dances which were performed sometimes for the amusement of the officers. He describes one ritual something like a maypole dance in which ribbons were wound about a post by Indian lads moving with an accuracy he was compelled to admire. He had less praise for the living quarters and for the hospital where men with amputated limbs lay about on benches or on the floor, some bleeding to death, some with skulls blown off and the upper part of the brain exposed; 'yet hardly a groan escaped from the poor miserable sufferers, some of whom seemed to endure the agony they were undergoing with all the stoical indifference and resolution ascribed to their North American brethren when put to the torture by their conquerors. The only cry I heard was for water.'[2]

[1] Hippisley, G., p. 311.   [2] Hippisley, G., p. 384.

Hardships were beyond belief; but the Angostura epoch was one in which contending forces in Bolívar's own nature and in the liberation movement were gathered and sorted. Characters were tested, failings discovered, wills tried. Pondering upon the truisms that 'arms destroy tyrants in vain unless we can establish a political order capable of repairing the havoc of revolution', and 'the military system is that of force, and force is not government . . .',[1] on February 15, 1819, he held a congress for which he knew that he had general approval. Dictated to his secretary as he sailed the Orinoco in a skiff, the speech in which he submitted his full and considered views on government is a literary and political master-piece, a slice of Socratic philosophizing adapted to the nineteenth century.[2]

Beginning modestly, Bolívar likened himself to a plaything and a straw blown on the revolutionary hurricane. 'I have been able to do neither good nor ill,' he said. Irresistible forces had determined events, and to attribute them to him would give him an un-deserved importance:

'Do you want to know who are responsible for past and present events? Consult the annals of Spain, America, and Venezuela. Examine the Laws of the Indies, the old colonial system, the influence of religion and foreign rule. Observe the first act of the republican government, the ferocity of our enemies, and our national character. . . .'

He insisted that it was necessary for him to surrender the supreme power of Venezuela into the hands of Congress, because the perpetuation of authority in a single individual had too often been the downfall of democratic governments. Nothing being more dangerous than to leave power for long in the hands of a single citizen, frequent elections were essential to popular systems. Otherwise people become used to obeying, the ruler to com-manding; whence arise tyranny and usurpation.

But this was to contradict what from practical experience he had already determined, that it is rare for a people to be capable of

---

[1] Lecuna, V., *Cartas del Libertador*, vol. 1, No. 142.
[2] Lecuna, V., *Proclamas* 83; *Selected Writings*, No. 70.

judging what is good for them. Caught in a cleft stick between the democratic ideal and the realities of human psychology he took refuge in a sense of history which he possessed to an unusual degree. Together with his intuitive understanding of men, it set him above the political scene and gave his utterances the ring of oracular certainty. The conflict continues throughout this long speech, implicit in the development of statement and counter-statement. It is the conflict of our times, just as Bolívar is typically a hero of our times, racked by doubts that would not have occurred to any European before the French revolution. And yet we are never uncertain about where his own final conviction lies: somewhere in the unexplored territory where tyranny can be used not as a means to masochism and self-indulgence but as a pause on the way to the ultimately desirable but ever-receding democratic form.

A tortuous Creole ambivalence is apparent in all he says. If America broke loose from the Spanish monarchy, Bolívar could see that the situation would be similar to that of the Roman Empire at the moment when its enormous mass collapsed in the ancient world. At that time each of its fragments formed an independent nation suited to its location or its interests. Nevertheless there was an important way in which the situation at that time differed from America's; for in the east the various members of the empire had eventually re-established their earlier links. Americans on the contrary had been unable to preserve even the vestiges of what had existed before. They were neither European nor Indian but an intermediate species between the aborigines and the Spaniards:

'Americans by birth and Europeans by law, we find ourselves faced with the anomaly—in the very country that gave us birth—of having to dispute our titles of ownership with the natives and of maintaining ourselves against the force of the invaders.'

The American situation was unusually complicated. The lot of the inhabitants had always been passive. Politically it had not even existed. People who had been slaves, who had not been allowed so much as the right 'to exercise active and domestic tyranny', must find it more than usually difficult to become free. This last point seems paradoxical, but Bolívar explained it by the limitless legal powers that exist in absolutist systems and which reduce even the subordinate authorities to the level of puppets obeying the master. The will of the despot himself becomes the supreme law, arbitrarily enforced by subordinates who enjoy the feeling of power that comes with delegated responsibility for civil, political, military, and even religious functions.

Here was the great difference between the ancient east and modern America. 'Persian satraps were in the last analysis Persians. The Pashas of the Grand Turks were Turks; the Sultans of Tartary were Tartars. China did not seek Mandarins in the cradle of Genghis Khan who conquered her.' America on the other hand received everything from Spain, so that her senior citizens had never any part—not even a tyrannical one—in their domestic affairs and internal administration and therefore they never learned to conduct public affairs. Nor had they enjoyed the glamour which the 'glitter of power' inspires in the eyes of the multitude and which Bolívar knew very well was exploitable in great revolutions

It is evident that Bolívar was speaking not for the Indians but for the Creoles. It was his own, the Creole situation that disturbed him, and his republic was not Washington's but Plato's where the abject situation of lower social orders is taken for granted. When he inveighs against slavery, it is the slavery of the middle classes to a foreign master that he is concerned with, not the slavery of the peon on his own family estate.

Bolívar went on to analyse how ancient and modern nations had often shaken off oppression but had rarely enjoyed liberty since they soon reverted to their former political vices: 'for it is the people rather than the governments that drag tyranny in their train.' Here speaks the spiritual aristocrat; but, alas for his peace of mind, he is bound by the temper of the times to support democracy. Only democracy, in his opinion, could establish absolute liberty; yet his thoughts continued to be heretical. Democratic governments, he frankly admitted, tended to be transitory, while monarchies endured for centuries. China, Sparta, Venice, the Roman Empire, France, Britain; they had all been, or still were, great; but they were all aristocracies or monarchies. What pernicious thinking was this that it should so gnaw at the mind of a dedicated revolutionary? By hook or by crook the aristocratic Bolívar was compelled to find some way of condemning aristocracy and monarchy or his ideals would collapse. But in the innermost sanctuary of his own mind he could never deny his disbelief in the multitude—especially such a multitude as existed in his homeland:

'The more I admire the excellence of the Federal Constitution of Venezuela, the more I am persuaded of the impossibility of applying it to our state. As I see it, it is a miracle that its model in North America continues to prosper and does not fall before the first difficulty or danger. Although that country is a unique model of political virtues and moral example; although it was cradled in liberty, reared and nurtured on pure freedom: I must emphasize . . . that this people is unique in the history of human kind; it is a miracle, I repeat, that a system so weak and complicated as the federal has been able to govern it in such difficult and delicate circumstances as those it has been through.'

He emphasized that the English-American way of arranging public affairs would not fit the Spanish American reality; that laws had to be adapted to peoples; that the most perfect system of government was that which would bring the greatest measure of happiness, social security, and political stability. Venezuela must, said Bolívar, have a republican regime with sovereignty residing in the people, with division of powers, civil liberty, abolition of slavery, of monarchy, and of special privileges. Venezuela must avoid the weakness of Athens with its 'absolute democracy'. He thought Solon had deceived the world and showed how hard it is to rule men by simple laws. Sparta on the other hand he praised for producing more real good than Athens. He admitted, however, that Pericles, though a usurper, was a 'useful citizen'. Though with no proper distribution of power, Rome had the most forceful of constitutions. Rome showed, indeed, that political virtue can ride above the defects of institutions.

In modern times there were the examples of the English and French revolutions. Rome and Great Britain were the most outstanding among ancient or modern nations, both having been born to command and to be free; and both succeeding not through brilliant forms but through solid structures:

'Therefore I recommend to you, Representatives, a study of the British Constitution, which seems destined to bring the greatest possible good to the peoples who adopt it. But perfect as it may be, I am very far from advising that it should be slavishly imitated. When I speak of the British government I refer only to its republican features. And indeed, can we designate as a pure monarchy a system that recognizes popular sovereignty, the division and balance of powers, civil liberty, liberty of conscience and the Press, and all that is sublime in politics? Can there be more liberty than this in any type of republic? And can any such make a greater demand upon the social situation?'

Bolívar thought that there would be no alteration in the fundamental laws of Venezuela if the British parliamentary system were adopted as a model. A hereditary senate, for instance, because it would ride above political storms, would be the binding element and the soul of the republic. In all governments there ought to be a neutralizing body such as the Roman senate and—in Bolívar's day—the British House of Lords, whose members could be trained from infancy for their high office. There was nothing anti-republican in such an idea for 'in all struggles, the calm of a third party is the organ of reconciliation', and thus the Venezuelan senate would be like a rainbow of harmony shining above the political arena, giving 'eternal stability' to the structure.

The British sovereign, moreover, was restrained from absolutism by having three formidable rivals: his cabinet, responsible to the people and to parliament, the senate (or House of Lords), and the Commons. Judges, by being subject to their own laws, were restrained from misappropriation of public funds. Application of the British Constitution to Venezuela, under a president elected by the people or their representatives, would be an important step toward the creation of a happy nation. (In a republic, however, the executive should be the strongest power, in a monarchy the legislative.)

Holding these views, why then did Bolívar later show so much resistance to the monarchist plans of San Martín and other South Americans? Monarchy—even limited monarchy—stuck in his throat though he longed to follow Britain's example. He feared power, yet knew that power was needed for controlling unruly members. Even more, he was afraid of the outward trappings of power, perhaps because he knew that by instinct he was attracted to them. Therefore he was prepared to curb the power of the populace by a hereditary chamber but was not prepared to accept any symbol—however stripped of real authority—of the ancient divinity of kings.

The speech goes on to extol moderation and patience, for Venezuela was not likely to achieve what had eluded humanity in the past. Undefined freedom, and absolute democracy, were the reefs on which all republican hopes had foundered. Only angels and not men, said Bolívar the mystic, can exist freely, tranquilly and happily. Venezuela should abandon her federal forms which do not suit her requirements, and also the triumvirate of executive power. A president should have enough authority to combat the ills that threatened the new republic. The legislative power should be separate from the executive. Tribunals should be reinforced by making the judges independent. A Holy Alliance should be formed of the Areopagus of Athens and the censors and domestic tribunals of Rome so that the idea of a people who can be not only strong and free but also virtuous might be revived. From Sparta should be borrowed her austerity; and a fourth power should rule moral life so that the Areopagus could supervise the education of children and national institutions, thus purifying whatever in the republic had become corrupt. Punishment should be meted out not only to those who violated the constitution but also to those who forfeited public respect. A moral power should be created which would revive the virtues of Greece and Rome. Citizens should be divided into active and passive, the doers and the knowers, each with their appointed tasks.

What a Utopia this was to be, this Venezuela! Bolívar's dream stopped only just short of a heaven upon earth, and yet through every word he uttered there ran that realism which could scarcely avoid seeing man as being so frequently the destroyer of his own happiness and virtue. Bolívar's greatness was to have known pessimism and to have transcended it, to have believed in the essential goodness of man in spite of his disbelief in man's practical ability to keep clear of disaster. So long as a true and virtuous idea existed, surely it could be compelled in the long run, however arduously, to triumph. But how to reconcile the need for force with the principle of freedom?

Bolívar's speech at Angostura made such an impression in the Hispano-American world that it was included in the first printing of the 1819 Argentine Constitution, glossed interestingly enough by the anonymous editor (who calls himself a Spaniard who loves his country and will never allow it to be outraged). He deplores Bolívar's condemnation of the 'apathetic' Spaniards who could not live under the 'sweet dominion of laws'. The footnote comments:

'None but Bolívar—in other words a cruel enemy of Spain—is capable of speaking thus of the Spaniards and of the glories of this heroic nation, the restorer and mother of the world's freedom in this century: witnesses to this statement being precisely France and England whom he praises so enthusiastically. What Bolívar calls Spanish apathy overthrew the throne of the conqueror of Europe, before whom those two nations trembled and who suffered his evil yoke until Spanish 'apathy' had given the call for freedom, had communicated its impulse to them, and had made them free. The political constitution of Spain—the most liberal in Europe and the most fitting to make man and society happy— speaks on her behalf. . . . It does seem, however, as if Bolívar is referring to the events of May 1814, during which, not because of their inability to live under the dominion of laws, but because of infamous advisers unworthy of the name of Spaniards, we lost our freedom. So his language may be excused.'[1]

[1] Footnote to *Constitución de las Provincias Unidas en Sud-América* (see Bibliography).

With this caveat the anonymous Spaniard justifies both his race and its enemies, thus gaining—as Bolívar and so many of the liberators would in the depths of their unconscious minds have longed to do—the best of both hemispheres.

5. THE ANDES CROSSING AND THE COLOMBIAN REPUBLIC

Bolívar's surrender of authority was not accepted by Congress. Asked to resume power until independence was established, he reorganized his troops and crossed the Cordillera to join Santander who was commanding the republicans in Nueva Granada. Mitre acknowledges this feat, second only to San Martín's, who must be given credit for pioneering the apparently impossible venture of traversing the Cordillera with an entire army. Bolívar had already crossed a spur of mountains from west to east with a small force, when he had defied his commanding officer and had marched from Ocaña to Mérida in 1813. But the present venture was on a very different scale. Bolívar's force included four infantry battalions, a rifle battalion, the Bravos of Páez, the British Legion, and cavalry. It was May of 1819 when they set out, and the seasonal rains had begun to fall with unwonted force. Rivers overflowed and small streams became raging torrents filled—to make matters worse—with the diminutive man-eating fish called *caribe* whose bite was more lethal than that of an alligator. The infantry had frequently to wade up to their waists in water and became so sodden that pause for rest was impossible. At the end of each day their beds were a sea of mud. Rafts made of rawhide carried the ammunition and baggage. Bolívar swam his horse constantly back and forth encouraging the men and ensuring that those who got into difficulties were helped. The English, being unused to the terrain, suffered the most, and progress was so slow that it took a whole month to reach the Andean foothills and make contact with Santander's force of 1,200 well-armed infantry and six hundred mounted plainsmen.

Now as they left the plains for the mountains the scene changed. The snowy peaks of the eastern range of the Cordillera appeared in the distance. The roads ran along the edges of precipices made the more treacherous by rain. Torrents had to be crossed on swinging bridges formed of tree trunks or cables. Where it was possible to ford them the current was so strong that the infantry had to pass two by two with their arms thrown round one another's shoulders, and anyone who lost his footing lost his life too. Bolívar was to be seen everywhere on horseback, carrying the weak and sickly or the women who accompanied the men. After four days' march the horses were exhausted and some squadrons of *llaneros* deserted on finding themselves on foot. Bolívar called a council of war and secured an agreement to carry on in spite of the difficulties, now augmented by the rarefied air which caused sickness and heart-pounding, leading in the end to apoplexy, stupor, and death. Soldiers had to beat one another to drive off the fatal drowsiness that accompanied this malady.

In this passage more than a hundred men died of cold, fifty of them English, although by now in the highlands the Venezuelans accustomed to the tropics suffered as much or more. No horse survived. The reserve supply of arms and even some of those the soldiers carried had to be abandoned. It was a mere skeleton of an army that reached the beautiful valley of Sogamoso in the heart of the province of Tunja on July 6, 1819. From this point Bolívar sent back help to the stragglers, collected horses, detached parties to scour the country round about, and communicated with a few guerrillas who still roamed there. The morale of the troops received encouragement from the buoyant spirits of Colonel James Rooke who now commanded the British Legion and whose optimism was irrepressible.

The enemy had no knowledge of the numbers available to Bolívar and decided to take up strong positions and remain on the defensive. On the morning of August 7 the patriots paused at Tunja and noticed that the royalists were heading for Boyacá. José María Barreiro, one of the most able and intelligent of the royalist officers (he was executed on Santander's orders later that year), was so shocked at the state of the patriot troops that he protested he could not fight against beggars. Yet it was here that the Bravos of Páez clashed with the Spanish Chausseurs in a bayonet charge that broke the royalists completely. The British Legion played an important part in this defeat, but Rooke had an arm amputated and died soon after. The story goes that as his arm fell he seized it in his other hand, lifted it up, and shouted in Spanish, 'Long live the fatherland!' The surgeon asked him in English, 'Which country, Ireland or England?', to which he replied, 'The one which is to give me burial.'[1] He had once remarked to Bolívar that he would follow the Liberator 'to the mouth of hell if it should be necessary'.

After the battle Bolívar proceeded to Santa Fé, but a plot to reinstate the defected General Mariño forced him to hurry to Angostura where on December 14, 1819, the republics of Venezuela and Nueva Granada were formally united under the title of the Republic of Gran Colombia, the seat of government being transferred provisionally to Rosario de Cúcuta on the frontier between the two provinces.

Hoping to spare more bloodshed, on November 25, 1820, at Trujillo, Bolívar made a six-months armistice with the Spaniards. Morillo was recalled and General Miguel de la Torre took command. But the armistice expired and in a decisive battle at Carabobo on June 24, 1821, Bolívar met and crushed de la Torre's troops who fled to Puerto Cabello where two years later they surrendered to Páez. An account of the battle was written by an officer of the British Legion:

'We halted at dusk on the 23rd at the foot of the ridge. The rain fell in torrents all night and reminded us of the night before Waterloo. Next morning the sky was cloudless when we stood to arms, and presently Bolívar sent us the order to advance. We were moving to get round the enemy's right flank, where his guns and infantry were partly hidden by trees and broken ground. Bolívar, after reconnoitring, ordered us to attack by a deep ravine between

[1] See Duarte Level, L., 'Campaña de Nueva Granada', in *Boletín de Historia*, quoted by Henao, J. M., and Arrubla, G., *History of Colombia*, p. 320.

the Spanish infantry and artillery. The enemy's guns opened fire
and our men began to fall. Meantime the Bravos de Apure had
advanced within pistol shot of the Spaniards, and received such a
murderous volley from 3,000 muskets that they broke and fled
back in disorder upon us.

'It was a critical moment, but we managed to keep our ground
till the fugitives had got through our ranks back into the ravine,
and then our grenadier company . . . formed up and poured in
their fire upon the Spaniards, who were only a few paces from
them. Checked by this volley, the enemy fell back a little, while
our men, pressing eagerly on, formed and delivered their fire,
company after company.

'Receding before our fire and the long line of British bayonets,
the Spaniards fell back to the position from which they had rushed
in pursuit of the Apure Bravos. But from thence they kept up a
tremendous fire upon us, which we returned as rapidly as we
could. As they outnumbered us in the ratio of four to one, and
were strongly posted and supported by guns, we waited for
reinforcements before storming their position. Not a man, however, came to help us, and after an hour passed in this manner our
ammunition failed. It then really seemed to be all over with us.
We tried as best we could to make signals of our distress. . . . Our
commanding officer apprised General Páez of our situation and
called on him to get us a supply of cartridges. It came at last, but
by this time many of our officers and men had fallen. . . . You may
imagine we were not long in breaking open the ammunition
boxes; the men numbered off anew, and after delivering a couple
of volleys we prepared to charge. At this moment our cavalry,
passing as before by our right flank, charged, with General Páez
at their head. They went on very gallantly, but soon came gallop-
ing back and passed again to our rear without having done any
execution on the enemy, while they themselves had suffered considerably.

'Why Bolívar at this time, and indeed during the period since
our first advance, sent us no support I have never been able to
guess. Whatever the motive, it is certain that the second and third

divisions of the army quietly looked on while we were being slaughtered, and made no attempt to help us. The curses of our men were loud and deep, but seeing that they must not expect any help they made up their minds to carry the enemy's position or perish. Out of nine hundred men we have not above six hundred left . . . the colours of the regiment had seven times changed hands and been literally cut to ribands and dyed with the blood of the gallant fellows who carried them. But in spite of all this the word was passed to charge with the bayonet, and on we went, keeping our line as steadily as on a parade day and with a loud "hurrah" we were upon them. I must do the Spaniards the justice of saying that they met us gallantly, and the struggle was for a brief time fierce, and the event doubtful. But the bayonet in the hands of British soldiers, more especially such a forlorn hope as we were, is irresistible. The Spaniards, five to one as they were, began to give ground, and at last broke and fled.

'Then it was, and not till then, that two companies of the Tiradores came to our help, and our cavalry, hitherto of little use, fiercely pursued the retreating enemy. . . . The remains of the corps passed before the Liberator with trailed arms at double quick, and received with a cheer, but without halting, the words, *"Salvadores de mi Patria!"* '[1]

The complaint of lack of support from Bolívar was natural enough from a single observer caught in the heat of battle. The strategy was intricate and Bolívar had at every moment to weigh up the dangers of sparing a battalion from one or other flank. In a letter to the President of the Colombian Congress he acknowledged that the British battalion, led by Colonel Thomas Ferrier, gave distinguished service together with Páez, who for his conduct was raised to the rank of 'General in Chief'.[2] Among those foreigners who fought were also the German Colonels John Uslar and Ludwig Flegel.

Bolívar gave his casualties as two hundred dead and wounded,

[1] Account published in a journal, *All the Year Round*, and quoted by Pilling, W., p. 479.

[2] Lecuna, V., *Cartas del Libertador*, vol. 2, No. 416.

which is an understatement. The royalists lost between a thousand and fifteen hundred men, besides 1,700 taken prisoner and another thousand who fled. Although there were bloody encounters still to come, this battle, which has been called the Colombian Waterloo, assured the independence of Venezuela and Nueva Granada.

Páez, together with Carlos Soublette and Mariano Montilla, continued successful, and on June 29 Bolívar entered Caracas for the second time in triumph. In August and September, at Cúcuta, the Constitution of Gran Colombia was adopted with Bolívar as President and Santander as Vice-President. Bolívar made two attempts to resign from his new post, saying that he wished freedom for all and for himself; and Mitre—in spite of frequently showing an Argentine prejudice against the Liberator in favour of San Martín, says of this occasion:

'. . . Though ambitious he was not a despot, and had no wish to be. He swore the Constitution and proclaimed it, and devoting himself to his military duties left the administration in the hands of the Vice-President. But on October 9, 1821, he procured the passage of a law by Congress which gave him absolute power over the army, and empowered him to organize, as he pleased, the Provinces he might liberate until he saw fit to place them under the Constitution of the Republic.'[1]

Bolívar seems to have no intention of usurping these absolute powers for longer than was necessary to keep order and to ensure that the sacrifices made by himself and his armies were not in vain. The Constitution itself was clear and precise, and it established the principle of Spanish American unity at a high level. O'Higgins recognized this when he wrote to Bolívar congratulating him on the event:

'The Union of two states into one has always caused wars and desolation and has never been either sincere or lasting. It has fallen to Venezuela and Nueva Granada to give others a glorious example of friendly fusion motivated by patriotism, politically advisable, dictated by wisdom, sanctioned by the popular will, and consecrated to the glory and prosperity of the Nation.'[2]

[1] Pilling, W., p. 404.   [2] Lecuna, V., *Bolívar y su Epoca*, vol. 1, p. 77.

Future events showed how unstable such a glorious example was to be. Even at the time there was no peace, for the Spaniards were still in Ecuador and Peru, and Bolívar was marching on Quito. To get there he had to traverse the region of Pasto which was a royalist stronghold and in a highly agitated state. Moreover, a strong Spanish fleet was off Guayaquil. Bolívar went ahead with his plans, however, and on April 7, 1822, the bloody battle of Bombóná left him in command of the field but with a Pyrrhic victory (800 dead and over a thousand wounded). Only a few days later Canterac inflicted a crushing defeat on the patriot General Domingo Tristan near Pisco and it was feared that the royalists might advance upon Lima. With a force said to number 6,000 men they did in fact reach a point only three days' march from the Peruvian capital. One British observer, Gilbert Farquhar Mathison, thought that San Martín's government had become so unpopular that 'a large portion of the inhabitants . . . would have hailed with pleasure the return of their old masters.'[1] It was given out that if the enemy drew nearer the patriots would abandon Lima and defend Callao. The government became so nervous that it prohibited the use of weapons and walking-sticks or of cloaks under which arms might be hidden, and a curfew was imposed. Undoubtedly another victory for Canterac at this moment would have been disastrous; but luckily for the patriot cause Sucre, marching from Guayaquil which had proclaimed its independence two years before, routed the enemy on May 24 at the battle of Pichincha, which opened the way to Quito. Sucre was one of the greatest of the liberation generals and Bolívar said of him that he had 'the best organized head' in Colombia. San Martín, who never met him, wrote of him that he was one of the most noteworthy men produced by the republic and of greater military skill than Bolívar.

Bolívar now gave instructions for organizing the recently liberated lands. Francisco Antonio Zea, appointed Minister Plenipotentiary in Europe, was accorded an enthusiastic reception by Wilberforce and other liberals in the City of London tavern, at

[1] Farquhar Mathison, G., p. 253 *et seq.*

which gathering the historian Sir James Mackintosh said, 'For me insurrection against liberty is the greatest of crimes, and insurrection against tyranny the greatest of virtues. Gentlemen, honour to General Bolívar and the Colombian Army!'[1] Zea was nevertheless unsuccessful in his mission of persuading the British to recognize the new republic; and in December 1822, evidently worried that commercial interests would suffer from this omission, a British businessman, James Henderson, sent Bolívar a copy of an 'Address to the South Americans and Mexicans, chiefly intended to dissuade them from conceding commercial privileges to other nations in prejudice of Great Britain, on account of the delay by her of their recognition; which delay is explained on the sound principles of national integrity and honour'.[2]

In Lima, in the meantime, San Martín had drawn up a draft Constitution for Peru, which was finally approved on November 12, 1823, and which was centralist and conservative in character.

As President of Colombia, Bolívar invited the governments of Mexico, Peru, Chile, and Buenos Aires to form a federation and to send plenipotentiaries to a congress in Panama or at any convenient spot. It was to 'serve as an advisory board in important conflicts, as a point of contact in common danger, as a faithful interpreter of public treaties whenever difficulties crop up, and—in short—as an arbiter in our disputes.'[3] Peru and Colombia became formally allied, and Colombia made a similar treaty with Mexico; but for the moment nothing further was done to advance the larger plan, though in the interests of continental unity Bolívar wrote to San Martín thanking him on behalf of Colombia for his and Sucre's aid and offering help in the liberation of Peru.

Bolívar's victories had exalted him and he had a strange vision which he embodied in a prose poem, *My Delirium on Chimborazo*:[4]

'I came wrapped in the mantle of the rainbow from whence the rushing Orinoco pays tribute to the god of waters. I had visited

---

[1] Lecuna, V., *Bolívar y su Epoca*, vol. 1, p. 93.
[2] Lecuna, V., *Bolívar y su Epoca*, vol. 1, p. 99.
[3] Levine, R., vol. 2, p. 175.   [4] Lecuna, V., *Proclamas*, Document 125.

the enchanted fountains of the Amazon and had longed to climb to the very watchtower of the universe. . . .'

He described how, following in the tracks of Humboldt but leaving him far behind, he reached the summit 'as if driven forward by the genius that moved me', and there fainted. Time spoke to him saying:

'I am father of the centuries, the arcanum of fame and of the secret, and my mother was eternity. Infinity marks the boundaries of my empire. There is no tomb for me, because I am more powerful than death. I look upon the past and the future, and the present moment trickles through my hands.'

An atom of creation, centuries, the universe itself, are as nothing to this arcane figure with his secret knowledge of the infinite, and Bolívar had better know it. Duly mortified and humbled, his proud nature was bound, nevertheless, to rebel against the certainty that he—who had climbed so high—must disappear. Time told him to observe and to learn, to hold in his memory all that he had seen and to pass on these truths to all men. It is a strange document to come from one of the world's great soldiers, a document full of grandeur, of deep and hidden meanings which Bolívar himself may scarcely have understood but which must have existed in that layer of the mind where logic gives way before inspired mysticism. Now he was forced to believe in revelation and to assume the role of prophet, for the task had been given him to be the teacher of his people. Henceforth his 'manifest destiny' was clear.

6. BOLÍVAR AND SAN MARTÍN: A CLASH OF PERSONALITIES

What did the feverish mystic look like at this time? General Miller gives a very full description:

'The person of General Bolívar is thin and somewhat below the middle size. He dresses in good taste, and has an easy military walk. He is a very bold rider and capable of undergoing great fatigue. His manners are good and his address unaffected but not very prepossessing. . . . His complexion is sallow; his hair, originally very black, is now mixed with grey. His eyes are dark and penetrating but generally downcast or turned askance when he speaks; his nose is well formed, his forehead high and broad, the lower part of the face is sharp; the expression of the countenance is care-worn, lowering, and, sometimes, rather fierce. His temper, spoiled by adulation, is fiery and capricious. His opinions of men and things are variable. He is rather prone to personal abuse, but makes ample amends to those who will put up with it. Towards such his resentments are not lasting. He is a passionate admirer of the fair sex, but jealous to excess. He is fond of waltzing, and is a very quick, but not a very graceful, dancer. His mind is of the most active description. . . . His voice is loud and harsh but he speaks eloquently on all subjects. . . . Although the cigar is almost universally used in South America, Bolívar never smokes, nor does he permit smoking in his presence. . . . Disinterested in the extreme with regard to pecuniary affairs, he is insatiably covetous of fame. Bolívar invariably speaks of England, of her institutions and her great men, in terms of admiration. He often dwells with great warmth upon the constancy, fidelity, and sterling merit of the English officers who have served in the cause of independence, under every varying event of the war. As a collateral proof of his predilection towards England, he has always had upon his personal staff a number of British subjects.'[1]

Such then, according to General Miller, did Bolívar appear in July 1822 when he was to come face to face with the taciturn and unflamboyant San Martín at their historic and controversial meeting in Guayaquil. The triumphant armies of north and south had converged upon Peru and the incredibly intricate pincer movement was complete. Guayaquil, which had been governed until then by an independent Junta under the poet José Olmedo,

[1] Miller, J., vol. 2, pp. 291-3.

became part of Gran Colombia, and here Bolívar awaited San Martín who wrote to him from Quito accepting the offer of troops for Peru and adding, 'We shall meet, and I have a suspicion that America will not forget the day we embrace.'[1] America did not, but the interview must bitterly have disappointed San Martín. There is no doubt that by this time Bolívar felt himself to be the head of the whole liberation movement; but it must also be said that San Martín seems to have behaved below his best, either because he was tired or because Bolívar's intense nervous energy overpowered him. The fullest account of the meeting we possess is the confidential report from José Gabriel Pérez, Secretary-General, to Pedro Gual, Minister of Foreign Affairs, dated from Bolívar's general headquarters in Guayaquil on July 29—three days after San Martín's arrival in the city.[2] The two men met on board ship, and, after an exchange of compliments which were evidently sincere on both sides, repaired to Bolívar's house. Here Pérez was disappointed in San Martín:

'. . . The Protector spoke only of what had already been the subject of their conversations, raising vague and unconnected questions on military and political matters without going deeply into any, shifting from one theme to another and mingling the serious with the trivial. If the character of the Protector is not as frivolous as appears in conversation, it must be supposed that he acted thus with a certain purpose. His Excellency is inclined to disbelieve that the Protector's character is what it appeared, but neither does it seem to him that he was calculating his words and behaviour.'

Pérez goes on to accuse San Martín of having twice used a coarse word (*pellejería*, literally a place where skins are cured but slang for fecklessness, its use by San Martín being probably no more than the result of his soldierly bluntness). It appears that the Protector had some complaints about disloyalty from his officers, and it is evident that he was feeling generally dispirited and had already decided to renounce his post and retire to Mendoza.

[1] Levine, R., vol. 2, p. 175.
[2] Lecuna, V., *Cartas del Libertador*, vol. 3, p. 60; *Selected Writings*, No. 150.

Before doing so, however, he was determined to lay the foundations for stable government in the form of a monarchy, since democracy was unsuited to Peru. On this point the views of the two men were totally at variance and Bolívar must have expressed himself forcibly, though he did not entirely condemn the monarchic scheme provided a Spanish American, and not a European, were crowned.

San Martín thought that Guayaquil would be a suitable place for the capital of a federation of Spanish American states, an idea of which he warmly approved especially in so far as it included mutual armed aid 'against ambitious and rebellious internal enemies'. He thought Chile would join the federation but had his doubts about Argentina because of her internal disunity.

Bolívar's own account to General Santander[1] is more flattering to San Martín, who impressed him as being 'very military in character, and he seems energetic, quick, and not dull. He has the kind of correct ideas that would please you but he does not seem to be subtle enough for sublimity either in ideas or practice.' Evidently Bolívar had every desire to show good will toward the Protector, and it may well be that San Martín was the more prejudiced of the two; especially since he would have heard of Bolívar's provocative words during a banquet in Quito when he had exclaimed, 'It will not be long before I shall be carrying the Colombian flag triumphantly to Argentina.' According to Mitre, five Argentine officers were present, and one of them proposed a counter toast, 'To the independence of America and of the Argentine Republic'. San Martín was also taken aback by certain theatrical flourishes in Guayaquil, and rejected a laurel wreath which an eighteen-year-old girl placed on his head, though—not to offend—he said he would keep it for the patriotic sentiment that had inspired it.

The meeting in Guayaquil included two interviews (one strictly private) and a banquet during which Bolívar, who suffered from no false modesty, proposed a toast to 'the two greatest men of South America—General San Martín and myself'. San Martín

[1] Lecuna, V., *Cartas del Libertador*, vol. 3, No. 494; *Selected Writings*, No. 152.

countered, 'To the speedy conclusion of the war, to the organization of the several republics on the continent, and to the health of the Liberator of Colombia'—thus showing disapproval of the plans to unite all Spanish America into one large republic (and seeming to contradict his praise for such a scheme made at the interview—his monarchical ideas he had at that moment tacitly put on one side), and gently suggesting that Bolívar should limit his sphere of influence to Colombia.

The ball that followed was not to San Martín's taste, and in the early hours of the morning he boarded a schooner on which his baggage had already been placed, and sailed away. From Callao he wrote to O'Higgins, 'The Liberator is not the man I took him to be.' But he gave no account of the discussion. Afterwards he said of Bolívar that his feats of arms entitled him to be considered the most remarkable man in South America. It seems that San Martín would have been willing to serve under the military command of Bolívar, but they were evidently temperamentally incompatible and at variance on the important question of the extent to which a democratic form could be imposed upon semifeudal countries. Though Bolívar rejected San Martín's plans for a limited monarchy, San Martín in his turn would not have tolerated Bolívar's suggestion of stabilizing the democratic form by making appointments for life. Each man was suspicious of the other in case ambition should triumph over idealism and good sense.

On returning to Peru, San Martín wrote to Bolívar telling him that the royalist forces were greatly superior to their own and concluding:

'My decision is irrevocable. I have convened the first Congress of Peru. The day after its installation I shall leave for Chile, convinced that my presence is the only obstacle that stops you from entering Peru with your army. It would have been the greatest happiness for me to have ended the war of independence under the orders of a general to whom America owes her freedom. Destiny has determined otherwise, and I must resign myself to it.'

With the letter he sent a fowling piece, a brace of pistols, and a war horse to carry Bolívar on his next campaign.[1] Utterly dispirited he had written to O'Higgins:

'I am tired of hearing men call me tyrant, that I wish to make myself King, Emperor, the Devil. On the other hand my health is broken, this climate is killing me. My youth was sacrificed to the service of Spain, my manhood to my own country. I think I have now the right to dispose of my old age.'[2]

It must have been with relief that at the installation of Congress he removed the bi-coloured sash that was his emblem of authority, and retired. Congress passed a vote of thanks to 'the first soldier of Liberty', and named him commander-in-chief of the land and sea forces of Peru with a pension of 12,000 dollars a year. San Martín accepted the title and the pension, but refused to serve, saying that his presence in Peru would be 'inconsistent with the dignity of Congress, and with my own. I have kept the promise I made to Peru, but if some day her liberty be in danger I shall glory in joining as a citizen in her defence.'

Thus did San Martín abdicate in favour of Bolívar, happy no doubt to know that the fate of Spanish America was in the hands of a proved soldier and patriot; sad that the two leaders could not come to any agreement about the future of their countries. The problem that exercised them both throughout their working lives was how to achieve a balance between democratic freedoms and a degree of control that would avoid anarchy or at least constant disturbances in the new and largely uneducated countries. It is a problem that has not grown less through the years; for the proportion of illiterate peasants in Spanish America is still high, the armies have still too strong a hold over the political affairs of many countries, and a new and growing middle class tends to demand rights while not being altogether willing to shoulder responsibilities. In Bolívar's day many of the constitutions were too weak to endure, but public opinion was suspicious of control that began to approach despotism. Bolívar's own hatred of

[1] The account of the relations between the two men is based on various sources including Pilling, W., pp. 419 *et seq.*, and Lecuna's introduction to Bolívar's *Selected Writings*. But very little is known except indirectly.

[2] Pilling, W., p. 427.

royalty was balanced against an awareness that his compatriots were unequal as yet to taking upon themselves the burden of democratic rule. He therefore opposed San Martín. San Martín in his turn had a horror of dictators, and opposed Bolívar in the belief that the latter wished to become one. Thus the two greatest figures in the Spanish American independence movement met and parted, the one defeated and sad, the other triumphant but unsure of what the future could hold for his politically immature country-men. Their preoccupations were alike. It was temperament alone, and perhaps some trick of language or outward form, that kept them apart. San Martín and Bolívar suffered equally—after this historic meeting—from the kind of anarchy they had both feared and predicted. Two years before his death, from his retirement in Boulogne, in September 1848, San Martín wrote the following illuminating letter to General Ramón Castilla, President of Peru:

'If America owes me any thanks it is for my retirement from Lima, a step that not only jeopardized my honour and reputation, but was the more grievous to me because I know that with the combined forces of Colombia the independence war would have been over during the year 1823. But this costly sacrifice, not the least of which was that I had to keep absolute silence (so necessary in those circumstances) as to the motives that obliged me to take this step, meant efforts which few can judge. . . . Returning to Lima, I went to live on a small farm which I possessed in Mendoza; not even by this complete retirement, nor by my having painstakingly severed all my former connexions, nor even by the guarantee that my conduct offered . . . could the mistrust the government had in me be allayed. . . . In these circumstances I became convinced that unfortunately I had become more en-tangled in the revolution [that is, the civil strife in Buenos Aires] than I had wished, and this would prevent me from taking an impartial line among the parties. Therefore, in order to get rid of every idea that I was ambitious to lead, I set out for Europe where I remained until 1829, when, encouraged by the government and by various friends who convinced me that the country could offer guarantees of order and tranquillity, I returned to Buenos Aires.

Unfortunately for me, when I arrived in that city I came upon the revolution of General Lavalle, and without disembarking I returned to Europe, preferring this new banishment to being forced to take part in civil disputes. At the advanced age of 71, my health completely ruined and almost blind from cataract, I had expected . . . to end my ailing life in that country; but events since February have presented the problem as to where I shall now rest my bones. . . .'[1]

Before he rested them at last, in a gesture that can be explained only by his total loss of contact with events in his own country, he directed that the sword which had seen him through the wars of independence should be presented to the Argentine dictator Juan Manuel de Rosas 'as a token of the satisfaction . . . I have felt on seeing the firmness with which he has upheld the republic's honour against . . . the foreigners who sought to humiliate her'.[2] Ironically, at the end, the liberator of Argentina paid homage to one of Argentina's most hated tyrants.

7. THE LAST PHASE OF THE WAR AND THE END OF THE LEGIONS

At the time of San Martín's retirement it was vitally necessary that Spanish Americans should unite, for the royalists were still not wholly defeated. After the meeting of the two liberators, Bolívar was forced into a defensive position; and in spite of much feasting of him in Lima, where he was invested with Peru's supreme military authority as ladies paraded side-saddle and flowers fluttered on the air, it was not until the middle of 1824 that the liberating army could be reorganized for its final drive against the royalists. Only in June of that year did a new campaign open with a march once more into the high Andes, toward Cerro de Pasco and Huanuco. This time the armies had the assistance of General

[1] Levene, R., vol. 2, p. 176.   [2] Quoted by Herring, H., p. 638.

Miller who had given loyal service to San Martín and now joined Bolívar. As the divisions climbed each by a different valley, Miller sent out his scouts to keep control of events. Behind the men a train of three hundred mules brought the ammunition, and six thousand head of cattle were herded upward for food. The trails were precipitous and slippery and the temperature below zero with winds and snow blowing bitterly down the ravines. Many suffered snow blindness, and breathing became so difficult that men lay down where they were and had to be killed as an example to others, for any lingering at these altitudes was fatal.

A month's march put the patriots in contact with the royalists under Canterac, and at Junín on August 6 the cavalry clashed in a battle of lance and sabre (not a shot was fired) which lasted only three-quarters of an hour and left 374 Spaniards dead on the field for a loss of 55 patriots. Fortunately for the latter they had spared their horses on the march to the highlands, using mules where possible and leading their more precious mounts. The royalists could scarcely have expected them to be fit enough to put up much of a fight and must have been astounded, after at first gaining the ascendancy, to be so decisively beaten. The supreme command of the cavalry was awarded to General Miller in gratitude for his part in the battle.

Bolívar at once returned to Lima, leaving Sucre to pursue the peninsular Spaniards in their retreat to Upper Peru. On December 9 Sucre won the battle of Ayacucho and forced Canterac to surrender. In the whole of Peru the Spaniards now held only Callao, and the war was virtually over. At the capitulation of Ayacucho the Spanish leaders were offered citizenship and the same rank in the Peruvian army as they had had in the Spanish: a generous gesture to be set against the stigma of 'war to the death'.

Bolívar now planned to send an expeditionary force to free Cuba and Puerto Rico but United States opposition was too strong and the fate of the Spanish Caribbean remained in abeyance. Both Castlereagh and Canning had had their eyes on the islands, and it was partly with Cuba in mind that Canning, in 1823, proposed to the United States that an agreement be signed whereby both parties would renounce all claims to the Spanish colonies and would refuse to see 'any portion of them transferred to any other power with indifference'. John Quincy Adams saw the trap and refused to sign. Cuba was an apple which by the force of gravitation ought, he felt sure, to fall into the lap of the U.S.A. So instead of collaborating with Canning he used the pretext that the Holy Alliance might be scheming to invade Spanish America to formulate his Monroe Doctrine, which virtually gave the U.S.A. paternal sway over the fortunes of the hemisphere and which was a landmark in the receding tide of British interests there.

With the fighting now virtually at an end, the British Legion (or Albion Battalion) was disbanded and the foremost of the legionaries were honoured with decorations: General Miller Hallowes, who served first with the Irish and distinguished himself at Carabobo; Thomas Manby who marched into Bogotá after the battle of Boyacá at the head of his column though not a man in it possessed a pair of shoes; William Miller himself; the German Usler; a number of Americans including Colonel Felix Jastran who was under fire at Carabobo and Ayacucho, and John Daniel Daniel who joined Brión's squadron in 1818. There were also, of course, those who became members of Bolívar's personal staff including O'Leary who married General Soublette's daughter, O'Connor, and William Ferguson and Belford Wilson who together, on a later occasion, performed the remarkable feat of marching 1,800 miles in nineteen days from Lima across the Andes to deliver the Bolivian Constitution into the hands of Sucre at Chuquisaca. Independently of their governments, for they had enlisted mostly after such service had been made illegal in 1819 at the request of the Spanish government, they had done, and were to do, much more for the liberation than the smallness of their numbers suggests. A whole century after independence, at the Pan-American Centennial Congress of 1926, Spanish Americans were still expressing their official gratitude:

'The Congress of Bolívar, Commemorative Congress of 1826, *considering*:

'That Great Britain lent to the Liberty of Spanish America not only the support of its diplomacy, represented by Canning, but also an appreciable contingent of blood, and it may be asserted that there was no battlefield in the War of Independence on which British blood was not shed.

'That the heroic collaboration is made more brilliant by the decisive bravery of the British Legion in the battle of Carabobo; by the admirable loyalty of the British Aides of Bolívar, whose model was Ferguson, killed in defence of the Liberator, at the post of duty; by the actions of MacGregor, Rooke, Brown, Guise and a hundred more; by the intrepid bravery of Cochrane and the battling constancy of William Miller of Peru.

'That later on the British heroes who survived the epopee of liberty, incorporated themselves in the life of our democracies and also set through their austerity and love for order and institutions the highest civic examples.

'That finally it was such Britishers as O'Leary, Miller, O'Connor and Stevenson who laid the basis of the history of Spanish America by collecting for posterity the first fragments of the immense Bolivian legend.

'*It is resolved*:

'That the Bolivarian Congress, commemorative of the Congress of 1826, gratefully pays tribute and homage to the memory of the British Heroes who gave their lives or fought without compensation except their love of Liberty and Glory, in favour of the Independence of Spanish America.'

'Few people', says Webster, quoting the above document, 'have been so generous in outlook after so long a lapse of time.'

8. THE CONGRESS OF PANAMA

On February 10, 1825, the Peruvian Congress met in Lima and Bolívar surrendered the dictatorial powers that had been conferred upon him the year before. He also refused the million pesos offered to him. In April he set out on a triumphal march through the provinces, and this gave him a chance to survey the whole territory and to arrange for land to be returned to the Indians—a reform that was incorporated into a decree issued in Cuzco in July when forced public service exclusively by Indians was abolished and all citizens were ordered to collaborate in public works. Bolívar also gave an impetus to mining and education. But what chiefly occupied his mind were his plans for the Congress of Panama. He hoped that it would be supported by all governments of ex-Spanish colonies in America. The Congress was destined to be incomplete, however, because Uruguay was the subject of a territorial dispute between Argentina and Brazil, and Paraguay was in the grip of dictator Francia with his isolationist policies. Bolivia had not yet become a separate country; but Gran Colombia, Peru, Mexico, Argentina, Chile, and Central America were all invited to attend. Bolívar did not expect the United States to be included, but Santander—supported by Mexico and Central America—issued an invitation in the belief that 'the cause of independence and freedom belongs not only to the former Spanish colonies but also to the United States of the North.' Bolívar could not without grave discourtesy have rescinded it but there is reason to think that he strongly disapproved, not because he was unfriendly to the United States but because he was thinking above all in Andean terms. He did, however, hope for British support at the Congress so that it should be strong enough to oppose the Holy Alliance.

Not all Spanish Americans were as enthusiastic about Britain, and on February 2, 1825, the Mexican Carlos María de Bustamante had sent Bolívar a letter in which he spoke bitterly of Britain's perfidy:

'. . . We should work for *ourselves*, without taking into account that England exists; the manoeuvres of that cabinet are tortuous. Let us remember that the Minister of that Nation excited the deputies of the Madrid Cortes to continue opposing the French army when it was on the point of passing the Bidasoa. They did so, counting Britain's help. And what happened? The promises were broken. England opted out and left them in the lurch. They have remained passive spectators of Spain's slavery and have given a sad asylum in Gibraltar to the liberal deputies who took flight, and a miserly help for them to live in penury in London. . . .'[1]

Bolívar's own views on the subject were reported in full by Captain Thomas Maling to Viscount Melville in a private and secret document dispatched in March 1825:

'. . . [France or Spain] can never obtain a permanent footing in our country. France has declared she will not tolerate popular governments, that revolutions have distracted Europe for the last thirty years, and that America can never see peace so long as she gives way to the popular cry of equality. And in truth I am of the opinion of France, for although no man is a greater advocate for the rights and liberties of mankind, which I have proved by devoting my fortune and the best years of my life to their attainment, still I must confess this country is not in a state to be governed by the *people*. . . . No country is more free than England under a well regulated monarchy; England is the envy of all countries in the world, and the pattern all would wish to follow in forming a new constitution and government. Of all countries South America is perhaps the least fitted for republican governments. What does the population consist of but Indians and Negroes, who are more ignorant than the vile race of Spaniards from whom we are just emancipated? A country represented and governed by such people must go to ruin. *We must look to England for relief*; we have no other resource; and you have not only my leave but my request that you will communicate our conversation, and bring the matter under the consideration of His Britannic Majesty's Government in any manner that may seem best to you, either officially or otherwise. You may say I never have been an enemy to monarchies upon general principles; on the contrary, I think it essential to the respectability and well being of new nations, and if any proposal ever comes from the British Cabinet for the establishment of a regular government, that is, of a monarchy or monarchies in the New World, they will find in me a steady and firm promoter of their views, perfectly

[1] Lecuna, V., *Bolívar y su Epoca*, p. 176.

ready to uphold the sovereign England may propose to place and support upon the throne.

'I know it has been said of me I wish to be a King, but it is not so. I would not accept the Crown for myself, for when I see this country made happy under a good and firm government, I shall again retire into private life. . . .

'The title of King would perhaps not be popular at first in South America, and therefore it might be as well to meet the prejudice by assuming that of "Inca" which the Indians are so much attached to. This enslaved and miserable country has hitherto only heard the name of King coupled with its miseries, and Spanish cruelties. . . . Democracy has its charms for the people, and in theory it appears plausible to have a free government which shall exclude all hereditary distinctions, but England is again our example; how infinitely more respectable your nation is, governed by its King, Lords and Commons, than that which prides itself upon an equality but with little temptation to exertion for the benefit of the state; indeed, I question much whether the present situation will continue very long in the United States. . . . If we are to have a new government, let it be modelled on yours. . . .'[1]

It is impossible to say whether this apparent reversal in Bolívar's attitude to a monarchy was mere flattery to Britain or whether his earlier condemnation arose rather from fear of having planted upon him one of the European dynasties whom he had reason to mistrust. In any case his admiration for Britain was so sincere that he could not envisage a Panama Congress without her support. He hoped to place before the assembled delegates a plan for a single rule of conduct to govern all Spanish American countries.[2] The New World was to consist of independent nations united by one law that would control their foreign relations and would provide them with the stabilizing force of a general and permanent congress. The existence of these new States would afford the necessary guarantees. Spain would make peace out of

---

[1] Foreign Office document 61/6, letter 277, in Webster, vol. 1, printed in full in H. W. V. Temperley, *Foreign Policy of Canning, 1822–1827*, p. 555.
[2] Lecuna, V., *Proclamas* No. 150; *Selected Writings*, No. 235.

respect for England, and the Holy Alliance would grant recognition to the infant nations. Domestic control would be preserved intact in and among the States. No one would be weaker or stronger than another but a perfect balance would be maintained. All States would come to the aid of any that might suffer at the hands of a foreign enemy or from anarchy within. Differences of birth and colour would cease to count, and Spanish America would no longer have anything to fear from Negroes or Indians. Social reform would be the result of freedom and peace, with Britain holding the balance.

Great Britain, according to Bolívar, would gain much from this arrangement. Her influence in Europe would grow and her decisions would have 'the force of destiny'. America would become a rich source of trade. America, moreover, would act as a pivot point in relations with Asia and Europe. The British would be given equal rights with Spanish American citizens, and Britain and Spanish America would in time become equals, so much so that British characteristics and customs would eventually be acquired by Spanish Americans. In the course of centuries it might even come about that one single federal nation would embrace the globe.

This union fondly dreamed of by Bolívar, if it had come into being, would have drawn Spanish America into the British commonwealth of nations. The possibility did exist at one moment of the independence wars, when British influence was strong in Argentina; but, as we have seen, Britain's short-sighted attitude succeeded in alienating the potential of good will that existed. Now once again, as preparations went ahead for the Panama Congress, Britain lost her opportunity through a curious timidity and fear of becoming involved with the emerging nations. Dispatches from C. M. Ricketts to George Canning,[1] written from Lima and labelled secret, note that Bolívar 'spoke handsomely' of Canning himself, whom he earnestly hoped would exert his powerful influence in an endeavour to heal the dissen-

[1] Foreign Office documents 61/7 and 8, letters 280, 281, 284, quoted by Webster, vol. I.

sions between Spain and South America; and he remarked:

'. . . that it was of course immaterial where the Congress might fix on assembling, but that it was a point of the utmost solicitude with him to induce Great Britain to assent to the appointment of a political agent to attend the meeting, after its deliberations had assumed some degree of form and consistency, in order that the whole plan might be consolidated through the wisdom of her counsels, and supported by her weight and influence. . . .'

And, when he heard of the appointment of a Minister Plenipotentiary from Britain:

'His Excellency at the same time requested me to state to you that on this occasion he could not withhold the expression of his anxious hope that Great Britain would not be a silent observer of the discussions which would arise in the Congress, since he was satisfied that they could not terminate in any practical good unless aided by your judicious and impartial counsels. The several States required to be upheld by the power and influence of Great Britain, without which no security could be expected, no consistency preserved, and no social compact maintained. All would be alike subjected to destruction by disputes with each other and by internal anarchy. Different interests were already propelling them; wars which might have been prevented unfortunately raged. . . . The respective classes of inhabitants began to feel that they had equal rights, and as the coloured population so far exceeded the white, the safety of the latter was threatened.

'Under the protection of Great Britain, the South American States would learn the measures most advisable to adopt for the general preservation and tranquillity. . . .'

(In the event, in spite of this urgent call for help, Britain's observer to the Congress remained passive.)

Bolívar's second formal and complete exposition of laws fitted to Spanish American needs (they had already been outlined in a letter to Santander in December 1825) was given in an address to the Bolivian Congress on May 25, 1826,[1] Bolivia having been declared an independent republic the year before. He wanted a

[1] Lecuna, V., *Proclamas* No. 153; *Selected Writings*, No. 251.

president for life and with power to nominate his successor, and this upset not only Santander but many republicans throughout Spanish America. Adding a further division to Montesquieu's three, but rejecting Benjamin Constant's Municipal Power, he divided the supreme authority into four: electoral, legislative, executive, and judicial. The concept of an electoral power (it was suggested that every ten citizens should have an elector to represent them) was based on the views of the Abbé Emmanuel-Josèph Sieyes. Bolívar's hope was that this system would favour not the moneyed but the knowledgeable and honest. All the same, servants and day labourers were excluded from his electorate, for which literacy and a trade were necessary qualifications.

His Panama Congress finally took place in June and July, unfortunately without the attendance of delegates from Chile and Argentina, the former refusing the invitation apparently out of jealousy, the latter because it had hoped that a discussion of the dispute with Brazil over territorial rights in the Banda Oriental (Uruguay) might be included in the agenda. One U.S. representative, Richard C. Anderson, died on the way; and the other, John Sergeant, arrived late. The British observer, Edward J. Dawkins, had been instructed to see that principles of maritime law favourable to Britain were respected; and he was also to make the best possible propaganda out of the belligerent attitude of the U.S.A. to the Cuban situation, contrasting it with Britain's sympathetic attitude to Bolívar's hopes for the island's liberation.

Bolívar proposed six points or principles, most of which are still held sacred by those members of the Organization of American States who dare for the sake of ideals defy the communist-fearing United States: (1) perpetual neutrality of all parties to the league and abandonment of all warlike acts; (2) adoption of the Monroe Doctrine (this seems a contradiction of Bolívar's desire to benefit from Britain's maturity but was in fact his way of safeguarding the corollary of point one—neutrality must work in both directions and could not be pledged by Spanish American countries if they were going to be fearful of infiltration from Europe. Bolívar did not seem to foresee any situation in which the U.S.A. might herself break the first principle and enter the Spanish American countries with bayonets drawn. Canning did, and tried to warn the Hispanic Americans of this); (3) the principle that disputes should be settled by international arbitration; (4) abolition of slavery; (5) safeguards to national sovereignty within the league; (6) common guarantees for the upholding of these principles.

Of all these points only the Monroe Doctrine is regarded as suspect in Latin America today—and that because the U.S.A. has not infrequently come under suspicion of breaking points 1 and 5. At the time of the Congress, however, events went against Bolívar and his vision proved to be far in advance of what the still immature countries were prepared to accept. The tardy arrival of the delegates suggested that they were not taking his plans very seriously; but the calibre of the Spanish Americans was high enough to have made the Congress valuable had it not been for the absence of the southern countries and perhaps the overbearing presence of the U.S.A. There were in the event too many red herrings.

The representatives of Colombia were Pedro Gual and Pedro Briceño Méndez, close friends of Bolívar. Peru sent two international jurists, José María de Pando and Manuel Pérez de Tuedela, but replaced them later by Manuel Lorenzo Vidaurre who had been President of the Supreme Court of Justice in Trujillo and a confidant of Bolívar. Mexico, more inclined to think of the problems as military ones, sent Generals José Mariano Michelenes and José Domínguez. Central America had a strong team: Pedro Molina, chief author of the Guatemalan Constitution and a supporter of his country's independence from Mexico; and an insurgent priest, Antonio Larrazábal, who had championed many liberal reforms including the right of all children, legitimate or otherwise, to citizenship.

A number of controversial subjects came up for discussion including perpetual confederation against Spain 'or any other power that may seek to dominate us'; the Monroe Doctrine, which Santander praised highly and which all countries approved in so far as it guaranteed non-intervention, but about which all had serious reservations because they suspected already that it would be applied onesidedly; and the freeing of Cuba and Puerto Rico. When Florida had been ceded to the U.S.A. in 1819 there were rumours that Britain might seize Cuba. By 1823 the U.S.A. was publicly admitting to a desire to annex the island and there was even talk of war with Britain should that country stand in the way. It was obvious, therefore, that the U.S.A. would never allow the liberating invasion of both Cuba and Puerto Rico to take place.

The U.S.A. tried to dominate the Congress economically as well as politically. It was proposed that no American nation should give favourable commercial or navigational terms to any foreign power that were not extended to all American countries. Such a clause, if passed, would have favoured the U.S.A. overwhelmingly, and its spirit was very different from a commercial treaty signed by Lucas Alamán with Britain in which the latter country agreed that Mexico should have the right to grant special privileges to other former Spanish colonies, whose fraternal links deserved to be recognized.

At the Panama Congress no action was taken on any important topic. A treaty of confederation was signed and a loose military pact arranged which did not meet with Bolívar's approval, though he was partly in favour of Mexico's wish for a military league which he thought Colombia and Guatemala could usefully join— these three nations being the most vulnerable to attack from the north.[1] By the same token he was against moving the seat of the league to Mexico which he considered too close to the United States.[2]

Manuel Lorenzo Vidaurre was the most optimistic of the delegates for he believed that once credentials had been exchanged there would be no representatives of separate nations but only of a united America. He even wanted to extend the powers of this Congress to ecclesiastical matters. He had in his[3] youth been an atheist but had been converted to Catholicism; a fact which in no

---

[1] Lecuna, V., *Cartas del Libertador*, vol. 6, No. 1043.
[2] Lecuna, V., *Cartas del Libertador*, vol. 6, No. 1054.
[3] Belaunde, V. A., p. 268.

way alienated him from Bolívar who had remained all his life—
and in spite of his schooling under Simón Rodríguez—a deeply
religious man. Bolívar did, however, think that religion should be
kept out of social organization and politics, and his message to the
Bolivian Congress had made this perfectly clear:

'Religion is the law of conscience. Any law imposed upon it
cancels it out, because if duty is made compulsory it robs faith of
any merit, which is the basis of religion. The sacred precepts and
dogmas are useful, enlightening, and metaphysically proven; we
ought all to profess them, but this duty is moral and not political.
Moreover, what religious rights has man on earth? They are in
heaven. . . .'[1]

The business of legislators, he believed, was to look after morals
in so far as these concern society, but they could and should not
legislate on the inner meaning of religion which is by nature
private.

Disgusted and disillusioned by the failure of the Congress to
give practical form to his ideals, Bolívar wrote on August 8 from
Lima to Páez:

'Believe me, my dear General, there is a great volcano opening
at our feet, and its rumblings are not poetical but physical and
terribly real. Nothing can persuade me that we can overcome the
vast difficulties that confront us. By some miracle we found ourselves at an accidental point of equilibrium, as when two wild
ocean waves meet at a given point and rest there, supporting each
other in a calm that seems real though it endures but an instant. . . .
I was that point, the waves were Venezuela and Cundinamarca,
and the support was somewhere between those two. The moment,
already past, was the constitutional period of the first election.
There will be no more calm now, no more waves, no further
point of union to create this great peace. Everything will sink
back into matter—the primitive bosom of creation. Yes, matter,
I say, because all will return to nothing.'[2]

Here speaks the mystical Bolívar of the dream on Chimborazo.

[1] Lecuna, V., *Obras Completas*, No. 153; *Selected Writings*, No. 251.
[2] Lecuna, V., *Cartas del Libertador*, No. 1041; *Selected Writings*, No. 251.

Here he is, an insatiable man of action, yet regarding the interplay of forces as real, and materiality as something apart; as nothing; as an illusion come to shatter his dream of truth. He would never indulge in the false humility of imagining that he—placed by that accidental miracle at the point of equilibrium—was an unnecessary ingredient for success for he believed himself to have been entrusted with the teaching of his people. The tragedy was that he would have to go. The moment of stability was already past and as usual he gave a correct prognosis of events:

'. . . Seditious cries will be heard on all sides. And what is worse, every word I say is *true*. You will ask, "Which side shall we support? In what ark shall we find salvation?" My answer is very simple: "Only look at the ocean you are about to furrow, in a frail ship with an inexpert pilot." Is is neither vanity nor any private and overriding conviction that dictates my course. It is the lack of a better. I think that if all Europe were to try to calm our storm it would only perpetuate our calamities. The Congress of Panama, an institution which might have been admirable if it had been more effective, is exactly like that mad Greek who tried from a rock to guide the ships that passed by. Its power will be a shadow and its decrees mere advice: no more.

'They write to tell me that many thinkers want a prince under a federal constitution. But where is this prince? And what political division would bring harmony? All this is ideal and absurd. You will tell me that my poor delirium of a constitution is of even less use and that it embodies every evil. I know this; but I must say something if I am not to remain tongue-tied in the midst of this conflict. . . .

'Of course the most sensible thing to do is vigorously to uphold the public authority in order that its force may appease passions and check abuses by means of the Press, or of pulpits, or of bayonets. The theory of principles is good in time of peace, but when agitation is rife, theories are like trying to rule our passions by the rules of Heaven, which, perfect as they are, have often no connexion with reality.'

Bolívar's faithful friend Pedro Gual did his utmost to salvage the work of the Panama Congress. Immediately upon its closure he went to Mexico and remained there until 1829. Other delegates, including the American (Sergeant) and an observer from the Netherlands (but not from Britain) gathered there; but Joel Poinsett, who was to have attended, was so sure that the Congress was doomed to fail that he did not take the trouble to turn up. Peru, when it saw that the Andean ideal was giving way to inter-americanism, opted out. The Mexican President, Guadalupe Victoria, did all he could to give life to the gathering—such as it was—which took place in Tacubaya, then on the outskirts of his capital. But with wars breaking out between former allies little could be expected. Between 1827 and 1829 Central America was beset by civil strife. Colombia and Peru were at daggers drawn. There were revolutions in Buenos Aires and Bolivia; and in Peru reactionary *caudillos* were in power. The last meeting in Tacubaya was held on October 9, 1828, with only Mexico, Central America, and Colombia represented. To cap it all, in Paraguay Francia was offering to help Spain win back the continent on condition that he (Francia) be appointed viceroy under what he called a 'perfected Jesuit system'.[1] It seemed the end of hope.

9. The Liberator Rejected

The failure of the Panama Congress marked the beginning of the decline of Bolívar's power. He had wanted to lead an American federation with Santander ruling Colombia and Sucre Bolivia. He had also wanted to control La Plata, Brazil, and Chile. But Santander, Sucre, and his own secretary, Briceño Méndez, tried to dissuade him from thus coming into conflict both with the Holy Alliance and with England. Bolívar did not agree that there was this danger, though he did have the fear that the Holy Alliance would try to support Brazil with troops, subjugate Spanish America, and destroy the revolution. However, he accepted the advice of his subordinates and refrained from touring

[1] Gómez Robledo, A., p. 101.

the southern half of the continent. In Lima he tried to insist that General de la Mar (who was highly thought of in the United States and who had replaced San Martín on the latter's retirement) should head the Peruvian government; but de la Mar, who was ill, refused, and Bolívar thought he might remain in Peru himself and give it the Constitution he had drawn up for Bolivia. He imagined himself more popular than he actually was; and this euphoria was encouraged by the advisers closest to him, who failed to read the signs correctly. Peruvians were beginning to resent Colombian intrusion in their affairs, and Bolívar's activities were suspect there. Unpopular as he was, however, the announcement made in August of 1826 that he was prepared to abandon the country to its own devices was by no means welcomed, since all serious-minded people realized that anarchy would follow. The army, the Church, and the fair sex all supported him:

'The matrons of the capital assembled in the consistorial saloons, and passed on to the palace to join their supplications to those of the stronger sex, hoping that, with the assistance of the Graces, they would be enabled to soften the hitherto inflexible determination of the Liberator. To these fair petitioners the Liberator gave the following reply: "Ladies! Silence is the only answer I ought to give those enchanting expressions. . . . When beauty speaks, what breast can resist it? I have been the soldier of beauty, because Liberty is bewitchingly beautiful; she diffuses happiness, and decorates the path of life with flowers." At the conclusion of this speech . . . the ladies crowded round Bolívar, and, after a long and animated discussion, "an angel voice" was heard to pronounce these words, "The Liberator remains!" Loud vivas and acclamations were the answer. The church bells were kept ringing all night. Joy took possession of every heart, and a grand ball concluded the scene. . . .'[1]

The result was that on August 16 his Constitution was approved and he was offered the presidency but refused, saying that there were Peruvians fully capable of holding that high office.

[1] Miller, J., vol. 2, p. 303.

Besides, he was needed elsewhere. Ever since 1824, when an order from Santander which provided for compulsory enlistment of men between the ages of sixteen and fifty had gone unheeded and Páez had been compelled to impress men into military service, affairs in Gran Colombia had been very unsettled. The following year Páez had sent Bolívar an urgent call to return and save his country. In March 1826 Bolívar reached Bogotá, but riots presently broke out in several cities including Caracas; and on May 3 Páez, who had been suspended from office by Congress for what was considered to be his arbitrary behaviour in relation to the enlistments, declared himself to be officially in command and came out in open rebellion against the legal authorities. Santander appeared to write sympathetically to Páez but made charges against him to Bolívar.[1]

Páez dreamed of creating an empire stretching from the Orinoco to Potosí and this was a plan that Bolívar found by no means unattractive. Therefore, although nervous that the *llanero* General was perhaps getting too big for his boots, he was determined not to act too harshly toward a man who had rendered invaluable service. He left Peru on September 3 and reached Guayaquil on the 12th. From there he sent a message to his Vice-President, Santander, and to Páez, suggesting in the most gentle and diplomatic terms that they should come to heel. Santander, realizing that Bolívar meant business, journeyed to meet him and they held a brief parley in Bogotá, after which Bolívar assumed extraordinary powers. Páez was by now in active rebellion and was supported by his Bravos; but Bolívar knew the plainsman's weakness, his essential simplicity and love of recognition. Arriving in Puerto Cabello on January 1, 1827, he acted quickly, offered a general amnesty, and declared Páez the saviour of his country. On the fourth he had a friendly meeting with the rebel and the two entered Caracas in triumph side by side. After a service in the cathedral fifteen youths symbolizing civic and military virtues received Bolívar and gave him two laurel wreaths, one for his triumph over the tyrants, and one for having averted civil war.

[1] Lecuna, V., *Documentos*, vol. 6, p. 216, letter of July 15, 1826.

Páez[1] describes how Bolívar turned and crowned him with one of these, dedicating the other to the 'illustrious Colombian people'. Six pennants, each inscribed with a military or civic virtue, were presented from Colombia, Peru, and Bolivia. The one inscribed 'Disinterestedness' Bolívar handed his father-in-law, the Marqués del Toro. To Cristóbal Mendoza, who had first given Bolívar the title of Liberator, he dedicated 'Probity', to Great Britain 'Politics', to Caracas 'Generosity', and to Páez 'Valour'. For himself he reserved the pennant labelled 'Constancy'. Páez and the crowds were enchanted.

In the meantime Bolívar and Santander had been re-elected President and Vice-President of Gran Colombia; but in February 1827 Bolívar resigned, hoping thus to quash all imputations of ambition and to spend the rest of his days quietly administering his estate. Santander, however, urged him to continue as constitutional president. Congress agreed that only in this way could agitation be quelled, though the decision was by no means unanimous. Even Beaufort Watts, the American chargé d'affaires in Bogotá, remonstrated that all would be lost without Bolívar. For this he was reprimanded by his government and it became evident later that both John Quincy Adams and his Secretary-of-State Henry Clay suspected Bolívar of treasuring inordinate ambitions. Certainly at the time Bolívar was quick to use Watts's statement to his own advantage. Reinforced by this support he decided to remain, and toward the end of the year went to Bogotá to take the oath. Before arriving he issued three decrees: one granting a general amnesty; another convoking a national convention in Ocaña; and a third establishing constitutional rule throughout Gran Colombia.

Sharp differences of opinion between him and Santander had already become apparent. Bolívar was an individualist, Santander a believer in institutions and legal forms which he was convinced were necessary in order to curb the natural ambitions of men. But paradoxically Bolívar had no trust in the populace, whose approval would be necessary if Santander's forms were to be

---

[1] Páez, J. A., vol. i, p. 373.

upheld; he therefore feared that if Santander got his way anarchy would ensue. Belaunde[1] thinks that Santander was right; but history has shown the contrary for the constitutions of America have never yet been able to prevent seizure of power by the unscrupulous. As early as 1817 a U.S. observer warned that the mere wish to establish a free government was insufficient; and Páez, quoting him, says that Creole leaders such as Pueyrredón, Monteagudo, Rivadavia, Belgrano (and no doubt Bolívar himself), agreed.[2]

At the time the Peruvian situation was so delicate that the Constitution was annulled after six weeks by a counter-revolution during which Bolívar's enemies abjured his code, deposed the council appointed by him, and organized a provisional government. A rebel army division embarked from Callao on March 17, 1827, and landed in the southern department of Colombia the following month, but the whole thing fizzled out with a peaceful submission to the authorities.

April 1827 saw an uprising in Chuquisaca during which Sucre was wounded. The rebels were put down but all foreign troops were ordered to leave Bolivia and Sucre resigned as President and returned to Venezuela. Gran Colombia now became divided into two parties, those who favoured Bolívar and those who, under Santander, were apprehensive of his apparent desire to imitate Napoleon. Differences between Santander and Bolívar became personal and bitter, so much so that Sucre wrote to each in turn tacitly accusing them of pettiness and begging them to put larger interests first.

The Convention of Ocaña sat during the spring of 1828 in the hope of reaching a decision about the national will. Here Bolívar decided once and for all to abandon his ideal of unity and to accept the fact that Gran Colombia could not survive, that Venezuela and Nueva Granada would be split into two separate countries with a federal tie between them. Ocaña failed because the military were stronger than the republicans and because Bolívar's supporters would not compromise as he himself would

[1] Belaunde, V. A., pp. 271–2. [2] Páez, J. A., vol. 1, p. 471.

221

have done. The only course now left to him was to assume supreme power. He had already said that the republic would have to confer immense authority upon him or it would collapse;[1] and he had told Páez that the destruction of Colombia seemed to him inevitable unless a strong government could be formed.[2] There is no reason, therefore, to suppose that he had been insincere in saying that he would give up his mandate as soon as peace had been established with Spain. But at the time he knew he was still necessary, though the sands were running low.

The fight between Bolivarists and anti-Bolivarists continued, and in September 1828 conspirators tried to kill the Liberator in the presidential palace in Bogotá but were foiled by William Ferguson who, defending the door against their entry, was stabbed to death as his chief escaped through a window. It was the last great sacrifice made by a British legionary for independence. Bolívar suspected Santander of having been involved in the plot and jailed him but later commuted the sentence to exile. (Santander returned to Nueva Granada in 1832 and served a constructive term as President.)

The idea of a monarchy still cropped up, and Páez especially saw such a plan as a tool with which he could defeat his enemies. Hence arose a secret plot which had the support of Briceño Méndez but was opposed by Bolívar, although Zea told him that the great powers would never recognize America's independence until a hereditary system was established—no matter what it might be called. If there had been times in the past when Bolívar expressed monarchical ideas to Britain, he now spoke otherwise to Patrick Campbell, the English *chargé d'affaires* in Bogotá:

'The British minister resident in the United States does me too much honour when he says that he has hopes for Colombia alone, since Colombia alone has a Bolívar. But he does not know that Bolívar's physical and political existence is much weakened and will soon end.

'What you are good enough to tell me about the new plan for

[1] Lecuna, V., *Cartas del Libertador*, vol. 7, No. 1289.
[2] Lecuna, V., *Cartas del Libertador*, vol. 7, No. 1409; *Selected Writings*, No. 285.

appointing a European prince to succeed me in authority does not surprise me, because something of the sort had been communicated to me with no little mystery and a certain reticence, my view being well known.

'I do not know what to say to you about this notion, which is fraught with innumerable difficulties. You must know that there is no objection on my part since I am determined to resign at the next congress. But who is to appease the ambition of our leaders and the fear of inequality among the common people? Do you not think that England would be jealous if a Bourbon prince were chosen? Would not all the new American nations oppose it, and also the United States which seems destined by Providence to plague America with torments in the name of freedom? I already seem to detect a general conspiracy against poor Colombia, which is too much envied by all the American republics. The whole Press would call for a fresh crusade against those guilty of treachery to freedom, of supporting the Bourbons, and of betraying the American system. In the south the Peruvians, on the Isthmus the Guatemalans and Mexicans, and in the Antilles the Americans and the liberals of all parties would kindle the flame of discord. Santo Domingo would not remain passive but would call upon her brothers to make common cause against a prince of France. Everyone would become our enemy, and Europe would do nothing to help us because it is not worth sacrificing a Holy Alliance for the New World.'[1]

Not so much kingship, then, as Bourbonship, was Bolívar's bogey. William Henry Harrison, who had been sent out as U.S. Minister in Colombia after the Watts affair, wrote to him under the assumption that he did have kingly aspirations, and lectured him on the perils of tyranny. Rightly or wrongly he suspected a Bolivarian-British conspiracy directed to placing a British prince on the throne. The Colombian government did not take kindly to Harrison's interference, and the latter thought it expedient to leave before he was expelled.[2]

---

[1] Lecuna, V., *Cartas del Libertador*, vol. 9, No. 1874; *Selected Writings*, No. 315.
[2] See Parks, E. Taylor, *Colombia and the United States 1765-1934*, pp. 153-8.

That Harrison had not grasped the true situation seems certain; for Bolívar, with a number of cards still in his hands, did nothing to pursue the monarchical plan. At the Colombian Congress of May 1830 he resigned the supreme command saying:

'. . . Banish any idea that I imagine I am indispensable to the republic. . . . If any one man becomes essential to a nation's survival, that nation does not deserve to exist and in the long run will not.'[1]

For twenty years, he reminded Congress, he had served as a soldier and ruler, during which time three republics had been formed and many civil uprisings suppressed. Now, he feared, men were beginning to regard him as an obstacle, and because of the mutterings and slander against him he would abdicate of his own free will.

In any case the state of his lungs was bad and the doctors were ordering him to a healthier climate. He decided upon Jamaica. How deep were the feelings of failure can be deduced from two statements made about this time. In a pamphlet called 'A Glance at Spanish America' which appeared in Quito in 1829 and is almost certainly by him[2] it is said that 'there is no faith in America, neither between men nor between nations. Treaties are only paper; constitutions, books; elections, squabbles; liberty, anarchy; and life a torment.' The sentiments were reiterated in a letter he wrote from Barranquilla to General Juan José Flores on November 9, 1830:

'I have arrived at only a few sure conclusions: 1. For us, America is ungovernable. 2. He who serves a revolution ploughs the sea. 3. The only thing we can do in America is to emigrate. 4. This country will eventually fall into the hands of the unbridled mob, and will proceed to almost imperceptible petty tyrannies of all complexions and races. 5. Devoured as we are by every kind of crime and annihilated by ferocity, Europeans will not go to the trouble of conquering us. 6. If it were possible for any part of the

---

[1] Lecuna, V., *Proclamas* No. 813; *Selected Writings*, No. 319.
[2] Lecuna, V., *Selected Writings*, vol. 2, No. 318.

world to revert to primordial chaos, that would be America's final state.'[1]

On December 1, 1830, he arrived at the villa of San Pedro Alejandrino near Santa Marta, Colombia, where he was so weak that his friends despaired of saving him. Though he rallied, his spirit still undaunted, he could travel no further. News of the assassination on June 4 of his trusted General Sucre in the mountains of Berruecos while he was on his way to join his wife and daughter in Quito, saddened him deeply. It was only by a trick of fate that Sucre had not reached Bogotá in time to accompany Bolívar on his last journey; had he done so, his life would have been spared.

Bolívar died on December 17th. A week previously he had addressed a brief proclamation to the people of Colombia:

'My last wishes are for the happiness of our native land. If my death will help to end party strife and to promote national unity, I shall go to my grave in peace.'[2]

On the same day he signed his last testament in the name of Almighty God to whom he commended his soul, affirming that he believed in the high and sovereign mystery of the Holy Trinity and all other doctrines of the Roman Catholic Church. Among other things he asked his executors to thank General Robert Wilson for the noble conduct of his son, Colonel Belford Wilson, who was with Bolívar during the last days of his life.[3] Thus on his deathbed Bolívar showed concern for two things which he had often been accused of spurning—friendship, which he valued greatly, and religion. Not a cent of public money was found in his possession; nor, did it seem to him, was a shred of his former power and glory left. 'He who serves a revolution ploughs the sea.'

Of all the Spanish American liberators, Bolívar was the least predictable. San Martín was more consistent, perhaps even the better soldier if it had not been for his reluctance to follow victories up to their fullest conclusion; but Bolívar had the

---

[1] Lecuna, V., *Cartas del Libertador*, No. 2074.
[2] Lecuna, V., *Selected Writings*, No. 325.
[3] Lecuna, V., *Cartas del Libertador*, vol. 9, No. 2103; *Selected Writings*, No. 327.

creative fire that attracts the imagination. He was both soldier and orator, an artist with a sense of occasion. He knew the importance of ceremony as an aid to impressing both foreigners and his people. He was not a man to hide his moods which were sometimes exaggerated and impassioned, but when a battle was on or a job had to be done theatricality was set aside. Opposed as he was by the ruthlessness of Andean geography, by treachery within his own ranks, and by sincere feelings on the part of many Creoles that they should remain loyal to their European origins, he would not otherwise have survived. Many have imitated Bolívar's flamboyance but have lacked the foundations on which this was based. Spanish America has inherited from the Liberator a predilection for showmanship that in him was counterbalanced by hard work and solid talent. Some in his lifetime saw only the poseur, and when he was exhausted from his many responsibilities, the lustre gone from his eyes, he could look as unprepossessing as some eye-witnesses, including Gustavo Hippisley, described him:

'Personal courage he is gifted with, even to a fault. He has, however, never yet achieved any action worthy of renown, or equal to the real intrepidity with which he is endowed; because reason, judgment, and even necessary discretion, have been wanting.... He has neither talent nor abilities for a general.... Tactics, movements, and manœuvre are as unknown to him as to the lowest of his troops....'[1]

It is true that these words were written during the Angostura period before the great victories. Even so, Bolívar had already impressive achievements behind him. But Hippisley would have seen these and future ones as the result of unworthy personal ambition and of the talent surrounding him. Bolívar, he was convinced, sought only 'a diadem to crown his brow' and kingship over Venezuela and Nueva Granada, from which high eminence he would once again have enslaved his country. Then 'the gallant Britons who aided him in the patriotic cause' would have been viewed 'with the utmost suspicion, disgust, and jealousy....'[2] Thus spoke Hippisley in his anger and hurt pride because his

[1] Hippisley, G., p. 461.   [2] Hippisley, G., p. 527.

service to the liberating army had not been more enthusiastically acknowledged. It was the opinion of many of Bolívar's enemies. As to his friends, there were those who willingly followed him through fire to certain death. Others, like Páez, believed him at the end to have been misguided and to have betrayed the principles that he had publicly announced, even to the extent of threatening his country with armed invasion.[1] But Páez, who campaigned with him, who was no time-server or fawner upon the great though he had an easily tickled vanity, who was as different from Bolívar as temperament and upbringing could combine to make him, and who came near quarrelling with him irreparably, may be allowed to speak his epitaph:

'Simón Bolívar belongs to the band of modern men whose equals are to be found only when we reach back to republican times of Greece and Rome. . . . In the midst of people who had no more tradition than the respect for an authority sanctioned by the acquiescence of three centuries of ignorance, superstition, and fanaticism, nor any political dogma but submission to an order of things supported by might and force, Bolívar succeeded in defying that power. . . .'[2]

If there is any truth in the allegation that he was an imitation Napoleon he played the part better than his instructor. He combined courtliness with soldierly toughness as only the Elizabethans had done before; and as strategist and orator he is probably equalled only by Churchill. He had a vision and he drove his delicate body to its limits in trying to achieve it. The times, and human nature itself, were against him.

[1] Páez, J. A., vol. 2, p. 24.   [2] Páez, J. A., vol. 2, p. 130.

CHAPTER III

THE MEXICAN INSURGENTS

1. HIDALGO AND ALLENDE

Whereas the independence wars in South America were instigated by aristocratic Creoles, and the Indian population played only a minor part in them, in Mexico the movement was led by merchants, miners, and village priests— men whose background was usually humble or middle-class.[1] Almost from the beginning the poorer peasants and Indians joined the mass movement. Paradoxically out of this genuine revolutionary material there arose (if briefly) the only empire formed of independence (one other, that of Maximilian, appearing later, also in Mexico, this time instigated by the strong right-wing opposition to Benito Juárez).

The Mexican rebellion was never planned from a military or strategic point of view. The South American leaders were trained soldiers, often experienced in European and North American campaigns, who knew how to take advantage even of the apparently insuperable barrier of the Cordillera. The first of the Mexican leaders, Miguel Hidalgo, was a priest with no experience of soldiering. He became commander-in-chief almost by accident, because the independence plot was discovered and had to be put into effect prematurely, and because the rabble mob preferred him to the young military captain Ignacio Allende. Fortunately for the Mexican movement there was no Cordillera to cross. The terrain

[1] The differences between Creole and popular independence thought, and the rift between the high clergy and the parish priests, is fully examined by Luis Villoro, who believes that the contradictory behaviour of certain Creoles and of the Army in Mexico can be explained by a shift of aims as time went on.

228

was broken and difficult but it presented no single barrier—rather a series of serrated ranges and fissured canyons. The strategy did not have to be closely coordinated; and in this landscape so ideal for guerrilla warfare, an ideal guerrilla leader—José María Morelos —arose to carry on Hidalgo's early, almost instinctive and largely uncontrolled protest.

The Mexican movement, though impelled by these militarily untrained elements, did nevertheless have the backing of a middle-class Creole organization known as *La Sociedad de los Guadalupes*. But, in contrast to the situation among the Creoles of South America, this rebellious group worked in close contact with the poor sections of the community and aimed primarily to abolish distinctions of caste and to achieve a fair distribution of land to the peasants. The aim of overthrowing the absolutist Spanish ruling oligarchy was only secondary. Friendly contact with Miguel Hidalgo was thus easy to establish and was effected as early as 1807 through the mediation of the formidable Doña Josefa Ortiz de Domínguez, wife of the *corregidor*, or chief magistrate, of Querétaro. Her help to the revolutionary movement was given in defiance of her husband, who stood so much in awe of her that he allowed the conspiracy to gain considerable momentum before he finally denounced it. His wife was thereupon imprisoned but was released after three years at her husband's request. More was to be heard of her later.

It is difficult to assess exactly the importance of the Guadalupe Creoles' activities in the early stages of rebellion but it is certain that unrest and conspiracies existed at various social levels. On the abdication of Ferdinand at Bayonne on May 5, 1808, the Viceroy, José Iturrigarai, was not unaverse to establishing a Junta on the usual loyal pattern; but he was helpless to act against the opposition of the *Real Audiencia*. As chief of the rebels there arose a rich sugar grower, Gabriel Yermo, who had the support of equally rich mine owners from Zacatecas and of allies in New Orleans. The Viceroy wanted to resign but was dissuaded by his wife and the town council, who pointed out that his military skill would be needed against the French should they land on Mexican soil, an event which seemed at the time to be by no means improbable. At the time of the tumult of Aranjuez in 1808 there had been a strong rumour circulating that the Spanish royal family thought of fleeing to Mexico, but at this time it looked more likely that the French might reach their long hand into the New World.

On the night of September 15, 1808, Iturrigarai was surprised in his bed by an armed throng who carried him off to the office of the Inquisition where an attempt was made to accuse him of heresy and of deceiving the people. He was then put on board a ship bound for Spain, where he was absolved of the stigma of treason but condemned to pay a heavy fine for corrupt administration.

Throughout Mexico patriot groups began to coalesce into what were euphemistically termed 'safety Juntas', though they were in fact centres for spy rings. The most serious conspiracy was in Valladolid, later Morelia, where a revolution was planned to break out on December 21, 1809. The plot was betrayed to the authorities through the indiscretion of a Franciscan, Vicente de Santa María. By a stroke of irony Agustín de Iturbide, then a very junior royalist officer but later to become Emperor of Mexico, was responsible for rounding up the ringleaders. A lawyer among them put their case so well that nothing could be proved against them except that they had organized public opinion to resist the French should Spain fall completely under Napoleon's sway. For so laudable a pastime they could not of course be shot.

The Archbishop, Francisco Javier de Lizana, was sympathetic to the liberal movement and even ordered arms from Britain with which to prepare a militia in case of need. He was made acting Viceroy, an office which he held from July 1809 until May 1810 when the new Viceroy, Francisco Javier Venegas, arrived. The Spanish authorities had by this time got wind of Lizana's real sentiments and saw to it that his activities came to a halt. He died, in any case, the following year. He had served a purpose because through his liberalism he had succeeded in quieting the agitators and the Spaniards thus gained two years' grace. But exactly on the anniversary of the uprising against Iturrigarai, on September 15, 1810, the real trouble began.

On September 13 the intendant of the city of Guanajuato, Juan Antonio Riaño, was informed of a plan to take all Europeans in his area by surprise. This conspiracy, led by Hidalgo, Allende, the brothers Ignacio and Juan Aldama and their friends, was due to break out during the Christmas festivities. It did not at its inception have the backing of the populace, which rallied to the liberal cause only later. This is clear from a letter sent to Hidalgo by Allende on August 31:

'We decided to act carefully concealing our aims, because if the movement were frankly revolutionary it would not be supported by the general mass of people. . . . Since the natives are indifferent to the word liberty it is necessary to make them believe that the rising is undertaken simply to favour King Ferdinand.'[1]

Even some of the accomplices of the leading insurgents were against a policy of outright rebellion and passed details of the plan to the authorities. A watch was set on Hidalgo and an order put out for his and Allende's arrest, but the latter intercepted it and hurried to the little town of Dolores where Hidalgo was curate. This white-haired, almost slovenly dressed man with bald pate and stooping shoulders seemed an unlikely revolutionary; but while engaged in the more or less innocent occupations of running a pottery and breeding silkworms (though the latter was illegal) he had been thinking seditious and possibly irreverent thoughts. His reading had been avid and ranged a good deal farther than the Church would have countenanced although he had held honoured posts as professor and then rector of the College of San Nicolás in Valladolid. It is likely that he even included in his studies something of the strategy of war.

He and Allende now held a quick conference and decided that the cry of independence must be given forthwith. With five volunteers and five more men impressed from the pottery to make the business appear a little more formidable, Hidalgo gathered up a picture of the brown Virgin of Guadalupe (a symbol beloved

---

[1] Quoted in Mancisidor, J., p. 54.

above all others among the *mestizos* and Indians) and gave his famous cry, the *Grito de Dolores*: 'Long live Religion. Long live our Most Holy Mother of Guadalupe. Long live Ferdinand VII. Long live America and death to the bad government.' This was too long-winded for the mob who changed it, with results unforeseen by Hidalgo and much bloodier than he at first intended, to 'Long live Our Lady of Guadalupe! Death to the Gachupines (Spaniards)!'

Europeans in Dolores were seized and the patriots marched first to San Miguel el Grande (now San Miguel de Allende), where Hidalgo was proclaimed General-in-Chief of the rebels, thence to Celaya. He had by now an army of about 6,000, mostly rabble armed with slings, arrows, clubs, lances, knives, and a few muskets; but including also some dragoons and regular infantry. Celaya, which could offer no serious resistance even to such troops as these, was mercilessly sacked and the patriots marched to Guanajuato where for the first time they met organized resistance from the royalists. So far the Viceroy had not taken the uprising very seriously. On the morning of September 17 he had issued a proclamation reminding people of the favours granted by the Cádiz government to those who had deposed the alleged traitor, Iturrigarai, and asking for a loan of twenty million pesos. Only when arms intended for Juan Antonio Riaño had been intercepted did he become aware of the seriousness of the situation. He then tried to gain the confidence of the Creoles by appointing one of their number—the Mexican-born Conde de la Cadena, a former supporter of independence—to command a royalist regiment. This was a shrewd move for many of the Creoles were lukewarm in their support of the insurgents and ready to meet the Spaniards half way. Venegas also sent a strong force to Querétaro where some citizens had been found with arms and had been arrested. Riaño, the able and upright provincial intendant, had retired to the Alhóndiga de Granaditas, a massive granary which stands today imposing the simple grandeur of its architecture on the beautiful colonial mining town. Here with a battalion of infantry, two companies of dragoons, almost all the Europeans in the neighbourhood, and food for more than five hundred people for three or four months, the royalists expected to be able to hold out until the Viceroy and the commandant of San Luis Potosí could send help. Certain as they were of their impregnability they nevertheless set to work strengthening their positions.

For many years Guanajuato had been groaning under a heavy tribute exacted because of its support of the Jesuits expelled in the eighteenth century. They had also been forced to work in the drains that kept the steep and narrow streets clear of water. The Spaniards, thinking to gain friends, now revoked this tribute and forced labour; but the people became cynical about the motives of this show of friendship. A display of force with a march-past of infantry had an even worse result. On September 28 a deputation from Hidalgo arrived at the Alhóndiga to deliver a note to Riaño. In the name of the Captain-General of America—for Hidalgo had been acclaimed thus on the fields of Celaya and had been authorized to proclaim independence though he had neither territory nor any formal government to support the high-sounding title—he asked the Europeans to capitulate and promised them mercy. 'I do not view the Spaniards as enemies,' he said, 'but only as obstacles to the success of our enterprise.' He offered to allow them to become prisoners with the rights of Mexican citizenship as soon as independence had been won. If they did not accept these terms, which included return of all properties as soon as the war was at an end, he would—he said—allow no quarter. Riaño replied that he did not fear the insurgents and was ready to lose his life but did not want to put his companions at any risk if they were unwilling. There was silence until one man called out, 'We shall conquer or die.' Riaño thereupon returned a message to Hidalgo that he would fight, but reminded him of his offer of mercy and asked protection for his family in case of disaster.

The Alhóndiga was connected to a silver *hacienda* called Dolores, and from here the Spaniards opened fire. With the Virgin of Guadalupe at their head, Hidalgo's troops rushed forward hurling stones. Some tried to break open the great doors of the Alhóndiga, and Riaño was killed. He had himself foretold success for Hidalgo. 'Bad!' he is reported to have said when he heard the news that the priest was leading the insurgents. 'If Hidalgo is in this, New Spain becomes independent.'[1]

Even without their respected intendant the royalists fought on. Hidalgo called one of his men to set fire to the Alhóndiga door. With a stone slab for shield and a lighted torch for weapon the peasant threw himself at the door and others followed. The fort commander was killed and the patriots gained the advantage; but behind, in the silver *hacienda*, Riaño's eldest son continued to fight and the slaughter was terrible.

After this costly victory Hidalgo began hastily and prematurely organizing a civil government but the university in Mexico City disowned him. The Inquisition called him a Judas and atheist and alleged that he had spread it about that one Pope was burning in hell. An edict of excommunication was issued against him and the clergy put into the mouth of the Virgin of Remedios—special protectress of the royalists—the words:

'My children: Your Mother, your Queen, your Patron and your General is among you as you flee from the sacrilegious hands of the heretic Hidalgo and his excommunicated henchmen; she is looking after her tender devotees. . . .'[2]

Now each side had its Virgin and one can imagine Guadalupe and Remedios at daggers drawn in heaven. The more sober royalists deplored the confusion of religion with politics; but there were always the superstitious, including the Bishop of Oaxaca who told his flock that the insurgents had 'wings, horns, fingernails, beaks, and tails like griffins'. Instinctive fears were given plenty to feed on. Hidalgo attempted, at least at first, to restrain the wild hatred he had loosed; but as Justo Sierra says:

'. . . freedom for them did not mean rights but drunkenness; theirs was not a normal attitude but an explosion of hatred and of delight; the mob was undisciplined and would not be contained;

---

[1] Bustamante, C. M., *Resúmen Histórico de la Revolución de los Estados Unidos Mexicanos*, p. 60.

[2] Mancisidor, J., p. 96.

it had the aspect of a force of nature unleashed in all its violence: a cloudburst, a hurricane, or a flood.'[1]

Mexican history has been like that, as if the terrain itself were constantly imposing some wildness, a certain cosmic element of utter abandon, upon men. The army that now marched on Valladolid had a nucleus of regulars including part of the Celaya infantry, a battalion from Guanajuato, a regiment of dragoons, two bronze cannon and two of wood; but mainly it was a horde of incensed and undisciplined peasants. Hidalgo's thoughts as he offered a mass of thanks in the cathedral (which he was able to do though the doors had at first been closed against him) must have been not a little confused. But he was spurred on by his devotees who tore down the excommunication notices pinned up to stay him and clamoured for their beloved curate.

It was here in Valladolid that José María Morelos came forward asking to become chaplain to the insurgent armies. He had been curate of two indigent villages where he had seen near-famine take toll of his flock. Now he hurried to Valladolid to see how the revolt was proceeding and to offer his services, for he had long admired Hidalgo and in after years said that he had based his own constitutional principles on the teaching of the curate of Dolores. Hidalgo gave him the task of capturing the castle of Acapulco and the whole Pacific coast, and Morelos marched off with his ecclesiastical retinue, a few old guns, and some lances.

Hidalgo had trouble in Valladolid because of an outbreak of poisoning among the Indians who were so incensed that they wreaked their vengeance on anything that came to hand. His command of the forces was, however, officially endorsed and he decided to march upon Mexico City. Allende tried to form some kind of army out of the rabble but events went against him. Hidalgo's undisciplined troops were met by 6,000 well-armed men and some artillery which had been gathered by Venegas to protect the capital. The Virgin of Remedios had been transferred there with all her jewels, and the Viceroy placed his mace of office at her feet in one of those theatrical gestures in which the wars of

[1] Sierra, Justo, *Evolución Política del Pueblo Mexicano*, p. 166.

independence abound. Hidalgo's forces were intercepted on October 30 by the Spaniards at a point called Monte de las Cruces, a mountain pass dotted with crosses marking the graves of bandits caught and crucified. The royalists were utterly defeated. Allende the strategist was all for pressing on; but Hidalgo, fearing that the lack of discipline of his troops would do the patriots no good, and realizing that a pincer movement was converging upon him (the efficient and ruthless General Félix Calleja was reported to be bringing a strong force of royalists south from San Luis Potosí), beat a hasty retreat. Hidalgo had good reason to fear this intrepid general. On November 7, quite accidentally, Calleja found himself about two leagues from Hidalgo's army at a village called Aculco. Here the patriots were routed and Hidalgo reached Guadalajara licking his wounds. Allende managed a more orderly retreat to Guanajuato, which he had however to evacuate on Calleja's approach. The populace, angered at being left at the mercy of the Spaniards, massacred 249 Europeans who had escaped the disaster of the Alhóndiga; and this cruel act was the excuse for retaliations by Calleja. There was no longer any pretence at obeying the rules of war.

Very severe measures were taken by the Viceroy to collect all arms including working implements from the populace, and any found with them were killed and their homes reduced to ashes. From now on it was a fight to the death on both sides but this did not prevent the rebellion from spreading to such areas as Veracruz and Oaxaca. According to Bustamante, a Negro called Lino gathered a mob and incited it to cut the throats of all the Europeans imprisoned in the Alhóndiga. Calleja and the Conde de la Cadena also ordered massacres until a certain Father Belaunzaran appeared, crucifix in hand, and pleaded in the name of God that they should desist. This did not prevent many executions.

In Guadalajara armed forces were massing and volunteers—mainly students and shopkeepers—were hurrying to the aid of the insurgents. The bishop, Juan Cruz Ruíz Cabañas y Crespo (the man responsible for many of the finest buildings in Guadalajara including the famous Cabañas orphanage which still functions as such and contains the magnificent revolutionary murals of José

Clemente Orozco) formed a regiment called the *Cruzada*, composed wholly of secular and religious priests. With a cry of 'Long live the Catholic faith', they charged the insurgents and there were more atrocities; but later Ruíz Cabañas went over to the patriot cause.

While in Guadalajara Hidalgo heard that a counter-attack was being launched against him and ordered mass slaughters. 'Whatever be the justice of a cause,' said Bustamante with reason, 'the means of defending it are not always fair if the monster of civil war erupts.'[1] And the civil war in Mexico was at least as bitter as any in the whole Spanish American struggle, partly because the Aztec tradition had left a legacy of fierce cruelties, partly because —as we have seen—Hidalgo's armies were more undisciplined than those of South America; and partly because the leaders, being priests, were not only divided in their loyalties but produced in their followers a peculiarly fierce brand of fanaticism. Padre Herrera of Tlaxcala, for example, is said by Bustamante to have cut off the ears of Indians and to have carried them about in his sombrero in order to frighten the peasants.

On January 14, 1811, Hidalgo received news that the royalists were approaching. He, Allende, and José Antonio Torres (a peasant who had risen in the patriot ranks) each headed a division and there was a dispute whether or not to give battle. Allende was against this but Hidalgo's argument unfortunately won. On the 16th Calleja and de la Cadena were engaged at a point called Puente de Calderón and at first got the worst of the encounter; but the accidental blowing up of a munitions cart caused panic among Hidalgo's men. The Conde de la Cadena was killed, but Calleja was victorious in a particularly horrible battle in which 'deer, wolves, and coyotes emerged terrified from their caves and became entangled with the men . . . as if by their astonishment they wished to show that the cruelty of wars among men was even greater than among beasts.'[2]

Hidalgo's army joined Allende's in Saltillo and together they determined to cross to the United States with money and their

[1] Bustamante, C. M., p. 38.   [2] Bustamante, C. M., p. 42.

best troops; but their plans were frustrated by the treachery of one, Ignacio Elizondo, who harboured some bitterness against Allende for not having raised him to the rank of general and who on March 21, 1811, overtook and attacked the patriots' carriage. In the resulting skirmish Allende's son was killed and the leaders all jailed. On May 6 documents were issued condemning Hidalgo, Allende, and Juan Aldama to death, and Hidalgo thereupon issued a proclamation in which he asked:

'Is it really necessary, Americans, that you should take up arms against your brothers, who feel obliged at the risk of their lives to free you from European tyranny lest you remain mere slaves? Do you not realize that this war is waged against them alone, and that it would therefore be a war without enemies, and would be all over in a day, if you did not help them to fight? Do not let yourselves be deceived, Americans, or allow them to mock you further by taking advantage of your good natures and gentle hearts to make you believe that we are God's enemies and want to overthrow His holy religion; for they try by lies and slanders to make us appear vile in your eyes. No. Americans will never depart by a hair's breadth from Catholic doctrines . . . we shall not allow strangers who might distort it to meddle in this continent. We are about to sacrifice our lives happily in its defence, protesting to the whole world that we have not wished to unsheathe our swords against those men whose pride and despotism we have suffered with the greatest patience for nearly three hundred years. During that time we have seen hospitality infringed and the most honourable bonds that ought to unite us shattered. We have been the plaything of their cruel ambition and the unhappy victims of their greed. We have been insulted and provoked by a continuous series of insults and outrages, and have been degraded to the low species of reptile. . . . Open your eyes; remember that the Europeans are trying to set Creole against Creole while they themselves look on from a safe distance. If things turn out favourably they will take the credit for having conquered us, and will mock and despise whatever is Creole. . . .'[1]

[1] Bustamante, C. M., p. 373.

When Hidalgo and the other prisoners arrived in Chihuahua to be tried, the viceregal authorities were forced to take drastic measures to prevent a tumult. People were allowed into the streets only if they did not gather in crowds. They were forbidden to go out onto the flat roofs in order to see better, to carry arms, or to shout or make 'imprudent comparisons'.[1] The first prisoners to be judged were shot on May 10, 1811. On June 6 came the turn, among others, of Mariano Hidalgo, Miguel's brother; and on June 26 Allende, Juan Aldama, and the Governor of the State of Nuevo León were all shot. (Juan Aldama's brother, Ignacio, had been shot a week earlier in Monclova.)

On May 7 Hidalgo's own trial had begun. He was accused of insulting the Inquisition, of having written seditious matter and of having encouraged insurrection. He confessed to having criticized the Inquisition and admitted having been responsible for massacres in Valladolid and Guadalajara but denied robbing churches. Tartly he drew attention to contradictions in the accusations. He was, he said, supposed to have denied the existence of hell yet at the same time to have suggested that one of the Popes had gone there! He was also accused of questioning the authority of the Bible, and yet of accepting the doctrines of Luther who believed the Bible to be the word of God. He insisted that he was a good Catholic who had fallen out with the Church merely because he had undertaken to free his country from oppression, to banish poverty, and to encourage cultivation of the fertile soil of Mexico.

It is alleged that as he afterwards languished in prison, sleepless and tormented, he repented of his more fanatical acts. There is evidence of his repentance even at the trial; for when asked whether he could have been sure that his independence movement would not end 'as it had begun', in 'absolute anarchy or equally in despotism', he replied that experience had shown him that it would end in one of these. He was then asked whether it was not great imprudence and temerity to hope that any good should arise from insurrection, and whether the only prudent course would not have been to wait upon the decision of the Cortes of the

---

[1] Mancisidor, J., p. 123.

Spanish monarchy to which deputies from all the provinces had been admitted. He agreed that this was so, that his movement had been both unjust and impolitic, and that he had brought incalculable ill to 'religion, custom, and the State, especially to America, to such an extent that the wisest and most vigilant government' could not repair the damage in many years. He asked both the Holy Office and the Viceroy to forgive his actions and impetuosity.[1]

A document also exists whose authenticity has been doubted but which seems to bear the marks of his style. In this he asks for pity for the destruction he caused, for the orphans he created and the blood he shed. He conjures up a picture of souls sunk in a bottomless pit solely through having followed his own erroneous teaching. He calls the revolutionary doctrines 'perverse', and begs his followers to lay down their arms, fearing neither prison nor death but only God who has power to consign souls to hell.

There were, however, so many uncertainties as to the state of Hidalgo's mind at the time of his execution on July 30, 1811, that nearly a year later the Holy Office ordered an investigation into the signs of repentance he might have manifested in order to determine whether they were to be taken seriously. As a result, on March 15, 1813, the official Inquisitor decided that 'since there was insufficient cause to absolve the memory and fame of Hidalgo, nor yet to condemn him, the proceedings should merely be filed.'[2] Thus ended, as far as the Church was concerned, a dispute which had begun as early as 1800 when a friar named Joaquín Huesca had first denounced Hidalgo to the Inquisition for 'wishing to change the government, for not very orthodox opinions manifest to various persons, the carelessness with which he conducted his ministry and his worldly behaviour'. At that time the declarations of witnesses seem to have been mutually contradictory, although there was reason to suspect that Hidalgo denied the virginity of the mother of Jesus; wished to do away with the rule of chastity

---

[1] *Procesos Inquisitorial y Militar Seguidos a D. Miguel Hidalgo y Costilla*, Instituto Nacional de Antropología e Historia, Mexico, 1960, pp. 245–7.

[2] See Medina, José Toribio, *Historia del Tribunal del Santo Oficio de la Inquisición en México*, Santiago, Chile, 1905, pp. 475–8.

among priests as being against Nature; philosophized upon the mechanism of the world; denied the existence of hell; and interpreted the Holy Scriptures according to whim. On the advice of certain witnesses who said that the accused had mended his ways, the charges were dropped.

The controversy about Hidalgo's repentance is complicated by the fact that many Mexicans cannot bear his revolutionary posture to go, would have felt less desirous of remaining.'[1] A rumour was also circulating at this time that the Inquisition, which had been and trial he was aghast at the fury he had unleashed and terrified of the consequences of victory. Bustamante, who admired him greatly, admits that when he found his enemies intractable he became hard to his most intimate friends, insufferable even to Allende. He was, says Bustamante, 'vigorous and terrible in battle but sweet and merciful in cold blood. . . . Hidalgo achieved much but would have achieved even more with a less intractable temperament.'[1] His positive achievements toward a liberal constitution were the freeing of slaves and the abolition of tributes imposed upon lower-caste citizens, especially Indians. He was executed before he could do more, but it should be remembered that Morelos never ceased to acknowledge that his own philosophy was founded on that of his teacher, the first of the insurgents.

The mystique that surrounds his name was given credence by the description of his execution by the commander of the firing squad. Lieutenant Pedro Armendáriz described how at ten in the morning of the day before the execution Hidalgo was led to the hospital chapel where he alternately prayed, confessed, and talked with great fortitude, 'so that it seemed that the end of his life was not at hand'. He continued thus until nine in the morning of the following day when, accompanied by some priests, twelve armed soldiers, and the Lieutenant, he was taken to the *corral* of the hospital. The march proceeded in complete silence. There was no priest to put him in the right mind for death since he did this for himself, all the while consulting a little book which he held in his right hand, there being a crucifix in his left. When he reached the

---

[1] Bustamante, C. M., p. 60.

stool which had been put ready for the execution he gave a priest the book and without a word sat down and allowed himself to be bound with musket slings. With the crucifix in both hands he faced the firing squad. The first line of soldiers opened fire. Three bullets hit him in the stomach; a fourth broke his arm. The pain made him bend his body a little so that the bandage round his head was loosened; and he fixed 'those beautiful eyes of his' upon his executioners. The shots from a second volley, though aimed at his head, struck him in the stomach. A few large tears fell but he made no other sign of pain and remained quiet, his gaze unmoving. When the third line of soldiers fired they trembled so—'like quicksilver'—that they missed their mark. 'In this difficult and unfortunate circumstance,' said Armendáriz, 'I made two soldiers shoot with their gun barrels at his heart, and so the matter ended.'[1]

2. JOSÉ MARÍA MORELOS

After the executions of Hidalgo and Allende the insurrection entered a new phase, with José María Morelos now leading in a less undisciplined, more thoughtful way. He was a squarely built man under five feet high, swart and with a tendency to corpulence, his hair thick and black and his nose out of joint through having come into contact with a tree when he was fleeing from a bull. In spite of his unlikely appearance he became a thorn in the royalist flesh, harrying them for five years without ever being able to gain a decisive victory over the better-equipped Calleja. After declaring himself for Hidalgo's cause, Morelos reached the Pacific coast with about a thousand men but was forced to retreat by the defenders of Acapulco. A trick lured him back and he was again repelled. However on May 24, 1811, he was able to capture Chilpancingo, inland from Acapulco, and he was then near enough to Mexico City to give the royalists cause for concern. Money and mails were being captured by the rebels; and Calleja, fortified by troops newly arrived from Spain, was therefore determined to put an end

[1] Quoted by Mancisidor, J., p. 130.

to his activities. Forced onto the defensive, Morelos decided to make his stand in Cuautla and there to prepare for a long siege. Cuautla stands in an open plain and was thus difficult to defend, but it had the advantage of being surrounded by fertile lands which would provide food for the troops and a favourable climate for those of them who came from the warm south; whereas it would be uncomfortably hot for Calleja's men, recruited mostly on the high plateau.

Morelos had a thousand infantry and two thousand cavalry, augmented by about a thousand local Indians whom he used for heavy labour. Calleja, dogged by ill health as he was, mustered all his strength in a determined bid to wipe out what he called this 'obstinate' force. Morelos' troops were suffering from water shortage, the rains breaking late that year, and from lack of grain; but they put up a show of bravado by organizing fiestas and dances that took place at points of the city exposed to enemy fire. Even Calleja had to admit that the spirit of the insurgents, and the defiant way in which they buried their dead with gay celebrations, were remarkable. Morelos, he said, was a second Mahomet. Myths began to spring up about the insurgent leader who was supposed even to have the power of raising men from the dead! Even without such trimmings, the reality was tough. Morelos suffered from ill health, especially from malaria and migraine so that he constantly wore round his forehead a white kerchief soaked in vinegar. There were threats to kill or poison him which he ignored. When his followers tried to alert him to possible treachery from a 'pot-bellied man in his own entourage', he replied, 'Though my illnesses have wasted me I'm the only pot-belly here.'[1]

From February 19 to May 2, 1812, he held on in spite of famine conditions; but a sortie by his aide, Mariano Matamoros, in search of food, failed, and it was decided to retreat. Calleja had ordered a pardon to be offered to Morelos, who is supposed to have replied, 'I concede the same indulgence to Calleja and his troops.' By 2 a.m. on the second of May the retreat had begun.

[1] Teja Zabre, A., *Morelos*, p. 62.

The royalists knew nothing until the insurgents gave away their positions through being forced to fire on a small detachment blocking their way. Cavalry was immediately sent in pursuit of them but they dispersed into the hills. The royalists treated the civil population badly, as a result of which Morelos soon gathered about eight hundred men who, thirsty for revenge, were once more a threat to the south. By the end of 1812 he was issuing a manifesto from Oaxaca, and in January of the following year was making his second assault on Acapulco which fell to the liberals in August. Here he made a tactical error, lingering too long on the coast and allowing Calleja to re-form and to mop up guerrilla troops threatening the capital. He reached Valladolid on December 22, but Iturbide, by now an officer of promise on the royalist side, launched a fierce attack upon him. Matamoros was captured and, in spite of strong protests from Morelos who offered an exchange of prisoners, he was shot in Valladolid early in 1814.

Previously, on March 16, 1812, a priest, José María Cos, a loyal patriot who nevertheless deplored the civil war, had drawn up a 'manifesto of the American nation to the European inhabitants of the continent', in which he outlined plans for peace and—if these should after all prove unacceptable—for war. Basically his peace plans depended upon both Spain and Spanish America being acknowledged as subject to the King but with equal rights, neither being dependent upon or subordinate to the other. When the sovereign was absent the inhabitants of the Spanish peninsula should have no right to appropriate supreme power or to represent the King in the dominions. The conspiracy against the Spaniards by the Americans was at this moment only right and proper—said Cos—since it was a service to the deposed King and a patriotic act. European Spaniards should therefore resign command of the army to a national and independent congress representing Ferdinand. If they did so they would receive full protection; and once independence had been declared all grudges would be forgotten. Americans would, indeed, be in a position to help their cousins in Spain.

The war plan stated that the struggle between Europeans and

Americans ought not to be more cruel than it would be between foreigners! Human rights should be upheld for it was against Christian morals to proceed with hate, rancour, or personal vengeance. If the sword and not reason must decide, then it should be wielded as humanely as possible. From this it followed that insurgent prisoners should not be treated as traitors or condemned to death.[1]

Here was a genuine attempt to put an end to the worst atrocities; but the Spaniards could not accept Cos's offer and on September 29, in a gesture intended to show that they were more advanced in their views than the insurgents, they approved their own liberal constitution for Mexico. Believing that the country would never implement it, the *Audiencia* complained to the Cortes in Madrid:

'... The great charter of the Spanish people ... has not remained effective in these unhappy times. . . . The pretence that it has . . . far from producing the happiness of this political unit, is incompatible with its very existence. . . . If the government is ruled by the general will of the people, it follows that we must adapt to it and do what is just . . . but here for some reason the contrary has happened, because patriotism and public virtue are lacking. The general will, already corrupt, has prevailed; and so also does independence which most of the inhabitants undoubtedly favour.'[2]

The *Audiencia* was evidently baffled by the continued determination of the insurgents to fight on. Taking a strong hand, in November 1813 the Cádiz regency appointed Calleja Viceroy. In the meantime Bustamante had given Morelos a project for a constitution. Ignacio López Rayón, one of the few original leaders who had escaped the fate of Hidalgo and Allende, had drawn up another insisting on division of powers as a basic principle. In May 1811 he had even gone so far as to occupy Zitácuaro, a town not far from Valladolid, with the object of establishing a national Junta there. Though his plans had been premature they had led to Cos's declaration and had maintained Creole hopes of establishing a legal patriot government. Finally, under the presidency of

---

[1] Bustamante, C. M., p. 380, *et seq.*   [2] Bustamante, C. M., p. 149.

Mariano Matamoros, a convocation had been called in Oaxaca for August 5, 1813. López Rayón made a request that the constitution be put to the general vote. Morelos issued a statement which may have been intended to quash an unpopular suggestion that he should be named monarch. He would, he said, on no account allow a 'tyrant government', even if he himself were elected to lead it.

On September 13 the Junta met in Chilpancingo and celebrated Mass. In the name of Morelos a statement was read which stressed the overriding necessity for appointing a supreme chief. Applause greeted the nomination of Morelos. According to Bustamante all this happened so quickly that it seemed a put-up job. Morelos retired modestly for half an hour while his qualifications were discussed, and the matter was settled. Bustamante believed that from that moment 'the bandage of error covered Morelos' eyes, and his scant experience of the world made him the victim of a plot concocted by the ambition of certain people who, flattering him and persuading him to serve as an instrument for their own ends, were so able to confuse him that he endorsed a project which only a short while before he had himself disapproved.'[1] This supposedly blinded man on the following day announced that the laws of the new republic 'should be such as to moderate both opulence and indigence by raising the wages of the poor, improving their habits, and lifting them above ignorance, plunder, and theft'.[2]

On November 6, 1813, in the name of the prehispanic Mexican kingdom of Anáhuac, a 'Solemn Declaration of Independence of North America' was made in the national palace of Chilpancingo:

'The Congress of Anáhuac, legitimately installed . . . in the city of Chilpancingo of North America, solemnly declares in the presence of the Lord God . . . that due to the present situation in Europe this land has regained the exercise of its usurped sovereignty; for which reason its dependence on the Spanish throne is broken and dissolved forever.'

[1] Bustamante, C. M., p. 185.
[2] Quoted in *México en la Cultura*, February 5, 1967, p. 2.

Generally known as the Congress of Chilpancingo, this assembly was empowered to frame whatever laws best suited 'its order and inner happiness', to make peace or war; to establish alliances with European nations and with the Pope, and to appoint ambassadors and consuls. It reaffirmed allegiance to the Catholic religion which it would 'protect with all its power, watching over the purity of the faith and the other dogmas and the preservation of the regular orders'. No other religion was to be tolerated either publicly or secretly. Any who directly or indirectly opposed independence, whether by protecting the European oppressors or by refusing to contribute to expenses, subsidies and pensions for continuing the war until independence became recognized by foreign countries, were guilty of high treason.[1]

A manifesto drawn up by the Congress accused the Spaniards of forcing upon Mexicans the dogma of infallibility so that 'like the Athenians' they were compelled to worship an unknown God; 'and thus we did not suspect that there were any other principles of government except the political fanaticism that blinded our reason . . .'[2]

But the priests, however politically and socially radical, never ceased to be orthodox Catholics and even to work for the reinstatement of the Jesuits. They were also in favour of forbidding any non-Catholic foreigners from becoming citizens of the republic.[3]

Congress was presently transferred to Uruapan and to Apatzingán, and in the latter town (already famous because of fierce resistance to the Spanish conquerors from its Tarascan Indian inhabitants) a provisional constitution was promulgated in October 1814. So controversial was it that an article even appeared in the *Mexican Gazette* under the title 'Rebels Deceived by Monstrous Constitution'; but accusations made in it were at once rebutted. Among more orthodox decrees, such as sovereignty residing in the people and division of powers, this constitution tried to institute an innovation which was somewhat like the arrangement operating until recently in Uruguay, of a presidential committee

---

[1] Bustamante, C. M., p. 386.   [2] Bustamante, C. M., p. 387.
[3] Sierra, Justo, *Evolución Política del Pueblo Mexicano*, p. 174.

with the head of state alternating among its members. Three people were to lead the government, each with equal authority and each occupying the presidential chair for four months. Every year congress would draw lots for one member of the committee to retire.

Vicente Guerrero, one of the more competent of the insurgent generals, joined Morelos; and the two of them, with the supporters of the new constitution, decided to make for Tehuacán where they hoped to set up a permanent seat of government. By the autumn of 1815 they had assembled a formidable army of 20,000 men, but their progress was stopped by Iturbide at Valladolid and again at a small nearby ranch called Puruarán. Morelos was particularly anxious that members of his congress should not be captured; but while covering their approach to Tehuacán—which they reached without mishap—he himself was ambushed and caught on November 5, taken to Mexico City, jailed and tried by the Inquisition. Sentence was passed that 'the presbyter Morelos is a formal heretic, disturber of the peace, perfidious, lascivious, hypocritical, an irreconcilable enemy of Christianity'[1]; but that, in view of his 'repentance', he would be pardoned and handed over to a military court, where he would be tried clad as a penitent with collarless cassock, making general confession and doing spiritual exercises. 'In the unexpected and highly unlikely event that his life should be spared'—not exactly a propitious preamble to a free trial—he was to be condemned to 'retirement for the rest of it in Africa at the pleasure of the General Inquisitor, with obligation to recite perpetual psalms and the Virgin's rosary every Friday in the year....'

During his trial he behaved so impeccably that even Calleja respected him. He refused his surgeon's offer to rescue him from enemy hands, since it would have been obvious who had helped him to escape. On December 22, 1815, he went to his death. A friar arrived to confess him but he asked instead for a curate, after which he refused to have his eyes bandaged, preferring to do the job himself. Asking for a crucifix he said, 'Lord, if I have done

---

[1] Bustamante, C. M., p. 236; see also Medina, José Toribio, p. 513.

well, thou knowest; and if ill, I abandon myself to thy infinite mercy.'[1] As he knelt, they shot him from the rear, twice to be sure. He had been a modest, reserved, intelligent leader, a good judge of men and a good soldier. He admitted the charge of lasciviousness in so far as he had two natural sons, but he seems to have pleaded guilty of nothing else and his record was less fanatical, more thoughtful and planned than Hidalgo's. The principles of government which he laid down have guided all Mexican reform movements since his day.

3. ITURBIDE AND THE EMPIRE

The deaths of Matamoros and Morelos left Vicente Guerrero, hero of the campaigns of the south, as the only leader strong enough to carry on the war. He was offered a pardon by the Spaniards but refused. At this time Calleja was boasting that, with his forces triumphant in north Mexico, the revolution was at an end and he thought it unnecessary that a newly appointed Viceroy, Juan Ruíz de Apodaca, Count of Venadito, should be sent to replace himself. But Venadito was met immediately upon arrival in the country in 1816 with ample testimony that the insurgents were still to be reckoned with. He was attacked and almost captured; an event which, had it taken place, would have caused the war to continue under Calleja with unabated terror. As it turned out, Venadito—a man of more moderate temper—won many insurgents back to the Spanish cause and was, precisely because of his mercy, the strongest leader the peninsular side had had. His arrival in Mexico encouraged the Bishop of Puebla to extol the virtues of Ferdinand VII and Pius VII, many clergy returned to the royalists, and Venadito showed unusual clemency toward prisoners. His wife is said to have healed the wounds of insurgent soldiers with her own hands.

At this time the patriot cause received important encouragement from the success of an expedition planned in London, which

[1] Bustamante, C. M., p. 241.

led to a landing of guerrilla fighters on the Gulf Coast and penetration inland. Though small in scale, its extraordinary audacity fired the insurgents to greater efforts. The moving spirit was Francisco Javier Mina, a Spanish guerrilla fighter and nephew of a famous Spanish liberal, Francisco Espoz y Mina. The young Mina was among liberals who escaped from the autocratic régime in Spain and went to London. Here, encouraged by other exiles, he decided to carry the struggle into Mexico. He went first to the United States where he collected a diminutive fleet, promising that he was going to wage war 'against tyranny, not against Spaniards'. In 1817, after difficulties because his ships were becalmed and an epidemic of yellow fever broke out among his men, he landed at the bar of Soto de Marina—a lonely part of the coast north of Tampico, where the royalists least expected him and where many patriots joined him. Immediately he issued a proclamation saying:

'Sane and sensible opinion in Spain is today convinced not only that it is impossible to reconquer America, but impolitic and contrary to its own interests, which are well understood. . . . Already one part of America has achieved her independence, and we can congratulate ourselves that liberal principles will sooner or later extend their blessings to the rest.'[1]

Mina's most loyal lieutenant was Servando Teresa de Mier, a friar who had a stormy career in and out of jail and who finally fought against Iturbide when the latter became emperor of Mexico. A number of British and other foreign troops also joined the expedition and these were formed into a 'guard of honour of the Mexican Congress'; but at a crucial moment many became dissatisfied, deserted, and fled to the United States. Mercenaries never proved themselves effective in Mexico as they had done in South America, and these misadventures reduced Mina's tiny force to a mere handful. Even so it succeeded in penetrating inland and harrying the Spaniards for some time before its leader was captured and shot.

In 1820 the whole temper of the insurgent leaders changed. The Spanish liberal constitution, proclaimed as the result of an uprising

[1] Bustamante, C. M., p. 317.

by Rafael del Riego on January 1, 1820, had seemed like the thin end of the wedge to reduce Roman Catholic influence in Spain and it therefore alienated some priests who would otherwise have been in favour of its general principles. But with its acceptance by Ferdinand in March it looked to the dissident Mexican clergy as if they could now get the best of both worlds—a liberal constitution under a Catholic king. In any case the original rebellion had never been against Ferdinand but against Napoleonic Spain (this was even truer in Mexico than in South America). Therefore, when the Spanish government, through the intermediation of the well-liked Venadito, offered Mexico a pardon, many revolutionaries were inclined to accept. The go-between in the negotiations was Iturbide, and he could count upon the more conservative clergy to support his hidden intention of quashing liberalism in Mexico. Thus with the approval of the insurgents he succeeded in suppressing the insurgent movement.

By now a trusted officer in the royalist forces, Iturbide had a long time earlier been called before the Viceroy to answer charges made against him by the citizens of Guanajuato concerning certain irregularities. As a result he had temporarily renounced his military command. Friends had rallied to his defence but enemies accused him of ambition, cruelty, and self-seeking. Whatever the truth of the matter, he had proved himself since that time to be an officer of considerable courage and skill, so much so that Calleja believed him to be the one person capable of liberating Mexico. From a military point of view he was in a different class from the self-trained or totally untrained priests.

Even though they were now a thing of the past, Iturbide was sorely hurt by the slanders and it is clear that by February 1821 he was planning to remove himself from the royalist camp and to free Mexico on his own account and on his own terms. The royalists suspected nothing of his double game. As their emissary he pressed Guerrero to accept the Spanish offer of pardon, and when Guerrero answered proudly, 'Independence or death,' Iturbide must secretly have been congratulating himself that he had already prepared the way for his transfer to the winning side.

When he finally and openly moved over to the insurgents, Guerrero and the other revolutionaries took him to their hearts, forgiving him his support of the royalists and giving him a position of honour in their ranks. His Plan of Iguala—it bears the stamp of his thinking more than that of the other signatories— was proclaimed on February 24, 1821, and was based on three guarantees: religion, unity between Mexicans and Europeans, and independence. These were symbolized in the Mexican flag: at first horizontal red, white, and green; but later changed to the vertical in order that the bands could be widened to make room in the centre for the ancient Aztec symbol of the eagle on the nopal cactus.

The Plan was an immediate success. Those Creoles who had previously opposed the revolution now saw a way of maintaining their own interests within a framework of independence. The fears of the clergy that religious faith was being upset were set at rest. The Spanish absolutists regarded the Plan as a safeguard against the imposition of the type of constitution Morelos had drawn up, and the constitutionalists themselves adhered to it for the sake of peace. Conquered at last, the royalists now held only the capital, the port of Veracruz, and its outlying fortress of San Juan de Ulúa.

Like San Martín and other favourers of imperialism in South America, Iturbide seems to have been convinced that only a limited monarchy would suit a politically immature nation and prevent civil wars and the seizure of power by ambitious despots. He described how Hidalgo had offered him a high rank in the insurgent armies and how he had declined because he thought the movement would lead only to disorder, massacres, and devastation. He believed that the aims of the conspirators were not independence and freedom but the extermination of all Europeans and their possessions, the upsetting of all humane and religious laws.

He may well have been right; but his own ambitions and his somewhat sycophantic desire to remain on good terms with all groups of Mexican society, were serious obstacles to establishing a form of monarchy based—as the Anglophile Lucas Alamán hoped—on the British model. There was a strange twist in the Plan in that—though it was the culmination of a mass movement of the poor and outcast such as never occurred on anything like the same scale in South America—it upheld the rights of the upper classes more deliberately and completely than any of the constitutions in the south.

On March 1 the Plan was formally approved. It declared Mexico independent; created a limited monarchy 'regulated according to the spirit of the constitution and exactly adapted to the country'; set up a Junta and a Regency to reign until an emperor could be found, and announced that Spanish laws were in force until new ones could be made. Iturbide, in the uniform of a royalist colonel, vowed allegiance to the Roman Catholic Church, to preserve independence, to maintain unity of Europeans and Mexicans, and to obey Ferdinand should he accept the constitution. Only then did he tear the colonel's epaulettes from his shoulders as a sign that he was no longer under orders from the royalists.

The Plan of Iguala, though generally popular, had its opponents. It was rumoured that Doña Josefa Ortíz de Domínguez, who had been a leader in the conspiratorial *Sociedad de los Guadalupes*, had participated in it. This she regarded as slander and her reply was forthright. She branded both Iturbide and Guerrero—formerly her hero—as traitors: Iturbide because he represented the clergy and the property-owners, Guerrero because he had compromised by accepting a political as distinct from a social independence.[1] In spite of opposition and suspicion, however, Iturbide succeeded in imposing his will upon the country and in maintaining the loyal approval of many of his royalist troops.

Royalist power was virtually at an end; and on July 30, 1821, the last Viceroy to be sent from Spain, Juan O'Donojú, arrived to replace Venadito. On reaching San Juan de Ulúa, O'Donojú found that the town of Veracruz was being threatened by the insurgents. He therefore hastened to proclaim his own peaceful and mediatory intentions. Iturbide was in Puebla where on

[1] See *México en la Cultura*, September 18, 1966, p. 1.

August 5, in the cathedral, the oath of independence was solemnly sworn; and there O'Donojú sent him two letters, addressing him as 'Commander in Chief of the Imperial Forces of the Three Guarantees', and in the second more simply as 'Friend'. Iturbide was anxious to come to terms, and allowed O'Donojú safe conduct as far as Córdoba where they met on August 24. Cornered, and in danger of being taken prisoner if he did not comply with Iturbide's plans, O'Donojú felt obliged to act beyond the authority the liberal Spanish government had conferred on him. He signed the agreement declaring Mexico an independent empire, the throne to be occupied either by Ferdinand or some other prince of the royal house of Spain.

On September 27 the Army of the Three Guarantees entered triumphantly into Mexico City—triumphantly in a sense that has scarcely been witnessed before or since, for Iturbide had not conquered O'Donojú nor had he tried to. What he had done was to fuse the aims of the two contending parties and to make it appear to each one that it—and not the bitter enemy—had got the better of the bargain. This was shrewd, but it left the whole purpose of the independence war unresolved. Mexico was free and yet not free—an autonomous empire in name but ruled almost equally by a viceroy and a one-time royalist colonel. Iturbide had not freed Mexico for the Creoles, still less for the ragged armies of Hidalgo, Morelos, and Guerrero, but for the aristocrats and for himself. Robertson gives details of the odd situation created by a division of power which had neither been approved by the Spanish Cortes nor fully accepted even by O'Donojú, who must have been taken aback, to say the least, when Iturbide assumed the right to occupy the viceregal seat in the cathedral. O'Donojú did not have long to ponder the situation however, for less than a month after the signing of Mexico's independence he was dead, probably from pleurisy, almost certainly not from foul play though it was inevitable that Iturbide should come under suspicion in some quarters.

In the Act of Independence of the Empire, signed the day after the army's triumphal entry into the capital, there was fulsome praise for Iturbide who was described as a genius above all admiration and praise. But in Spanish America people were watching events with some trepidation. Bolívar acknowledged Iturbide's achievement but his words may have had more in them of diplomacy than sincerity. By November 16 he was confiding his fears to San Martín, saying that now more than ever it was important to complete the expulsion of Spaniards from the whole continent in order that Americans could join together against any new enemy or new method that might be used to undermine the Creoles. It was not the empire as such that he feared so much as the possible importation of a European prince to occupy its throne. On November 22 he wrote to General Carlos Soublette pointing out that if a Bourbon were established in Mexico it would be to his advantage to maintain close relations with his princely relatives and with other potentates in Europe. In their own interests they would want to help and support the Mexican throne, which would do all in its power to restrain Colombia whose republican system would seem a threat to monarchy. The Mexicans would therefore spy upon Colombia and would even hope to invade South America or at least to split and weaken the liberals there.

Bolívar was thinking historically, in terms of the power wielded by great European dynasties in the past. It happened that his conclusions coincided with those of the populace who feared a monarchy as such. Therefore if Iturbide were to create one against public opinion he would have to adopt methods unpopular with the man in the street. And he did indeed in November 1821 put forward a scheme whereby deputies to Congress should be elected by, and should represent, different classes in proportions which ensured an oligarchic rather than a democratic rule: nobility 3; government officials 24; clergy 18; the intelligentsia 18; labourers, miners, artisans, merchants, 10 each; the army, navy, and miscellaneous people 9 each. Even supposing the intelligentsia to have been entirely liberal which it was not, this would give a majority to the nineteenth-century Mexican equivalent of the Establishment.

Thus Iturbide managed to ingratiate himself with those sectors in whose hands power lay. Basil Hall, passing through Mexico at that time, described how the Mexican Cortes met on February 24, 1822, and how one of its first acts was an edict permitting any who wished to do so to leave the country and allowing the export of specie at a duty of only three and a half per cent. This measure had been promised by Iturbide and Hall said that his good faith 'gave great confidence to the mercantile capitalists and probably decided many to remain in the country who, had they been less at liberty to go, would have felt less desirous of remaining.'[1] A rumour was also circulating at this time that the Inquisition, which had been abolished by the Constitution before Ferdinand's release from France, might probably be re-established—a prospect which Hall said was 'no less grateful to the hopes of the clergy than a free export of specie was to the merchants'. With his usual diplomatic dexterity Iturbide had 'contrived to bring all parties into the best possible humour with himself personally'.

All but the recalcitrantly liberal, that is; and Iturbide remained in power rather because his presence was deemed expedient than because he held the popular imagination. Now, to set the cat among the pigeons, came news from Spain that on February 13 the Cortes had rejected the plan for an empire. Opponents of Iturbide stepped in with proposals for a republic on South American lines. Iturbide countered with a better plan: if the Bourbons would have nothing to do with it, he would himself take the imperial crown. In fairness it must be remarked that the suggestion was first mooted not by Iturbide but by Manuel Félix Fernández who as a youth of twenty-two had distinguished himself during the siege of Cuautla. Later, rather than submit to the Spaniards, this sturdy patriot subsisted on wild berries in the mountains about Orizaba, until in good faith he was able to join Iturbide in whom he thought to put his trust; but this proved ill-founded. Eventually, changing his name to Guadalupe Victoria in honour of the patron saint of Mexico and the victory he felt sure would come, he became the first constitutional President of Mexico.

[1] Hall, Basil, p. 274.

All that was for the future. For the present, Iturbide held the stage and his supporters included many influential people such as José Joaquín Fernández de Lizardi, author of some biting satires; the liberal Valentín Gómez Farías; the conservative Lucas Alamán; and Manuel López de Santa Anna who was afterwards to become Iturbide's most dangerous opponent. (Among those against the imperial plan was Fray Servando Teresa de Mier.) In his monarchical aspirations Iturbide was therefore supported by a cross-section of all parties. Since he had offered the throne to Ferdinand and it had been refused, there seemed nobody capable of occupying it but himself.

On May 18, 1822, Iturbide was proclaimed Emperor under the title Agustín I. Once again it was a chance for the same crowd of ragged peasants who had supported Hidalgo with 'Death to the Gachupines'. Now they thronged about Iturbide proclaiming him as loudly but for opposite reasons and in a contrary cause. The Mexican independence movement had come full circle, and from a hatred of all things Spanish was now fawning upon a man who had spent his youth supporting Spain and who had signed an act of independence in collusion with the last Spanish Viceroy and supporting conservative elements.

Three days later, in defiance of the fact that the Congress electing him did not assemble a quorum, Iturbide became the constitutional emperor of Mexico. Quarrelling with Congress, which tried to assert its rights, he dismissed most of its members and installed new ones of his own choosing. The coronation ceremony took place on July 21 in Mexico City cathedral. Iturbide wrote to Bolívar informing him of events and saying, whether with real or feigned humility there is no means of telling, that he was far from considering the crown a blessing since it placed an oppressive weight upon him; but that he had agreed in the end in order to avoid ills to his country, which was on the point of succumbing once more to anarchy.

The Mexican treasury was depleted, and now that the first flush of success was wearing off Iturbide was not popular—especially in Central America which it had been assumed would become part of the new empire. In South America feelings were mixed. Iturbide's letter of justification was uncomfortably reminiscent of some formulations of Bolívar's own; and though the latter was thoroughly suspicious of the Mexican Emperor's intentions he must also have been compelled to see in the situation that same dilemma that had so beset the South Americans—the choice between anarchy and formal republicanism on the one hand, and despotism with order on the other.

At home, enemies of Iturbide soon became impatient. They felt strong because they could count on the support of Congress, the Masons (who had become a growing power in the land and who disliked his autocratic brand of Catholicism), and the Press. The country was bankrupt, agriculture unproductive, mining at a standstill, and there were rumours of conspiracies. On August 26 arrests were made, Bustamante and Fray Teresa de Mier among others being thrown into jail. Guadalupe Victoria fled again into the forests, and soon even Fernández de Lizardi had turned against the Emperor and was on the side of Congress, whose powers were becoming daily more restricted. To cap it all, on September 15 Guatemala and El Salvador signed their own separate declarations of independence and Mexico was obliged to send in troops to bring them to heel. In the end, of all Central America, only Chiapas and Yucatán elected to remain with Mexico, though Iturbide would have liked to extend his domain not only to the Isthmus of Panama but to the Caribbean islands as well, especially Cuba.

By the end of the year Iturbide had dismissed General Santa Anna for having failed to capture Ulúa which was still in the possession of Spanish royalists. He thus mortally offended a man who was as proud and ambitious as himself. Santa Anna now saw in Iturbide only an unjust despot who was paralysing commerce, agriculture, and mining, exiling good men, and imprisoning others. Enlisting the help of Guadalupe Victoria, he formulated the 'Plan of Veracruz' to restore to Mexico the freedom she had lost under the Emperor. Guerrero and Nicolás Bravo (later to become Vice-President of the Republic) soon joined the dissident faction. Various plans and manifestos were drawn up proclaiming a republic. Opinion quickly gathered against the Empire which only shortly before had looked so strong; and by the end of February 1823 Iturbide was in control only of Mexico City and its immediate surroundings. Once it became clear that he was not after all the only available leader and that there were men of great military as well as civic talent ranged against him, the enmity that had been smouldering now flamed. The suddenness of his débâcle must have surprised him but he had no illusions about his waning power and in March he hastily convened Congress and placed before it his Act of Abdication. He no longer wanted the crown, he said, and he was tired of bloodshed. He surrendered power not because he was afraid but because he had achieved his purpose and could be of no further use to the cause he served. Mexico had no foreign enemies, and as for internal ones, his presence in the country was likely only to increase dissension.

His abdication was accepted and many must have sighed with relief when the Emperor was got rid of so cheaply, the cost being a pension of 25,000 pesos. Some urged that the sum be reduced, and others that he be executed forthwith, for there were real fears that Mexico would know no peace while an ex-emperor remained at large. However, on May 11, 1823, he was put on board a merchantman bound for Leghorn.

The following year, on the pretext that his sons needed an English schooling, Iturbide transferred to London and thence to Bath. His eldest son was sent to Ampleforth and, encouraged by the friends he still possessed in Mexico, Iturbide began to plan a return to his native land. The Foreign Office was informed that he wished to establish in Mexico a constitution similar to that of the British. Canning was cautious and preferred to avoid a meeting with the former emperor. There was no reason to suppose that the British government was in collusion with him or had any knowledge of his sudden departure from Europe. Nor had the French any part in it. He was acting alone. On May 11, 1824, he sailed from Southampton in the British vessel *Spring*, bound for Mexico and Peru and carrying with him much money and jewels. There was even a rumour that Spain, angry at Mexico's independence, had appointed him viceroy!

Why did Iturbide want to return? He said himself that his only object was to support Mexican freedom and independence with his voice and sword. Perhaps he could not bear to hear of his enemy Santa Anna now heading the revolutionaries and proclaiming the 'Constituent Congress' of 1824, with its ostensible—but only ostensible—republican affiliations, and with the support of Miguel Ramos Arizpe (who had been a member of the Cádiz Cortes in 1812), Valentín Gómez Farías, and Servando Teresa de Mier. (None of these men was apparently aware at this date of Santa Anna's autocratic leanings.)

In Mexico, on April 28, 1824, an edict was passed sentencing Iturbide to immediate death should he return to his native shores. The news did not reach him and so in all innocence he landed in Tamaulipas where he was seized, taken to Padilla, and executed on July 19. Justo Sierra wrote of this event:

'It was a political act, not a just one. Iturbide had done his country a supreme service which cannot be belittled by calling it an act of treason against Spain. He did not rise to the heights his work demanded, but neither did he deserve the scaffold for reward. If the nation could have spoken, it would have absolved him.'[1]

Posthumously it did; for in November 1833 Congress declared him one of the founders of Mexican independence; and his remains were transferred to Mexico City cathedral where he had been crowned. During the second empire Maximilian promised members of the Iturbide family high positions in the State, named some of his heirs princes and princesses, and considered making one of them—Agustín—his own heir. But in 1925 the left-wing President Calles did not think fit to move Iturbide's body to the Independence monument where the remains of Hidalgo, Matamoros, Mina, Morelos, Bravo, and Guerrero were deposited. Present-day Mexicans squirm if they hear him called 'liberator'; in a revolutionary country an emperor could never be that!

[1] Sierra, Justo, p. 201.

Iturbide was probably neither quite so despicable nor yet so noble as he has been painted. He had courage and was a clever diplomatist but was fundamentally a vainer and smaller man than Bolívar, and a far less upright one than San Martín; though he may be given credit for believing that his double-dealings were, in the true Machiavellian sense, necessary for his country's good.

4. MEXICO'S FOREIGN RELATIONS

In 1824, with the election of Guadalupe Victoria to the presidential chair of a new republic, the United States began to show increased interest in the potentially rich and by no means negligible land to the south. Britain had never been as influential there as in South America, and Mexico's independence had been won with less assistance from foreign powers—the popular impulse having been greater. But now the power of the United States was growing formidably, at least in the view of Europeans. Narciso de Heredia, Count of Ofalia, who was at the time Spanish Minister of Justice, had a good deal to say on the subject to the British Minister in Madrid:

'[He] went into a long dissertation upon the growing influence and power of the United States of America, expressing it as his opinion that if a separation took place between Spain and her Colonies, Mexico at least, if not the greater part of the other South American Colonies, would ultimately fall under the dominion of the United States; that the Spanish character, he was sorry to say, could not maintain a very long struggle against the energy, activity, and enterprise of the race that sprung from the British Isles; that the Mexicans were Spaniards, the Americans, English; that *old* England would do well to reflect that a *new* England was rising rapidly on the other side of the Atlantic, which, ere a century elapsed, would probably exceed her in population in the proportion of at least three or four to one. How would she be able to resist such a rival in all that constituted her present greatness and prosperity? He said that . . . in lending ourselves to the separation of the Colonies from Spain, we were only hastening the arrival of that day when the star of our prosperity must pale before that of our powerful, ambitious and enterprising descendants. . . .'[1]

The Count's fear were well founded, for already Joel Poinsett, who had been critical of the Emperor Agustín I (calling him exceptionally immoral in a not very moral society, arbitrary, tyrannical, and unscrupulous) had been campaigning for the formation of a general American federation from which all European powers, but especially Great Britain, should be excluded. According to H. G. Ward, writing confidentially to George Canning on September 30, 1828,[2] Poinsett was having considerable success by methods which the British deplored. He tried to infiltrate Panamerican ideas into the Masonic lodges which he was influential in establishing (the first meeting of the York Lodge in Mexico City was held in his house). The York lodges, supported by the American, were allegedly liberal and opposed to the Scottish lodges. A conspiracy to reinstate Spanish rule in Mexico led to a strong Yorkist counter-attack. Lucas Alamán, called by Vasconcelos 'the only Foreign Minister Mexico has ever possessed', became the butt of Yorkist attacks and, under the pressure of slanders that he was undemocratic, reactionary, and despotic (and of course Anglophile, which was true), he was forced to resign. At the end of 1827 peninsular Spaniards were expelled from the country and Guadalupe Victoria had gone over to the Yorkists though the Scottish lodges still counted on the support of his Vice-President, Nicolás Bravo.

According to Ward, General Victoria at first disliked Poinsett and had to be persuaded by Ward himself to treat him civilly. The legislatures of the States of Veracruz and Michoacán petitioned the central government to have the American deported. Evidently many Mexicans agreed with the British view that Poinsett's only interest was to keep Mexico in a state of confusion 'because it

[1] Sir William à Court, British Minister in Madrid, to George Canning, quoted in Webster, vol. 2, letter No. 549; Foreign Office document 72/285.

[2] Foreign Office Letter No. 256 (F.O. 50/14), Mexico, September 30, 1825, quoted by Webster, vol. 1.

possesses such great advantages over the United States that if it offered the guarantees of social order it would attract the emigrants from Europe to its own favoured soil and soon eclipse the greatness of the north'.[1] (At this time, we must remember, Mexico possessed what are now the south-western United States.)

In spite of the strong feelings against him, Poinsett was so successful that Ward soon regretted having championed the cause of his rival. The battle which had already begun in 1823 with the first formulation of the Monroe Doctrine was now engaged in earnest, and the fate of Spanish America was to be bound up henceforth with the policies of the United States. Since Poinsett's day the United States has been wooed for the material aid it can provide, hated for its interventionism, suspected because of its inbuilt inability to put itself in the position of Spanish American peoples with their different philosophical outlook and way of life. Between the two worlds of Washington and Bolívar, Mexico stands as a buffer. With the presidency of Guadalupe Victoria the Mexican independence struggle technically came to an end. The fight was henceforth to be for economic and social freedoms.

[1] Quoted in *Mexico and Mr. Poinsett, Reply to a British Pamphlet*, Philadelphia December 21, 1829. In this spirited reply the U.S.A. defends its own attitude toward Mexico and Spanish America.

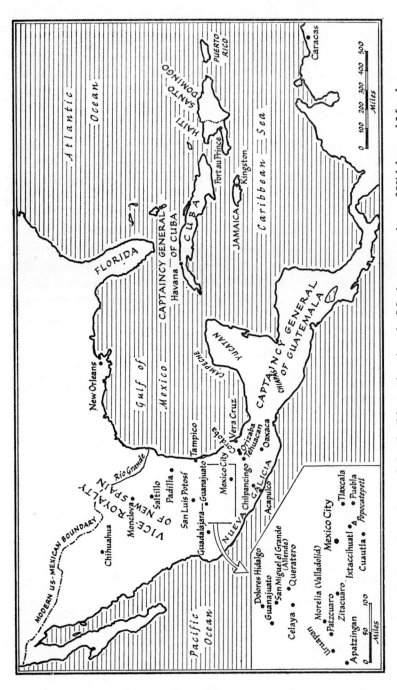

5. Region of Mexico and the Caribbean showing the Mexican campaigns of Hidalgo and Morelos

PART THREE

The Aftermath of Independence

CHAPTER I

THE PROBLEM

1. A HISTORICAL SKETCH

The decades after independence were not encouraging and they gave ample proof that Bolívar had had every reason to fear that power would fall into hands that were either incompetent or malevolent. There was little wonder that he had wanted to keep it to himself, whom he trusted even if others did not. Everywhere the picture was the same: of *caudillos*—strong men with few if any scruples—seeking power; of legality mocked; and of petty nationalism and wars among the countries that had once stood firmly united in the freedom movement.[1] During the active phase of independence differences of opinion had been subordinated to a common aim. Once the immediate danger was past and the republics were technically in being, the fragile nature of the alliance became evident. There was a deep cleavage in the Spanish-Indian character that led to weaknesses in the legal, political, and philosophical structure. Men of noble ideals were at the mercy of shoddier minds than their own.

Details of post-independence history are beyond the scope of this book, but a brief survey shows the kind of problems that bedevilled progress everywhere. In Mexico, Santa Anna's dictatorial tendencies were opposed by liberals who held power briefly in 1833 and 1834, after which Santa Anna staged a come-

[1] Such narrow nationalism was only to be expected in view of the faulty communications inherited from colonial days. After independence letters from Buenos Aires to Mexico had to go via London unless they could wait for the few ships that plied up and down the Pacific—not more than once or twice yearly (see Ward, H. G., vol. 1, footnote p. 143).

back and continued as a skilful commander in the war against the United States (1845) which concerned the rights of U.S. citizens who had settled in Texas (then part of Mexico). This dispute finally ended with Mexico losing approximately half her territory. There followed the episode of the French imposition of the Emperor Maximilian (1864–7) who was supported by the Mexican right wing against the liberals; the triumph of Benito Juárez and his austere reforms which harked back to Morelos; the long dictatorship of Porfirio Díaz (on and off from 1876 to 1910); revolution which reverted once more to the principles of Morelos; and eventual stability under the paternal and technocratic rule of the *Partido Revolucionario Institucional*. In Central America there had been attempts (encouraged by the U.S.A. and Mexico) to form a union, but in 1838 the area split into five small countries: Guatemala, El Salvador, Nicaragua, Honduras, and Costa Rica.

In Bolívar's lands Gran Colombia was broken into several quarrelsome republics. Venezuela had separated from the confederation and was presided over intermittently until 1863 by Páez either directly in the presidential chair or through intermediaries, including Soublette. There followed a series of unscrupulous dictators which continued through into the present century and ended only with the death of Juan Vicente Gómez who had ruled with an iron hand from 1908 until 1935. When in 1945 the *Acción Democrática* party seized power and instituted universal suffrage and equal voting rights for all adult citizens the cry went up that the long-yearned-for egalitarian ideal had been fulfilled. However a military coup soon overthrew the government of the novelist Rómulo Gallegos; and it was not until 1958 that the dictatorship of General Marco Pérez Jiménez was ended. The right wing and the liberals both allege that since then progress has been bedevilled by subversive action by communists infiltrating from Cuba.

Ecuador had also split off from the federation and in 1830 the almost illiterate and thoroughly autocratic Juan José Flores became the republic's first President. Territorial disputes with Colombia and economic difficulties marred his administration and after periods in and out of power he was forced to leave the country in 1845. Presidents and constitutions then followed one another in quick succession and there was no stability until the theocratic government of Gabriel García Moreno which lasted from 1861 to 1875, when he was assassinated by a Colombian. The succeeding series of liberal presidents had to contend with a tottering economy and its attendant social problems.

Bolivia's first President was General Sucre, who resigned in 1828 and was succeeded by Andrés de Santa Cruz who immediately abolished Bolívar's 1826 Constitution. Santa Cruz succeeded in uniting Bolivia and Peru in a confederation; but Chile, believing her interests to be threatened, declared war and defeated the combined Bolivian and Peruvian armies at Yungay in 1839. The government of Santa Cruz fell. Wars against Peru and Chile, and finally the meaningless Chaco war of 1932 against Paraguay, weakened the country still further.

Peru was in such economic straits that a settled political order was impossible. As we have seen, the union with Bolivia and the protectorship of Santa Cruz (1836–9) brought only war and defeat. Not until Ramón Castilla came to power in 1845 was any attempt made to solve economic problems by, for example, exploiting Pacific guano deposits, building the two important railway lines between Arica and Tacna and from Lima to Callao, and colonizing the section of the Amazon basin that fell within the country's territory. Another farsighted president, José Balta (1868–72), continued the work of constructing railways in the high Andes, but progress was seriously checked by a war in which Chile once again confronted Peru and Bolivia between 1879 and 1884. The basic dispute—concerning possession of the Atacama desert with its nitrate deposits—was settled in 1884 by the Treaty of Ancón, which gave the province of Tarapaca (formerly Peruvian) to Chile; and by a treaty between Bolivia and Chile which in 1904 deprived Bolivia of her former possessions around Antafogasta. The settlement was rounded off in 1929 when the U.S.A., called in to arbitrate, gave Tacna to Peru and Arica to Chile.

As to Colombia itself, Santander, who had returned from exile in 1832 to become its President, found himself at the head of a small nation known for a time as Nueva Granada, and opposed by a series of *caudillos* ending with José Hilario López (1849–53) who pursued some liberal policies which were evidently too advanced for the country since they led only to civil war and more dictatorships. By the time Nueva Granada was reshaped in 1863 into the United States of Colombia, it had become used to living in a permanent state of semi-civil war. The once liberal but later conservative Rafael Nuñez (in power on and off from 1880 until 1898) could control the country only by dictatorial methods. In 1903 Colombia lost the territory of Panama which became an independent republic.

In the south, Paraguay was in the grip of the dictator Francia until his death in 1840. Carlos Antonio López, who followed him, pursued some enlightened policies, but his son Francisco Solano López (1862–70: he inherited the presidency as if it had been a monarchy) provoked a disastrous war against Argentina, Uruguay, and Brazil which cost the country half its population and plunged it into chaos. There was some limited progress thereafter, stopped once again by the war of the Chaco against Bolivia.

In Chile seven years of anarchy following upon the resignation of O'Higgins in 1823 were brought to an end by Diego Portales, who defeated the idealistic but ineffective liberals at the battle of Lircay (1830). Portales organized the country and gave it a constitutional form, establishing an austere but highly efficient government. However, the dispute between Chile and the Peruvian-Bolivian federation and the resulting war were not popular in all quarters; and Portales, held responsible, was assassinated in Valparaíso in 1837. After him came a series of able presidents including Manuel Bulnes (1841–51) and Manuel Montt (1851–61). By the end of the century Chile had been transformed into an orderly republic which was not upset even by the long war against Peru and Bolivia.

Argentine rivalries between federalists and centralists had produced civil wars intermittently until Juan Manuel de Rosas took command of government in 1829. His régime lasted until 1853 and was filled with terror and repression. Many important families were compelled to flee the country before he was finally overthrown by Justo José de Urquiza, governor of the province of Entre Ríos, Rosas escaping to Britain where he died in 1877. Urquiza tried to form a government but people feared that he would set himself up as another dictator; and it was only after a bitter struggle that he was elected the first President under a new Constitution in May 1853; but Buenos Aires resigned from the Argentine confederation in protest. Subsequent events continued to revolve about federalist-centralist rivalries, with the forceful, contradictory Domingo Faustino Sarmiento confronting the more sober Bartolomé Mitre. The situation created at this period contained so many elements endemic to Spanish America that we shall examine it presently in greater detail.

Uruguay, which was to become one of the most stable of Spanish American republics, was in its early days beset by rivalry with Buenos Aires and by a struggle between the *colorados*, who were followers of the left-wing Artigas, and the *blancos*, who included the ruling classes, merchants, and clergy. Only with the era of José Batlle y Ordoñez (1903–15 with an interruption) were rivalries curbed and an enlightened social and economic programme put into effect.

Even this thumbnail sketch of the history of the countries after independence shows that they were suffering profound difficulties in coming to terms with themselves. The problem was to build a philosophical and legal infrastructure to which the political machinery could be smoothly geared. It was largely a struggle between absolutism and liberalism, a struggle which dominated not only the political scene but also the social ethic (complicated by racial prejudices), the legal structure, and the whole philosophical background without which there could be no consistency of aim.

2. ABSOLUTISM VERSUS LIBERALISM

The nineteenth-century confrontation between absolutism and

liberalism was by no means peculiar to Spanish America. In Spain the clash between them had been brought to a head by the Napoleonic invasion but it had existed earlier. In 1797 men who were accused of favouring republican ideas were banished to jails in La Guaira where they formed around them a group of intellectuals, including Creoles, to study the philosophical basis of liberalism. Thus the conservatives in Spain gave unwitting encouragement to the spread of liberalism in the New World. In Spain itself the confrontation was to continue throughout the vacillating half-reign, half-exile of Ferdinand. When he was restored to the throne in 1814 and reverted to absolute rule, those Spaniards who had defended the 1812 liberal Constitution were forced to emigrate and many of them found refuge in London where they publicized the cause of the rebellious colonies in books and journals. José María Blanco y Crespo, generally known as Blanco White (he was of Irish descent), who became a close friend of Andrés Bello, founded *El Español Constitucional* with a clearly formulated aim:

'Being Spaniards we hope and desire that the American colonies should not separate from the metropolis and that they should remain united under the protection of liberal constitutions and laws. But we are men before we are Spaniards, and we believe it is right for these colonies to resist absolutism.'[1]

A similar spirit animated many Spaniards who remained at home, including Rafael del Riego who in 1819 refused to command a powerful force destined for La Plata because he could not fight against brothers in a common cause. Next year the stand taken by himself and others forced Ferdinand for a time to return to the 1812 Constitution, but in 1823 del Riego was accused of high treason and hanged. Had the liberal movement triumphed—and it was by no means negligible—the need for the colonies to split off from the parent would have been less overriding.

The contrast between the violence of the Spanish American independence wars and the briefer, more conventionally fought

[1] Quoted by Enrique de Gandía in his preface to Sarmiento's *Obras Selectas*, vol. 2, p. xxx.

revolution of the New England States against Britain tells its own story. Separation of the North American colonies from Britain was made ideologically easier because of Britain's own tradition of free thought; whereas liberal Spaniards on both sides of the Atlantic had a greater weight of autocratic tradition to contend against (not to mention the admixture with equally autocratic Indian *caciquismo*, or bossism). Blanco White[1] had much to say about 'the struggle between enterprising genius and constituent ignorance' that had gone on in Spain for generations, with more or less open rebellion against it in the universities; for 'a mind once set on "the proper study of mankind" must be weak indeed not to extend its views beyond the limits prescribed by the ignorance of a despot. . . .' And he tells how he fitted up a small room for his *'prohibited books'*, which could lie there in perfect concealment. 'The Breviary alone . . . is kept upon the table. . . .'

The Spanish world was restricted by a number of intellectual taboos, whereas the Anglo-Saxon colonists had already a clear idea of the shape that political freedom could take, and their Constitution could be written readily and naturally. Attempts by the Spanish Creoles to imitate it were doomed to fail because a parliamentary-congressional system was beyond the area's experience. To pretend otherwise was to perpetuate a dangerous self-delusion. Freedom did not exist merely because its shape had been drawn on paper.

In any case it was not at all certain that the liberators were over-anxious to establish a democracy based on universal suffrage. In a very general way liberalism was supposed to be necessarily equated with democracy, despotism with tyranny; whereas a more careful look at nineteenth-century ideologies will show that the brand of liberalism then current was capable of working only if

[1] White, Blanco (Doblado, Leucadio), *Letters from Spain*, London, Henry Colburn and Co., 1822, pp. 114 and 134. In a letter attached to the copy of this book in the Kensington and Chelsea Central Library the donor notes that Shelley took 'a warm interest in the movements toward political liberty in Spain'—a reminder that the liberals in Spain and Spanish America had the support of English intellectuals of the time.

political power (including power bestowed by the franchise) was limited to the privileged, educated sections of society. If, as it often did, liberalism ameliorated or professed to ameliorate the lot of the underprivileged, it was forced to do so through the exercise of such overbearing persuasion that its methods verged, subtly and unnoticed sometimes, upon those of despotism.[1] The uneducated were usually presumed to be incapable of exercising a vote, and—as O'Higgins said—if they would not take happiness it would have to be forced upon them for 'By God they shall be happy!' Popular sovereignty was a laudable theory. In practice very few people really believed that it could work. There was, moreover, deeply embedded in the Spanish and Indian characters, a liking for the dogma of the divine right of kings; though logical argument could always sidestep the issue by presuming that this right was revoked if abused. Even the ancient Nahua-speaking Mexican priests, virtually unassailable in their divine prerogatives, could be demoted (at least in theory) if they were proved not to have the good of the people at heart.

The choice, then, was not between the outer forms of democracy and dictatorship, but between attitudes of tolerance and compassion which might arise in either. The populace was not always on the side of its own welfare, and its fickleness could be noted in the behaviour of the Mexican rabble who first shouted 'death to the Gachupines' and then 'vivas' to a Gapuchin-lover, Iturbide; in the crowd's distaste for O'Higgins, San Martín, and Bolívar once the fighting phase was over, though in retrospect there seems little evidence to suggest that any of them seriously intended to betray the aims they had stood for. That a despotism could be enlightened was demonstrated by Bolívar's self-searching, by San Martín's iron but kindly rule over his assembled hosts before the Andean crossing and his austere self-effacement at the time of his resignation, and by the success of the autocratic Portales in Chile. That enlightened liberalism could fail was shown

---

[1] For an analysis of the differences between nineteenth-century liberalism and modern mass democracy, see chapter 5 of Barraclough, Geoffrey: *An Introduction to Contemporary History*, Pelican Books, London, 1967.

by the disastrous results of José Hilario López's attempts at reforms in Nueva Granada.

It would be superfluous to draw attention to the obvious dangers of condoning a despot because his views happen to agree with one's own. It is easy to answer charges of violence and repression with the argument that the ends may sometimes justify the means. Nevertheless any oversimplification of the political issues, any reliance upon facile slogans and weighted vocabulary—including such words as fascist, communist, reactionary, élite, and the like—do nothing but obscure the true situation and make such concepts as liberalism or freedom more than ever difficult to define. If political freedom is taken, in its crudest form, to mean that every individual in a country is to influence the political situation directly, it is—as the liberators perfectly well knew—unworkable and undesirable. It can be argued that the impractical nature of such an objective was one of the factors leading to the gradual conversion of nineteenth-century liberalism into planned social welfare states. In any case, within the framework of either of these forms, the most that the individual can expect is to become part of an aggregate movement in such a way that the total politico-social scene is a reflection of a country's average understanding. The Chilean Valentín Letelier, for instance, said that the will of each individual contributes to the fulfilment of social laws, conservatives retarding them, liberals hastening them, and so on. Such a situation creates a kind of rough collective freedom which we have come to equate with democracy and which has a good deal to do with tolerance; but in practice it leaves each member of the group (especially those individuals who are more likely than the conformists to produce ideas of a revolutionary nature and to initiate new trends where established ones have petrified) impotent to effect any change. The most democratic countries become in the end conservative, and revolutions are carried out usually in conditions of tyranny or at least of the strong arm.

The more usual and more workable meaning of freedom in the political sense, and the one that Bolívar seems to have intended, is that there shall be equal opportunities for developing talent regardless of race, colour, or other irrelevancies. Unfortunately for theory, throughout history there have been despots who knew the way to such a felicitous situation better than the men they ruled. It sticks in the gullet of twentieth-century man to admit that power does not always corrupt. It was difficult enough even for the age of the liberators. In Spanish America there were those who believed in formal democracy at all costs, and those who thought that it was necessary, quite possibly through an enlightened dictatorship, to prepare the ground carefully beforehand. Even the 'aggregate will' tolerated all kinds of tyrannies such as those of Rosas, Francia, Rivadavia, Santa Anna, and Porfirio Díaz to name but a few. In modern times there have been many examples of a genuinely democratic machinery leading only to a stalemate; as for instance in the battles waged between Presidents Frei in Chile or Bealunde in Peru against an opposition in congress. The Mexican multi-party system with one party overwhelmingly dominant—though technically less 'democratic'—has turned out to be a more workable arrangement.[1]

Wherever the onetime colonies formed into republics (most Spanish American independence writers use the words democracy and republic interchangeably), there came a moment when dictatorships seemed inevitable, so much so that Alberdi actually saw Rosas as a typical product of the American soil. Pàez said that three kinds of actor appeared on the scene at independence: ex-military leaders who tended to severity and tyranny; those who had taken no part in the fighting but wanted to rule and slandered their former comrades; and those whom we would nowadays call the 'Establishment', determined to block encroachment upon their traditional 'rights'. In the atmosphere of mutual mistrust among these groups, dictators flourished, time-servers often got the pick of the jobs, and the revolution atrophied. Spanish America's misfortune was that she fought for liberty in an age

---

[1] Both the defects and virtues of the Mexican system are examined in an interesting way by Pablo González Casanova in *La Democracia en México*, Ediciones Era, Mexico City, 1967.

when democratic principles had become part of current orthodoxy but before any of her component nations could reasonably be expected to apply them.

In this situation one man, Domingo Faustino Sarmiento, found himself at the centre between two opposed trends. He was born in 1811, just as the independence wars were beginning. Enmity with the Argentine despots, the *caudillo* Juan Facundo Quiroga whose character he analyses in his most important book, and the dictator Juan Manuel de Rosas, sent him at various times into voluntary exile in Chile where people found his egoism insupportable and dubbed him *Don Yo* (Mister I). His journalistic work on *El Mercurio* of Valparaíso (of which he became editor) and *El Nacional* in Santiago, which he founded, was, however, sufficient to establish his professional reputation. In 1851 he joined an uprising in Montevideo which was led by an old friend and now a confirmed enemy of dictator Rosas, Justo José de Urquiza, who later—as the chronic enmity between Montevideo and Buenos Aires reached a climax—also fought against Mitre. Sarmiento could not align himself wholeheartedly with Urquiza, who paid him the left-handed compliment of putting him in charge of a paltry army bulletin; but his sharp pen made even of this unpromising medium an effective propaganda weapon. In it he attacked the British because of their policy of protecting Rosas. 'The Rosas government defies all the rules known to Christian governments,' he pronounced when the British were making arrangements to carry the dictator into exile in a ship of the Royal Navy:

'An Englishman studying it with a conscience formed by parliament, Habeas Corpus, justice, and freedom of the Press, must regard it as monstrous, absurd, and detestable; if not, he is no Englishman. An Englishman who looks upon it from the point of view of mercantile interests ought to be hostile to it since it refused to open rivers to navigation and because its whole policy is hostile to European interests and influence. . . . Why should a government so contrary to what English education has taught Your Excellency to think good, fair, legitimate, and lawful, be perpetuated in Buenos Aires, and yet Your Excellency would not dream of imagining that anyone should think it good for England?'[1]

In 1868 Sarmiento became President of Argentina. He improved communications and port works and was a progressive educationalist; but above all he put an end to the power of the *caudillos* of his time; made peace with Urquiza, and drove General López Jordán, responsible for the latter's assassination, into exile. However, open enmity arose between Mitre and himself after he had placed his own candidate in the presidential chair in the election of 1874. Complicated manœuvres by both parties established a precedent favouring illegality, and successive presidents kept or broke the law according to their personal convenience. Sarmiento died in 1888 with Argentina's internal problems as bad as they had ever been in spite of the flow of polemic that had come from his pen. His republicanism had been constantly baulked by his ruthlessness, and his career was an epitome of the difficulties of Spanish America to establish any kind of workable liberalism. Sarmiento, who understood that the struggle between liberal and autocrat had its roots in the situation in Spain, failed to recognize the autocrat in himself. This was particularly strange because he had deep insight into the workings of those typical Spanish American autocrats, the strong-armed *caudillos* of the pampas: men who so closely resembled leaders in other parts of Spanish America—including for example the Bolivian bandit Mariano Melgarejo who actually stormed himself into the presidency of his country for four years, or Pancho Villa in twentieth-century Mexico—that they may be considered endemic in the area. In his own land, Sarmiento wrote bitterly, elections never solved anything because everything was settled by force, and he attributed the lawlessness of the provinces to the commercial success of Buenos Aires and the relative poverty of outlying districts. *Caudillos* arose to protect local interests; and this they did with great severity, not out of any Machiavellian cunning but because of an instinct to survive. Many, indeed, held progressive views,

[1] Sarmiento, D. F., *Obras Selectas*, vol. 3, p. 240.

but these were constantly sidetracked by absolutist tendencies. Rogue idealists like Facundo and Villa bore the banner of freedom but killed mercilessly and in cold blood in order to obtain it. The poetic instinct of the people thereupon idealized these killers whom they both feared and admired. Facundo Quiroga became a public figure before he was a thief; and he stole only when force of circumstance compelled. He made himself strong in his native province of La Rioja and, rampaging through the land, reached Buenos Aires and made a pact with Rosas but was assassinated, very likely with the dictator-president's connivance. He believed in nothing but had, said Sarmiento, the power of a Caesar, a Tamerlaine, a Mahomet:

'He was born thus and it is no fault of his. He lowered himself in the social scale in order that he might lead, dominate, fight the power of the city and the police. When offered a place in the army he spurned it because he had no patience to wait for promotion, because there was so much servility, there were so many regulations blocking personal independence, so many generals bearing down upon him, a splendid uniform restricting his movements, tactics governing every step. All this was insufferable. The life on horseback, the life of dangers and strong emotions steeled his spirit and hardened his heart. He had an unconquerable and instinctive hatred for the laws that had persecuted him, for the judges who condemned him, for the whole society and organization from which he had been excluded from childhood and which he is prejudiced against and despises. . . . He is the natural man who has not yet learned to dominate or conceal his passions but who displays them openly, surrendering himself to their impetuosity. . . . Facundo is a type of primitive barbarian. He knows no kind of discipline. His anger is that of a wild beast. . . .'[1]

Facundo was far from believing in progress through material things alone, 'which of themselves have nothing to say because they know nothing and are worthless'. In this he has Sarmiento's approval. Sarmiento's hatred of the *caudillo* is indeed so modified by admiration that one has the impression that his hatred is

[1] Sarmiento, D. F., *Facundo*, pp. 90–4.

doctrinaire, unconvincing even to himself. He understood the
caudillo to the point of identifying with him, almost loving him.
All the same, he was convinced that there could be no compromise with such a man. Things had reached a pitch of absurdity,
with petty dictators imposing their wills upon countries created
specifically for freedom, without which their split from Spain
could mean nothing. Therefore Sarmiento had to destroy his
admiration and was forced into violating one half of his nature.
In spite of himself he was compelled to put more trust in Europe
than in the America to which he belonged:

'It is no use stopping to inspect the nature, objective, and aim
of the revolution of independence. Throughout America these
were one and the same . . . European ideas. . . .'

And again:

'Except in an external symbol, independence from the king was
interesting and intelligible only for Argentine cities; for the
countryside it was strange and without influence. . . . For the
countryside the revolution presented the problem of how to evade
authority.'[1]

And the city was of course European. It was the countryside
that revealed an original, New World character which, for all
Sarmiento's Americanism, did not appeal to him; for in the
countryside each man was his own authority, each a *caudillo* in
embryo who lived without reference to the law. Evading
authority, the countryman became the very source of authoritarianism. Liberalism was meaningless for him because liberalism
is an answer to problems of living in dense communities whose
freedom and anarchy must be nicely poised, each member giving
and taking for the sake of the majority. The country knew no law
of the majority, only of the strong. And on a continent largely
under-populated, where cities were few and legal vigilance
over vast and broken areas impossible, it was the strong who
triumphed. If, like O'Higgins, potential dictators sought to model
themselves on the virtuous tyrants of the past (O'Higgins had his
own father to look up to), they might advance the principles of

[1] Sarmiento, D. F., *Facundo*, pp. 33 and 61.

the Enlightenment better than any number of theory-ridden republicans; but always and only so long as they could maintain a precarious popularity against those who insisted that democracy should conform to the book.

3. RACE ANTAGONISMS

The dichotomy of Spanish American thought was nowhere more evident than in its attitude to race. If the liberation movement originated in the cities and had very little to do with the country-side, it did nonetheless make some attempts to alter the social structure and to improve the lot of the Indians and poor *mestizos*, particularly by redistributing land and abolishing tributes. The liberation was at least partly aimed at freeing the Indians whose bondage was distressing for conscientious upper-class Creoles to behold. San Martín, talking to the Araucanians, said, 'I am an Indian too', which was untrue; but consciously or unconsciously he was identifying himself with them. In a more practical way, when he was a member of the liberal Cortes of Cádiz, José Joaquín Olmedo, the Colombian poet, spoke against the system of the *mita* or Indian tribute; and in 1802 Mariano Moreno had written his thesis for the degree of doctor of law on the forced service of native labour. Many of the liberators were also hoping to revive interest in the ancient Indian past. Of course neither Miranda, Bolívar, nor San Martín ever really intended to revert to the tradition of ancient civilizations; but it is significant that there was a proposal to reconstruct the Inca temple of Paca Cámac so that it might serve as a symbol for the new nations. Even Andrés Bello, in many ways more European than any of them, used an Inca prophecy and a chorus of virgin priestesses to the Sun in his *Repertorio Americano*; and in his *Alocución a la Poesía* he described the legend of Huitaca, goddess of water, and Nen-queteba, child of the Sun. Bello had studied native sources—the chronicles of the early friars, and accounts of the old religions. He fell under the spell of Humboldt and studied Andean geography, flora, and fauna. He revived the legend of the elderly Alonso de Ledesma who anticipated Cervantes by going alone, with only his lance, onto a beach at La Guaira there to confront the mighty pirate, Drake. As we can see from these examples, the Indianness was never local. It belonged to the hemisphere just as the liberation movement did.

For all that, there seemed to be a gap between the new European culture and whatever of the old was worth conserving; and the liberators stood straddled precariously across the chasm. In the nineteenth century research had not yet established that long before they had petrified into totalitarian forms or degenerated into mass slaughters the native religions were beautiful and wise. Judged in the light of knowledge available at that time it must have seemed that the Indian heritage ran directly counter to the establishment of a Utopia on earth. The utopian dream came from elsewhere—from Columbus, from the early friars, from the principles of the French revolution. In spite, therefore, of safeguards for the Indians written into the various constitutions, there was a strong body of post-independence opinion which wished deliberately to leave the pure indigenous American beyond the pale and which looked down also on the half-breeds, especially upon those who, like the pampa *gauchos*, acquired a crude cultural tradition of their own and were thus a collective threat to the European Creoles.

An assessment of the position of the Indians at the time of independence was made by General Miller:

'Even the Indian character speedily underwent a perceptible change. Accustomed to be deceived, and consequently to deceive, they could neither speak the truth, nor believe in the truth when it was spoken to them. Although these poor people had been entitled by law to the privileges of citizens, yet such was their distrust of the cruel whites that they considered the abolition of the tribute and the *mita* to be some kind of trap to ensnare them in the commission of a fault. Most of the priesthood abstained from every endeavour to dispel this illusion, because general freedom would do away with the system of *pongos*, or domestic servitude, by which these pastors, as well as the *caciques*, benefit most materially. Thus the best-intended decrees in favour of the aborigines will be slow in producing the proper effect. Prejudices and timidity on their own part, and the interest of those who still keep up the delusion, in order to profit by the gratuitous labour of others, will combine to counteract the most benevolent views of the patriotic government. Time itself must be seconded by philanthropic and strong efforts on the part of prefects of departments, governors of provinces, and other principal authorities, and positive benefits must be conferred on the Indians, and actually felt as such by them, in order to produce the proper impression.'[1]

As Prefect of Potosí, General Miller did much to implement government decrees intended to ameliorate the conditions of the Indians; but the climate of the time was against him and his efforts had little overall effect. Sarmiento, among others, was imbued with the European tendency to regard his own culture as the only one and to spurn the indigenous Indian as dirty and degenerate. Though he quoted Castlereagh with approval as saying that attempts to capture distant lands are fruitless unless the conqueror first seeks the good will of the people, he was quite willing to forfeit the good will of the indigenous American whom he regarded as unworthy of the consideration given to even the lowliest of human beings. He thought it a disastrous mistake for the Spaniards to have mixed with the Indians, for they were now left with the task of 'correcting' their Indianness and of climbing back up the racial and intellectual ladder until they were once again on a level with other European peoples. There was, Sarmiento believed, no possible point of contact between a civilized and a savage race. Where the former entered, the latter disappeared. The rights of man were written for the civilized and not for barbarians whose customs included human sacrifice and cannibalism.[2]

Sarmiento was not alone among liberals of his day in despising

[1] Miller, J., vol. 2, p. 248.
[2] Quoted by Enrique de Gandía in Sarmiento's *Obras Selectas*, vol. 27, p. xlix.

the indigenous peoples. 'Would any man among us boast of being a pure Indian?' asked Juan Bautista Alberdi. 'Would he marry his sister or his daughter to an Araucanian princeling in preference to an English shoemaker?'[1] He divided Americans into natives or savages on the one hand, and Europeans who believed in Christ on the other. He seems to have taken for granted the myth of Creole inferiority when he said that Americans have conquered Europe in battle but not in thought or industry. He believed that his country could be saved only if it absorbed foreign elements. He had no use for the *gaucho*, the half-caste, or the common Latin American labourer, who must all be raised to a European level. Thus a hierarchy was established in which the Indian was lower than the Creole but the Creole was in his turn lower than the European. Racial prejudice became linked with a more general one against the very fact of being born in the New World. Trade treaties seemed more desirable if signed by foreigners. Railways were built by Europeans. Legislation must favour the outsider. And all this not because there can be no isolated nation on earth but because the European is in himself better, more civilized, worthier to be perpetuated. Alberdi had no faith in the *mestizo* and little in the Creole and yet he laid it down that the law should not discriminate between class or person, blood or birth. Contradictions arising from ambivalence of this kind became embodied in one after another of the constitutions and were inherent in the thought of those who drew them up. They created an intolerable tension from which perhaps only Mexico—with her enormous pride in the indigenous cultures—has become really free (though Mexico has done so by weighing the balance heavily in favour of the Indian and against the foreigner—especially the Spaniard—the Gachupín).

Paradoxically many Spaniards of colonial times were more interested in and tolerant of the Indian cultures than some post-independence liberals. There had been a long history of compassion toward them, from the days of the first friars to set foot in the New World, down to such men as Ambrosio O'Higgins whose

[1] Alberdi, J. B., *Bases*, p. 67.

tolerance and understanding were inherited by his son. In a draft letter written in 1837 Bernardo O'Higgins put forward a plan for establishing an Indian nation west of the Rockies:

'One of the first objects which occupied my father's becoming a public man was the amelioration of the condition of the indigenous inhabitants of the New World, frequently designated "the Red Race", and the first public school I ever entered was one founded by him for the education of the sons of the Araucanian *caciques*. . . . I have during the last thirteen years reflected with as much intensity and devotion on the prospect of being instrumental towards establishing an Empire inhabited solely by the aborigines of America, and where with the blessings conferred by Christianity and Civilization that race would have an opportunity of proving that in all respects they are not inferior to any other race which inhabits the globe. I have anxiously looked at the map of the world with that in view, and was rejoiced to find that a space existed that is most admirably suited to the object. . . . The space to which I allude lies between latitude 32 and 54° N. latitude and between the Rocky Mountains and the Pacific Ocean, and which territory is now in the actual and undisturbed possession of independent tribes of Indians with the exception of a few thousands under the management of Missionaries in New California. Its dominion over these Missions the Mexican nation would I am convinced resign with pleasure for the important object of acquiring Christian neighbours whose peaceable conduct would be guaranteed by the governments of the United States and England. . . .'[1]

Failing any such solution, which might have restored pride and unity to the American aborigines, the problem continued extremely complex; and without condoning the way in which they high-handedly wrote off the Indian and any possibility of educating him, we can see that in a certain aspect of the problem and in their historical time Sarmiento and Alberdi were right. The native Indians, or even the *mestizos*, could never have taken

---

[1] This proposition is quoted in full in an appendix to Collier, Simon, *Ideas and Politics of Chilean Independence, 1808–1833*, Cambridge University Press, 1967, p. 369.

over the European inheritance ready made. From the first it was evident that the kind of freedom that would best suit Spanish America could not be copied from Europe or Anglo-Saxon North America; though, being Creoles with more European in them than American, the liberators were often baffled by the inability of the *mestizo*-indigenous population to give practical expression to ideas inherited from the French revolution.

4. LAW

The result of the dichotomy was that Spanish America was split into four social groups: Spanish Creoles, *mestizos*, pure Indians, and foreigners. Each group was prejudiced against the other and each had a different view of what was or was not ethical and permissible by law. The Europeans were the original lawmakers and thus benefited from regulations which they knew and understood. To the Creole the purpose of law was to create an environment in which safeguards to life and property inherited from Europe could continue, but law was also to be used as a bulwark protecting him against foreigners who appeared to have an unfair advantage in talent, initiative, and social standing. To the Indian the law seemed an imposition from above, keeping him exactly where he was. To the *mestizo* it was a joke, a device to be used when circumstances were favourable, otherwise to be ignored. For to the *mestizo* the law represented a way of catching him always in the wrong. He was supposed to be European enough to understand it, Indian enough to evade it. It was only sensible, then, for him to use it for his convenience. *Mestizaje* became synonymous with trickery.

There were those who realized that law was the result, not the cause, of a country's ethos:

'English law is free because the Englishman is free. Do not copy his law but his personality: that is, his customs and how he is—if life *can* in fact be copied.'[1]

[1] Alberdi, J. B., p. 60.

Alberdi, whose work formed the basis of the Argentine Constitution of 1853, was not alone in his admiration for the British,
whose language was that of 'liberty, industry, and order' and
should be preferred over Latin in the teaching curriculum; and
whose legal system was the most enviable in the world. Many
Spanish Americans, while lured by the theoretical attraction of
the French legal code and by the democratic idealism of the
American, turned often and longingly to Britain because they
admired not so much the system as the result. The difficulty was,
how to embody in a Latin constitution the spirit of a law that was
so flexible. There was the danger on the one hand of falling into a
loose, almost 'Churchy' moralizing, but on the other of perpetuating a precise, logical dogmatism insufficiently elastic to deal
with people's day-to-day behaviour. As an example of the former
tendency we may take the style of Argentina's 1815 *Estatuo
Provisional*:

'Every man must happily shoulder whatever sacrifice is demanded by the nation . . . even to life itself (except in the case of
foreigners); must deserve the title of "good man" by being a good
father, son, brother, and friend.'[1]

A fair example of dogmatism can be found in those laws
directed against the entry of foreigners just at a time when foreign
immigration might have been of the greatest use to the new
countries; as, for example, one of the principles enunciated by
Morelos at the Congress of Chilpancingo: 'the only foreigners
who will be tolerated are skilled mechanics, politically unattached
and capable of instructing in their trades.' This was the kind of
apparently unexceptionable law—one that exists, indeed, in a
large number of modern countries—which at the time caused
either stultification of effort toward material progress, or alterna-
tively gross demands for monopolistic arrangements by foreigners
who were forced to make doubly sure of protecting their precarious investments.

The man who tried most persistently to steer a middle course
between legal idealism and legal logic was Andrés Bello, who in

[1] Quoted in Lugones, L., p. 136.

any society would have been exceptional for the breadth of his interests. Born in 1781, he was slightly older than Bolívar whom he tutored, but he did not die until 1865, so that he spanned both the active phase of the independence wars and the period of the formation of the new republic. With Bolívar and López Méndez he was sent to London as a representative of the Caracas revolutionary Junta. He remained there for nineteen years during which time he suffered penury until he was presented by Blanco White to William Hamilton (then Secretary of State for India), whose children he taught. Hamilton introduced him to the Scottish school of philosophers which he found much to his taste. Studying mainly in the British Museum, he acquired a taste for cosmology, comparative religion, law, linguistics (which for him included a study of the great classics of world literature), philosophy, and the theory of knowledge. In 1829 Chile invited him to establish a sound basis for government, and he made his home in that country though remaining loyal to his native Venezuela. With Bolívar and Alberdi, he believed that European institutions could not be adopted unaltered in a part of the world that was geographically and historically so different. His desire that South America should retain its unique personality extended to an insistence that proper use should be made of the Spanish idiom (thoughts, he said, are dyed in the colour of a language) and of grammar. It was fallacious, however, to take it for granted that Spanish America possessed one common language merely because it had inherited Castilian; for in Bellos' day distortions in the purity of academic rules and vocabulary were already diversifying daily usage. Sarmiento thought him a dry classicist, but this was to do him an injustice. He insisted on purity but did not forbid new words provided they were apt and aesthetic.

Just as linguistics was for him a mainly practical study, so also was philosophy. Its aim, he said, was to know the human spirit and to orientate its actions. In his inaugural speech as first rector of Chile's university he insisted that the pursuit of science and literature carry their own reward, being both a delightful exercise and a sure way of improving moral character. Since they weaken the pull of the senses and the vicissitudes of fortune, they are the best preparation for adversity. All life, he said, is a unity. Soul and conscience, actions and political forces, industry and the arts, are interlocked in such a way that none can develop without the rest. All aspects of history are, he believed, so connected that the indigenous and the European would be able to blend in the Americas without detriment to either.

So it was that a scholar steeped in the methods of European thought was able to value the indigenous; for Bello felt the juxtaposition not as a clash but as a positive challenge to create a new, fused world. To help in its achievement this man who was by nature a retiring scholar was obliged to enter the hurly-burly of the political arena. At the time of independence Chilean governments had been forced to impose all kinds of restrictions in an attempt to restore order, but these caused only more chaos. Because of theoretical loyalty to a democratic ideal, people with insufficient education were given responsible posts, but they were incapable of controlling the internal squabbles that arose. Bello saw the need for establishing a sound administrative and legal base without which it was impossible to give any social guarantees; and he therefore set about formulating the civil code, which he did with great thoroughness.

Many examples of merciful but largely ineffective laws were to be found among the earliest ones promulgated for the Indies. Charles V had said that since God created the Indians free men it was wrong to subject them to Christian masters. In spite of this, *encomiendas* were approved throughout Spanish America on the pretext that they afforded paternal protection to the natives. The *encomiendas* gave rise to the *mita*, virtually forced labour which reduced men to slaves. Expeditions were even made to the Chiloé archipelago to seize the inhabitants and take them off to Santiago for sale in the marketplace. As Bello said, synthesizing the arguments of José Hipólito Salas, a contemporary in the University of Chile:

'What use were the measures dictated so earnestly and often by the kings of Spain to relieve the oppressed Indians? Absolutely none. And yet the Laws of the Indies have been and continue to be praised as an example of the wisdom and humanity of the government that drew them up, and as a proof of the broadmindedness of Spanish colonial legislation compared to all other nations'. The wording of the laws of the Indies is very well-meaning and humane, but the safeguards were ineffective; and given the colonial constitutions they could not be otherwise. Spain had to turn a blind eye to the wretched state of the Indians.'[1]

Bello therefore set out to create a constitution that did not merely sound liberal but which would work. In his *Principles of the Rights of Man* he defined a nation or state as 'a society of men which has for its object the preservation and happiness of its associates; which is governed by positive laws arising from itself; and which owns a portion of territory'.[2] Men being by nature equal, so also were the collections of men of which world society is made. It followed that the weakest republic should enjoy the same rights as the most powerful. Every nation had a right to make its own laws and to defend them by war; though peace is the natural state and one of the results of civilization is the love of peace and justice.

Bello noticed that the part of the old colonial laws that had most effect was that which benefited the mother country precisely by keeping the Indians in a state of servility. 'In order that there should be no abuses, men were deprived of their rights.'[3] Therefore Bello saw the independence wars as a demand that men should administer their own affairs instead of receiving their laws from elsewhere. He was confident that Spanish America was capable of self-government provided the correct juridical framework, fitted to its situation, could be found. In his view Spanish America could not have inherited republican ideas from the mother country, where they did not exist; though Spain possessed much that was generous, heroic, and independent.

On the subject of written constitutions he was in two minds.

[1] Bello, Andrés, vol. xix, p. 313.
[2] Bello, Andrés, facsimile edition of his *Principios de Derechos de Jentes*, p. 10.
[3] Bello, Andrés, vol. xiv, p. 453.

He understood that often the written law failed to express the real will of a society because it tended to be dictated by a single man or faction. On the other hand he felt that the chaotic state of Spanish America necessitated clear-cut regulations with no possibility of double interpretations. Thus in his civil code, Article Two states categorically that custom does not constitute law except in those cases where the law specifically states that it does. In other words he ruled out the influence upon law of precedent which plays so important a part in the British system.

It was one of Bello's chief contentions that in framing laws for a country the whole situation—philosophical, historical, geographical—had to be taken into account. Whereas he knew the importance of the indigenous elements in Spanish America, he did not make the mistake of belittling the European. He saw the Chilean nation not as an abstraction but as a section of humanity moulded by specific circumstances as hardly factual as the mountains and valleys and rivers, the plants and animals, the various races that composed it, together with its moral, political, social, and poetic-literary background. It was partly for this reason that he was against philosophical systematization, which he felt created a strait-jacket for thought and prevented a healthy empiricism. During his years in Britain he had acquired a liking for the common-sense view. Because of the Spanish heritage of written laws, however, he could not go so far as to do away with written codes; and so his legislation became as rigid as any other in Spanish America—and as much an excuse for quibbles, prevarications, and lying. It seemed to be Spanish America's fate that, even when revolutions did not shatter them more suddenly, the best intentions of its best minds tended to be interpreted so rigidly as to become their opposites.

There is no need to detail the vicissitudes of all the various constitutions of Spanish America, which because of their un-workableness were made and remade as quickly as the ink was dry on the paper. Only the Mexican kept a continuous thread through the violent changes that shook the country during the reforms of Benito Juárez in the sixties of last century and the revolution of

1910. But in this case it is precisely the continuity—the periodic return to the principles of Morelos which reappear every fifty years like the fires lighted by the ancients to keep the Sun alive and the world turning—which draws attention to the extraordinary aberrations that had taken place in the intervening periods. During a full century it proved totally impossible to put the logically impeccable formulations into effect. Independence was bedevilled by economic subservience to greater powers; religious toleration by rather less than other-worldly behaviour of the clergy;[1] the franchise by frankly bullying methods; law by bribery and nepotism; abolition of judicial torture by tolerance of thug methods among the police. (By now many of these lapses are either dead or dying under a régime of prosperity and no little international dignity; and Mexico is here singled out merely as a convenient example of the way in which mature laws have turned sour in Spanish America.)

There was never any question that the work of men of the calibre of Bello, Alberdi, Morelos, and other lawmakers was unappreciated; but their influence was weakened by an attitude of mind which took root first because of the divisions we have already noted in the social organization, and later through a tendency for Spanish Americans to do what the world expected of them. The bad reputation once on record was not easily expunged. Only in the last decade or so has there been greater participation in world affairs and a chance for Spanish Americans to contribute effectively to the international legal code, which they have done much to rationalize. On the whole their international legal status has been higher than their national, and reforms in individual countries may therefore be expected to come not by direct attack but obliquely through loyalty to such principles as non-intervention and self-determination in the larger world.

---

[1] But for a very interesting account of the Church's part in the economy, which was by no means as grasping as is sometimes made out, see Costeloe, M. P., *Church Wealth in Mexico*, Cambridge University Press, 1967.

CHAPTER II

UNITY AND DISUNITY ACROSS THE CONTINENTAL DIVIDE

1. PANAMERICANISM

The first man to dream of a great Panamerican union, though of course he did not call it that, was the Franciscan Bartolomé de las Casas, whose *Leyes de Indias* envisage an America made whole by the Roman Catholic faith. Much later, toward the end of the eighteenth century, Count Aranda substituted the idea of political for religious unity and gave Charles III secret advice on the subject. During the 1821-2 session of the Madrid Cortes Lucas Alamán and other Spanish American deputies proposed a Hispano-American federation of the mother country and her former colonies. Bolívar, at his Panama Congress, tried to shape a united America freed from European domination, but from the outset his plans were bedevilled by international jealousies and United States dominance.

The Monroe Doctrine, first formulated three years before Bolívar's Congress, seemed designed to create a power block capable of acting as a western counterpoise to the Holy Alliance. On December 2, 1823, President Monroe told Congress:

'. . . the occasion has been judged proper for asserting as a principle in which the rights and interests of the United States are involved, that the American continents, by the free and independent condition which they have assumed and maintain, are henceforth not to be considered as subject for future colonization by any European powers. . . . We owe it, therefore, to candour, and to the amicable relations existing between the United States

293

and those powers, to declare that we should consider any attempt on their part to extend their system to any portion of this hemisphere as dangerous to our peace and safety. With the existing colonies or dependencies of any European power we have not interfered and shall not interfere. . . .'[1]

The Tsar of Russia had originally intended his own alliance to be bound by Christian charity and peaceful intentions toward all nations. But Britain, more pragmatic and practical, could see in Alexander's project nothing but an obstacle to much-needed change; though for a time she was persuaded to join the great concert of European powers which under Metternich was trying to stabilize the political situation. In the long run, however, Britain was unable to accept the doctrine proposed by Russia, Austria, and Prussia, that 'States which have undergone a change of government due to revolution, the results of which threaten other states, *ipso facto* cease to be members of the European Alliance. . . . If, owing to such alterations, immediate danger threatens to other States, the Powers bind themselves, by peaceful means, or if need be by arms, to bring back the guilty State into the bosom of the Great Alliance.' This was a doctrine almost exactly parallel to what Monroe was proposing; for although theoretically his formulation merely warned European powers against forcibly interposing themselves on the American continent, the doctrine was almost from the beginning used as a pretext for restoring the *status quo* after any upheavals or outright revolutions in Latin America. Thus Britain—politically, militarily, and navally strong—became the repository of European liberalism in opposition to the authoritarianism arising from Alexander's failed Christian-liberal vision; while on the other side of the Atlantic the politically inexpert and militarily exhausted countries of Spanish America became the real but almost wholly ineffective repositories of liberalism, against the United States which (its constitution and the Gettysburg address notwithstanding) was actually more concerned—once Spanish dominance had been

[1] Quoted in Royal Institute of International Affairs, *The Republic of South America*, p. 319.

removed from the Americas—with maintaining the *status quo* (at least so long as existing régimes were favourable to its own interests). In 1805 Jefferson officially announced that it was necessary for the United States to take possession of Cuba; and the Monroe Doctrine was created at least in part to make its annexation easy and to prevent any revolution from taking place there.

The Doctrine and the Holy Alliance were bulwarks of conservatism; but whereas in Europe conservatism had strong and healthy opposition, in the Americas it was countered by little more tangible than dreams. However, American conservatism had this to commend it: that it was liberal in its aims so long as these were intended to refer to home affairs, and conservative only in so far as it was felt necessary to put up a resistance to the anarchic elements in Spanish America. (There was already ample evidence that these could be more than merely locally dangerous.)

The situation led many people both within and outside the United States into an assumption that the issue was one of young, liberal America against worn-out, conservative Europe, and not of liberalism against conservatism wherever the two might be found. If it was not obvious to many at the time that Britain, with her mistrust of Spain's scheming to restore the colonial system in the Americas, was a more genuine ally than the United States working under the umbrella of the Doctrine, this was because Britain's unconcealed commercial ambitions were also thoroughly suspect. No wonder, then, that Spanish Americans became wary of all foreigners and were hereafter continually imagining ulterior motives behind shows of friendship.

After Bolívar's failed Congress there were a number of specifically Latin American meetings called in the forties, fifties, and sixties of last century to discuss intervention by France and the United States in the area's affairs. A congress was held in Lima at the end of 1847, one in Santiago in 1856, and one in Lima in 1864–5, but the kind of U.S. intervention to which exception was being taken continued even into our own century when, under cover of the Monroe Doctrine, U.S. marines at various times occupied the Dominican Republic, Haiti, and Nicaragua. (America's sins of omission and commission and her positive achievements in inter-American relations are listed impartially by Gordon Connell-Smith.[1])

Theodore Roosevelt's corollary to the original Monroe Doctrine made it yet more unpopular because it appeared to give the United States a free hand to police the hemisphere whenever it felt inclined. The corollary reads:

'Chronic wrongdoing, or an impotence which results in the general loosening of the ties of civilized society, may in America, as elsewhere, ultimately require intervention by some civilized nation, and in the Western Hemisphere the adherence of the United States to the Monroe Doctrine may force the United States, however reluctantly, in flagrant cases of wrongdoing or impotence, to the exercise of an international police power.'[2]

Friendly collaboration between Latin America and the United States has been dependent on recognition that the republics to the south are not infants needing protection but nations in their own right. Whether by intent or merely by clumsiness, the wording of the corollary seemed to imply that the United States was civilized, the rest of the hemisphere somehow not, and it therefore confirmed Latin American suspicions that they were still regarded as being in tutelage to the north. Even as late as 1959 the Chairman of the Senate Foreign Relations Committee thought that this kind of bad manners was a more important cause of his country's unpopularity than anything material. Long before, in 1884, as a curtain-raiser to the First International Conference of American States, delegates had been taken on a conducted tour of east-coast industrial cities. Apart from the tactlessness of this display, Latin Americans thought they detected a plot to limit the sphere of their activities. The Argentine delegate, Dr. Sáenz Peña, was foremost in condemning exclusive policies. 'Let America be for mankind,' he said with a Bolívarian flourish.

[1] Connell-Smith, G., *The Inter-American System*, London, Oxford University Press, 1966.
[2] Quoted in *The Republics of South America*, edited by the Royal Institute of International Affairs, p. 320.

Deliberately, or from inadequate knowledge of the Spanish American point of view, U.S. policy had from the first run counter to the internationalism advocated by Bolívar. Jefferson had said, for instance:

'The European nations constitute a separate division of the globe; their localities make them part of a distinct system; they have a set of interests of their own in which it is our business never to engage ourselves. America has a hemisphere to itself. It must have a separate system of interest which must not be subordinated to those of Europe.'[1]

Throughout the whole of the independence struggle this had never been the Spanish American view. Plans for an area grouping have been in terms of an Andean or a Colombian or a Latin American unity and not in terms of the hemisphere as a whole. In other words, the people south of the Río Grande have felt themselves to be capable of adhering naturally to one another (at least in theory) but they have not excluded communication with any other part of the globe; they have not felt themselves bound by an arbitrary cutting of the round apple of the world into two longitudinal hemispheres.

It was not surprising, then, that in 1889, when all Latin American governments except Santo Domingo sent delegates to Washington to discuss a common customs union, the motion was defeated because it appeared to favour nobody but the United States. This conference did, however, succeed in creating the International Bureau of American Republics, the formation of which is generally taken to mark the birth of what has been called the 'Interamerican System', and which Woodrow Wilson converted into the Panamerican Union. It was surely a clerical error that caused it to be listed in the Washington telephone directory under 'U.S. government offices'; but its nickname, 'the ministry of colonial affairs', could scarcely help but stick.

Panamerican conferences now became the fashion, and were held in Mexico City (1902), Río de Janeiro (1906), and Buenos Aires (1910). The outbreak of the First World War interrupted the

[1] Quoted in Connell-Smith, Gordon, p. 2.

series. Ever since the shots fired at Maximilian's execution told the world that Latin America would have no more imposition from foreign powers at least in so unashamed a form as an imperial take-over, there had appeared to be no danger of any European country attempting to annex new territories in the hemisphere. Apart from Canada, the little corners reserved to Britain had gone by default, for who, in any case, could want the Mosquito Coast except lunatics prepared to fell timber in a tropical graveyard? Latin America was therefore considerably shaken when British Intelligence officers intercepted what came to be known as the Zimmermann note, in which the German Minister in Mexico suggested that, if Germany were victorious, Mexico should have all the territory lost to the U.S.A. in the mid-nineteenth century. Germany's plans went awry. Eight Latin American republics were persuaded to declare war on Germany, and seven to break diplomatic relations. Mexico, together with Argentina, Chile, and Colombia, remained officially neutral although sympathy was strongly pro-ally.

After the war Panamerican conferences were renewed, one being held in Santiago in 1923. Several countries were absent for no better reason than that, having no diplomatic representation in Washington at the time, they had not been able to join the deliberations of the Council of the Panamerican Union which fixed the agenda. Albeit accidentally, this fact aggravated the old criticism that the Union was American-controlled.

At the following conference, in Havana in 1928, there was some difference of opinion about the exact meaning that should be given to the term 'non-intervention', which has been a cornerstone of Latin American international policy; and the rift between the U.S.A. and other American countries widened. In Montevideo in 1933 Cordell Hull's exposition of Roosevelt's 'good-neighbour policy' was soon identified in Latin American minds with the 'big stick'.

The Second World War gave the U.S.A. a chance to wipe her sullied slate clean, and she joined with the rest of the hemisphere in pressing for a three-hundred-mile 'safety belt' round American shores. Though the battle of the River Plate put an end to the illusion that hemisphere neutrality could be maintained, the presence of the U.S.A. was a safeguard to the weaker nations and ensured that essential imports could reach them. The U.S.A. naturally seized upon trading advantages which she has held ever since, though her overwhelming percentage both of exports and imports has been diminishing slightly in recent years.

At the Chapultepec congress held in Mexico in 1945 Spanish Americans expressed resentment that they had not been consulted about the Dumbarton Oaks project to create a modern substitute for the League of Nations. 'If tomorrow's international order is to be established taking into account only the opinion of the great powers,' said President Avila Camacho, 'this whole war will turn out in the long run to be a huge and grotesque lie.'[1]

Finally came the Bogotá conference of 1948 at which, in the midst of rioting, the Organization of American States came into being. In this body, which is a regional organization functioning within the United Nations, the U.S.A. has not always been able to maintain a dominant role. Strong countries such as Mexico, Brazil, Argentina, and Chile stand together in condemning interventionist policies even when these masquerade as a proposed peace force to keep order in such turbulent places as Cuba or the Dominican Republic. Nevertheless the Latin American sector within the O.A.S. has continued to regard as suspect the manner in which governments topple the moment they obstruct, or even appear to obstruct, U.S. policies. When Argentina failed to support such policies in 1962, the Frondizi government fell. A similar fate had already befallen Arbenz in Guatemala in 1954 and was to be suffered by João Goulart in Brazil in 1964 and Juan Bosch in the Dominican Republic in 1965.

During all these years the Monroe Doctrine had been altering its character. From being no more than a statement of U.S. overseas policy, it had now become a weapon wielded by government to prevent almost any kind of foreign intervention however oblique. Latin Americans felt it necessary to insist that they had

[1] Quoted by Gómez Robledo, A., p. 198.

never given their consent to the Doctrine, which they in no way equate (as some U.S. ambassadors to the area have tried to do) with their treasured twin doctrines of self-determination and non-intervention. Revival of the Doctrine in 1960 when President Eisenhower—faced with Khrushchev's declared intention of making Cuba a Soviet enclave in the hemisphere—said that the Doctrine was as valid today as in 1832, met with little sympathy among Spanish Americans.

Dislike of the Monroe Doctrine also threw a shadow over the well-intentioned Alliance for Progress established under the Charter of Punta del Este in 1961 at a special ministerial meeting of the Interamerican Economic and Social Council. The Alliance was intended as a kind of Marshall Plan for the Americas and it recommended that comprehensive national programmes for economic and social development, 'aimed at the achievement of self-sustaining growth, be carried out in accordance with democratic principles'. The U.S.A. was to provide assistance including the financing of national improvement programmes, and Latin American governments were to put forward their own development plans. Success has been meagre, due partly to the inefficiency of Latin American governments. 'We can't', said Dean Acheson, scolding them, 'have the Latin American countries screaming for worms like a bunch of young robins in a nest. We must see some progress from them first.' It would seem a reasonable demand except for the fact that blame for some of the regress has not unplausibly been laid at the benefactor's door. In the first five years of the Alliance, the U.S.A. distributed four billion (American) dollars, much of it to dictatorships of the right. In spite of this massive injection of wealth the economic growth rate was not maintained and there were signs that the rich had become richer, the poor poorer. Mexico has been an exception; and it is interesting that Mexico has received relatively little from the Alliance funds—much less than Brazil, Chile, or Colombia.

One current joke makes play of the fact that *Alianza para el Progreso* can mean Alliance *for* Progress or Alliance *stops* Progress. It will, however, be disastrous if Latin Americans merely use the

United States as their whipping boy. Simon G. Hanson diagnoses a double malady: 'prescriptioneering in the United States for improvement of relations with Latin America', and 'sloganeering' in Latin America as 'a substitute for meaningful appraisal and action'.[1] The same author censures Latin American countries for begging and—what is more—for demanding charity as a right. Luis Quintanilla, a distinguished Mexican, has also criticized Latin Americans for mendicancy: 'It is unpardonable for the weak through conformity or cowardice to renounce their own dignity.'[2]

Self-criticism apart, Spanish Americans are dubious about the enthusiasm shown by the U.S.A. toward their plans for economic integration. In the early days of the Economic Commission for Latin America the U.S.A. poured a good deal of cold water on the mere suggestion of a planned economy, but with the emergence of the Alliance for Progress planning became fashionable. If economic integration is to have the result desired by Latin Americans it must naturally be organized in such a way that it will benefit their own companies in preference to North American ones. At a Punta del Este summit conference in 1967 President Lyndon Johnson's pledge for aid for 'long-term, common action' designed to further the economic growth of the hemisphere, 'including the creation of a common market to be completed by 1985', was met with less than the expected warmth. On his return home President Díaz Ordaz of Mexico told his people in a television broadcast that Latin American integration must be made to benefit Latin American companies. This statement, following immediately upon a conference which had achieved some show of unanimity, and coming from a President who had expressed warm appreciation of U.S. friendship toward his country, shows that Latin Americans will not easily lose their fears of being exploited by richer powers.

---

[1] Hanson, S. G., *Five Years of the Alliance for Progress: an Appraisal*, Washington, Inter-American Affairs Press, 1967, p. 27.
[2] *Chicago Tribune*, June 9, 1965.

2. SPANISH AMERICAN ORIGINALITY

One of the chief differences between Latin America and the United States is that the former has been more apt to regard economics as secondary to such invisible assets as laziness, cheerfulness, and the ability not to worry. To churn out endless gadgets for insatiable consumers, kept constantly titillated by advertising plugs, is clearly not the aim of Latin American nations however much their broadcasting systems have fallen into ways of American big business; but neither is sitting in the sun in perpetual *siesta* while highly respectable pickpockets, heavy with the insignia of office, are allowed to walk away with whatever wealth may be snatched from the forced labour of peasants. *Siestas* can in any case be a cold pastime at ten thousand feet. So on the one hand material success is spurned, on the other it is grasped sometimes by methods that are scarcely 'spiritual'.

It is essential, however, that 'spirituality' should have lip-service paid to it. No law, no custom in Spanish America could be established unless it were based upon the philosophical doctrines inherited not only from Bolívar and the other liberators, but further back from the very discoverers of the New World. Enrique de Gandía, in a preface to an edition of *Facundo*, synthesized the New World point of view:

'The study of ideas explains even the most obscure facts and puts us in touch with the infinite currents that have moulded humanity. These currents usually emanated from the Old World, from Greece, Rome, Spain, and other parts of Europe. Then, after 1492 when global history began, ideas were born and proliferated also in America, whence they returned to Europe to throw new light on the tragedies of men of the Old World. The world of Columbus completely transformed and gave us back the classical and medieval spiritual baggage of humanity. This was the greatest and most sublime transformation in history. Century after century, and by means of Spanish liberalism, ideas which ancient philosophers had thought of as dreams were turned into reality and with new wings were swept round the world like a living gift from God. We made the miracle of freedom possible, and by America's example we gave freedom to other enslaved men who trembled still beneath the bludgeon of despots. America possesses this glory because she was born of freedom and lives and will live through it. Men created her and men will defend her eternally. This is her greatest treasure, her spirit, and her destiny. Without freedom there is no aim for man, and with freedom man raises himself majestically into the bosom of God.'[1]

It was expected that this miracle of freedom—this spirituality—would be the great contribution of the New World to humanity, and at the outset there was no inkling of a doubt that it could be achieved. It was conceived of as a deep and holy attribute fully satisfying to the religious and compatible with the dogmas of the Church.

But soon a division became evident. The racial rift in Spanish American society is matched by a deep cleavage in the attitude toward spiritual things. On the one hand there has been the strong tradition of Roman Catholicism; on the other a devotion to ideals leading toward modern socialism. When, one by one, the countries wrote into their earliest constitutions an affirmation of loyalty to the Roman Church they were pledging themselves to support a spiritually hierarchic system which was evidently in some degree bound to conflict with aims of equality: the more so since in the complex racial and social environment the popular mind had strangely fused ancient goddesses and Christian Virgins, strengthening both. Roman Catholicism in Mexico or Peru is far from being the same thing as Roman Catholicism in Rome. There is even a case for saying that the Roman Catholic Church has been the downfall of democracy in Spanish America; although it is equally arguable that without the Church the area would have been in danger of collapsing into cynicism. (Much of the criticism levelled at the Church can be accounted for by simple envy: it did often manage to be an efficient banking and business

---

[1] Gandía, Enrique de, in Sarmiento's *Obras Completas*, vol. 2, pp. cxvi *et seq.*

organization when the politicians were still hamstrung between idealism and corruption.)

A counterbalance to the Church—it would be better to say a counterbalance to an other-worldly, hierarchic mysticism which at least in theory denied the flesh and ignored its comforts and its pains—was provided by positivism which was used by the first generation of post-independence intellectuals as a weapon to coerce people into questioning old and deep-rooted superstitions. Sometimes the positivists professed to be anti-religious but they could not kill the religious spirit in themselves and they did not even try. Sarmiento, for instance, was a religious man who believed that there was nothing wrong with faith as such but only with the clergy whom he saw as enemies of progress. He thought there was nothing more detrimental to true religion than weak governments which impose faith and Catholicism by violence. These force Catholics to turn to atheism because political despotism suppresses freedom. True religion, Sarmiento believed, was the only teacher society should have. The aim of Christianity was not to achieve undying happiness but to spread culture, bringing an element of compassion into customs and thus restraining the passions of men. Though dogmas never changed, mankind did, and religion must therefore move with the times. He thought that the Jesuit order was pure totalitarianism and was therefore opposed to true Christianity. The Inquisition had deprived Spain of the benefits of Renaissance humanism, and in the Americas religion was a queer blend of Christian and Indian which he deplored. Sarmiento, in short, like Miranda in pre-independence times and like Juárez in Mexico, had no use for outward forms; and it is one of the anomalies of Spanish America that the external symbols of Roman Catholicism—the crossings and the incense and the genuflexions—have survived not only scorn but active persecution.

Indian-*mestizo* influences on the one hand and pure Spanish Creole on the other have tended to perpetuate a natural propensity for hierarchic forms—whether of church, politics, or society—and a liking for dogmatism. To the radical Spanish Americans the only way out seemed to be a complete change of loyalties, and rejection both of Spanish and Indian forms in favour of that seemingly so successful and so utterly different world—the Anglo-Saxon. Alberdi thought that without Britain and the United States freedom would vanish, and in a poetic flight he likened a country without Englishmen to a forest without birds. Usually, however, he was more apt to overlook any colourful, singing, poetic aspects of the Anglo-Saxon character in favour of its drier but success-attracting puritan virtue—industry—which seemed to him a force for stability and calm. Most Spanish American intellectuals, indeed, found it easy, in extolling Anglo-Saxon virtues, to forget Shakespeare and remember only the steam engine. Thus Manuel Vicente Villarán could inveigh against decorative and literary trends in education inherited from Spain which prevented his countrymen from turning to farming, mining, and other useful occupations. In the context in which he was speaking Villarán had a point, for useful occupations had come to be regarded as beneath the dignity of educated (and, by implication, white) Peruvians. The servants, virtually the slaves who were of course the Indians, existed to perform tasks of that kind. The upper classes were then free to pursue a genteel metaphysic. It was impossible for Villarán or any of his contemporaries to see that it was feasible to achieve a blend of elegance and industry, thought and muscle, sensibility and sound economy.

Those who sympathized with Villarán in deploring the impractical word-weaving of the salons were strongly attracted to positivism, but positivism was interpreted in a wide variety of ways many of which would probably have been unrecognizable to Comte and his European followers. Spanish Americans seized upon it not so much from a conviction that it was true, as because it seemed a handy instrument by which to achieve freedom as it was then interpreted. They were using it as a means and not as an end, as expediency and not as science. Positivism seemed to them to provide the kind of dialectic that would convince the more educated people that worn-out dogmas were useless, that mysticism could result in nothing but airy fancies, and that hard industry of the Anglo-Saxon type would bring its due reward. Of course everything must be based on science. It must, that is, be proven. And yet at the same time the useful could be allowed to take precedence over the true.

Positivism, through its insistence on the scientific method, put a taboo upon an area of human experience that had a special emotional attraction for Spanish Americans. Therefore it became necessary to create a uniquely Spanish American union between positivism and mysticism. True, the Peruvian positivist Manuel González Prada poured scorn on the repressive tendencies of religion. Science, he said, never anathematized any man for proving that a straight line is the shortest distance between two points, nor did it ever torture those who dared to say that the earth revolved round the sun. But he did not notice that his positivist science had rejected any investigation that could not be measured with a tangible rule. How, for instance, measure the 'justice' and 'kindness' which a new type of knight errant dreamed up by another positivist, the Chilean Juan Enrique Lagarrigue, was to dispense to the humble and suffering?

Positivism was a necessary phase in the process of self-probing. For all its limitations it helped to loosen the shackles of the Inquisition and bring the dreamers down to earth. But it was only one small step toward the kind of liberty which Spanish Americans desired, and after the positivists a new generation arose which believed that true liberalism could be established only if man himself were transformed:

'. . . It was not the form of government that was important to them, but rather the content. They attempted to transform man himself. Liberalism was not just a political banner but a programme to educate the Hispanic American, to make of him a man different from the one the colony had produced.'[1]

The mysticism lurking within Spanish American positivism led directly to popularization of such anti-positivist movements as Rosicrucianism which influenced the Nicaraguan poet Rubén Darío and, in our day, Jorge Luis Borges in Argentina. It led to

[1] Zea, L., p. 68.

the 'cosmic man' painted by the Mexican revolutionary muralist José Clemente Orozco, rising heavenward out of a cupola as he transcends the three 'partial' men: the sleeper, the thinker or meditator, and the emotional man—the man filled with wonder.[1] It led to the systems of Antonio Caso and José Vasconcelos which said that the most important force in the universe was cosmic energy organized and directed on three different levels of existence: the material, the vital, and the spiritual.[2] It was represented by such men as Ignacio Pudencio Bustillo, professor of legal philosophy in the Sucre University law school between 1918 and 1921, who believed that the scientific method as it was practised in his day was incapable of discovering all aspects of truth, that a whole world existed beyond the reach of scientific instruments and which could not be investigated by methods of experiment open to science. Nevertheless he warned against the intuitive inclinations of Bergson and William James which slipped easily into fantasy. He hoped that a way would be found to combine the two kinds of investigation, physical and metaphysical.

José Enrique Rodó went still further in his reaction against pure positivism, likening the material world to Caliban, the spiritual to Ariel, and roundly condemning the former in a polemic directed chiefly against the United States. Rodó agreed with Renan that democracy and idealism are incompatible, that democracy is equivalent to materialism: that is, to Caliban. He fulminated against the United States for having made an automaton of man. To him, good taste and the moral sense are equivalent, and in the U.S.A. he recognized many virtues (including inventiveness and the ability to create a solid substratum for spiritual life), but not these. Life in the United States, he thought, had no aim outside itself, its prosperity being equalled only by its inability to understand where human destiny lies. Such a civilization produces an extraordinary sense of insufficiency and emptiness. After all the centuries of Greek and Christian

---

[1] See Echavarría, S., *Orozco*, in the series *Jalisco en el Arte* (bilingual), Planeación S.A., Guadalajara, Mexico, pp. 54–7.

[2] See *México en la Cultura*, Nov. 13, 1966.

civilization we reach the rock bottom of materialism, bereft of all tradition, mindless of the future, interested only in the moment, in the egoism of personal and collective well-being. Rodó believed that British utilitarianism was redeemed from these depths by a practical flair and emotional sensibility. The latter, he thought, was unfortunately not transferred to American soil, where the ideals of beauty and truth failed to inspire the austere Pilgrim Fathers who wanted a more immediate return for effort. For Rodó the highest reaches of American thought are to be found in Benjamin Franklin whose philosophy is based on the 'mediocrity of honesty and the utility of prudence'. 'Pushing to the front', worldly success, thus became the aim of American life.[1]

Following upon Rodó and trying to provide a practical alternative to America's 'mediocrity of honesty', a movement arose during the thirties and forties of the present century which was known as the 'Andean'. It was small, and its aims have been superseded by the drive toward economic unity that better fits twentieth-century trends. In its time, however, it marked a significant return to Bolívar's original ideals. It affirmed that a civilization could be built that need not be based upon the patterns of culture established in Europe during the Renaissance and penetrating gradually to the whole of the western world.[2] These patterns included the kind of economic organization that we take for granted today, together with religious, philosophical, and artistic schools even when these appear to break with tradition; for according to the Spanish American view the break arises out of the tradition itself and its revolutionary impulse ties it to the old as effectively as conformity does.

This European tradition (including of course the American-Anglo-Saxon) was so strong that all other peoples of the world gradually became intoxicated by it, hypnotized, totally subservient to it; and this is the view not only of the small Andean group as such but also of leading intellectuals such as Leopoldo Zea, Pablo

[1] Rodó, J. E., *Ariel*, pp. 87–93.
[2] See Cosani Sologuren, A., *Los Andes, Cuna de una Nueva Civilización*, in *Humanismo*, March–April and May–June 1953, Mexico.

González Casanova, and Octavio Paz. Nevertheless the endurance of some Amerindian peoples in the face of terrible passive suffering is evidence, according to many, that there is another strength, another line of culture, behind the European. Thus Spanish Americans live according to European patterns but their spirit is other and free. The Spanish American is neither Indian nor western but the result of tension between the two. The ideas that arise in Spanish American minds as these tensions increase are so strange to the western world that they appear clownish, even lunatic. Therefore the Spanish American keeps them to himself, and speaks of them only in private among trusted friends. They are coded in satire and song: in the words (often unexpectedly profound) and the rhythms of the Argentine tango, in the *roto* philosophy embodied in the lyrics of the Chilean *cueca*, in the Mexican *corrido*, in the cartoons of humorists such as the satirical José Guadalupe Posada and Abel Quesada, in the early and wholly Mexican films of Cantinflas before he was taken up by the American industry; and not (whatever their excellence, artistically speaking) in the novels and short stories of people like Borges in Argentina or Carlos Fuentes in Mexico, which fall within the European-North-American tradition. A study of folk and 'pop' art in Spanish America might yield more understanding of what the area is about than any amount of scrutiny of ministerial speeches or the art forms of the intelligentsia.

Spanish Americans may be apt to exaggerate their differences from the rest of the world, their un-European-ness, their only semi-Indianness, their separateness from Anglo-Saxon America. There *is* a difference, there *is* something specifically Spanish American which is unmistakable wherever it is met with; but it has not yet become sufficiently articulate to be raised into a formalized style, to be discussed, to be analysed, to be pointed to as one would to Palladian or Gothic, saying '*This* is Spanish American.' It may possibly be that its very nature is hidden; and yet in some ways it is as sharply incised as the outline of a maguey cactus or a *huaso* on his horse.

The western cultural-political-economic tradition swirls about

Spanish Americans and by its sheer centripetal force sucks them in. But there is another force that resents the compulsion put upon the area to take sides in the world power struggle, to be either democratic or communist, for or against 'free enterprise'. Might there not, Spanish Americans suspect, be some other arrangement that fits neither the one nor the other? The question is particularly pertinent when, as frequently seems to happen, the powers turn out to be moving in convergent directions. Democracy equated with the crew-cut and the attitude that each man is as good as his brother has a way of forcing the nonconformist to become society's renegade. The obverse of the regimented, brain-washed repeater of slogans is the hippie.

Still worse, when one of the octopus-armed private companies from the United States carries with it into Spanish America not only its business efficiencies but a complexity of interests so ramified that all the resources of a foreign government, its security and espionage services and its armed forces, are brought in to support it, then private enterprise becomes foreign invasion; and it is this factor which nullifies the argument that the foreign companies bring prosperity to the countries they invade by providing jobs and by teaching skills. So they do, but at a price. Given the present international industrial set-up, therefore, there is no reason why a nation should not, as Mexico for instance to a large extent has done, form itself into a corporate business enterprise which can operate frankly through its own loan banks, which enlists its best entrepreneurs and economists, and which behaves like any international corporation. To call this trend communist or Marxist is stretching a good many points, particularly in Spanish America where there is no cult of conformity to favour regimentation. In the U.S.A. it is important to be a 'regular guy'. In Spanish America every member of the crowd aspires to be a separate and distinguishable individual and a potential aristocrat. Thus the meaning of 'all men are created equal' is turned inside out. The titles of '*Don*', '*Licenciado*', '*Maestro*' replace the old aristocratic ones; and their proliferation, far from rendering them meaningless, establishes the princely and inestimable value of the spirit locked in the human skull. Nature, Rodó believed, is hierarchic. If so, men by their sense of goodness, of taste, or right action, will fit naturally into the niches to which they belong.

There is no question of egalitarianism here. A true democracy would, according to Rodó, be based on the supremacy of intelligence and virtue. The good thus engendered would descend upon the multitude in an effusion of love. According to him our civilization has received a double inheritance: from Christianity a sense of equality somewhat vitiated by asceticism and denial of spiritual selectivity; and from the classical cultures a sense of order, of hierarchy, of respect for genius, vitiated in its turn by an aristocratic disdain for the humble and weak. He believed that in future these two tendencies would fuse into an 'immortal formula', and democracy would triumph: a democracy not levelling into mediocrity but disseminating art and refinement. This is not the kind of democracy which feeds on the utilitarian, the material; and Latin Americans, said Rodó, must renounce their 'Nordomania'— their kowtowing to all that is Anglo-Saxon—and must have faith in themselves.[1]

It is part of the price paid for an individualistic political arrangement that it should be relatively easy to avoid punishment for graft, nepotism, and general political dishonesty. Each man is a test unto himself. If he rises to honour and nobility it is not because he is compelled by law but because his private conscience will have nothing to do with the alternative. A nation may go to the devil, but the individual has a chance of becoming the new man of whom Vasconcelos and Orozco and Rodó dreamed. Even Spanish American Marxists, when they are driven to select between individualism and the State, seem to have a bias toward the former. That is why Marxism has taken such unconventional forms in places like Chile, Venezuela, and Mexico, and why the communist party is weaker than might be expected and often collapses under the disruptive force of rivalries in its ranks.

A modern, efficiently organized factory was being opened in one Spanish American country. The foreign Press had been

[1] Rodó, J. E., *Ariel*, pp. 74-7.

invited, and the workers paraded in impeccable uniforms. The machines were pristine and their attendants seemed welded each to his particular lever which he threw in and out of gear to split-second timing. One correspondent wondered aloud whether this happy-go-lucky country was in danger of falling a prey to fascism. 'Oh no,' said his companion. 'You can always trust these people to make a mess of things!' It was intended as a compliment. 'Making a mess of things' is a privilege that may be costly; it ensures that the individual takes precedence over those abstractions 'the man in the street', the 'voter', the 'citizen'. For whomever the liberators fought, it was not for these. It is perhaps the one salvation of Latin American dictatorships that they are incapable of imposing a fascist type of brain-washed conformity upon the masses; for the simple and pathetic reason that the masses count for nothing at all. A peasant tilling his acre of maize on the outer margins of civilization can be allowed to think as he will; and so even can a factory worker whose union is controlled by leaders appointed by the dictator. Horrors and brutality there may be: conformity not quite.

In Spanish American history villain and hero have been locked in a battle not so much with one another as with man's inability to make up his mind where he is going. How to resolve the drama—how to achieve freedom without extending freedom to the intolerant and destructive; how to prevent democracy from becoming the rule of the mob; how to police without repression, to reconcile freedom with discipline—these were the problems the liberation movement was concerned to solve. They are implicit in much of the soul-searching committed by Simón Bolívar to paper as he poured out his tense, embittered, aspiring thoughts to correspondents in both hemispheres; in San Martín's shilly-shallying after what should have been decisive victories; even in the self-contradictions of tyrants like Iturbide in Mexico or Francia in Paraguay. They are implicit in the situations that exist today, in one way or another, in almost every country in Spanish America; in those with dictatorial rulers and in those where stability has been lost through weakness leading to political anarchy and economic inflation; even in those that have established equilibrium on a high governmental level but not in the substratum.

It is not that the liberators were wrong: on the contrary, they saw the difficulties clearly. It is rather that their practical aims have been mishandled by theorists who have failed to legislate for human nature. The ideals of the liberators still hold, and they stand for a not impossible unity yet to be created.

Date	Europe	Argentina and South-east	Chile
1808	Tumult of Aranjuez. Charles IV and Ferdinand VII abdicate. Joseph Bonaparte on Spanish throne. Canning British Foreign Secretary since 1807.	Montevideo repudiates viceregal authority.	
1809	End of Canning's term as Foreign Secretary		
1810		Liberal Junta in Buenos Aires. Asunción recognizes Spanish regency.	Liberal Junta.
1811	British and Spanish armies victorious at Albuera. Spanish Cortes give Spanish Indies equal representation.	Conservative triunverato in Buenos Aires. Paraguay declares independence under Francia.	
1812	Liberal constitution in Spain. Castlereagh British Foreign Secretary.	San Martín returns from Europe to Buenos Aires. Royalists defeated near Tucumán.	Coup by José Miguel Carrera.
1813	Joseph Bonaparte routed by British and Spanish armies at Vitoria.	Buenos Aires 'assembly of 1813'.	
1814	Napoleon abdicates. Ferdinand restored to Spanish throne.	After patriot failure to push liberation northward, San Martín goes to Cuyo.	Patriots defeated at Cancha Rayada and Rancagua.
1815	Battle of Waterloo.		
1816	Miranda dies in jail in Cádiz.		
1817			Andes Crossing by San Martín. Liberals victorious at Chacabuco. Chile declares independence.
1818			Chilean patriots defeated at Chancha Rayada but victorious at Maipú. O'Higgins gives Chile a provisional plan of government.
1819			Expedition to free Peru sails from Valparaíso.
1820	Liberal Codex accepted in Spain.		
1821	Death of Napoleon.		
1822	Death of Castlereagh. Canning becomes British Foreign Secretary.	José Miguel Carrera shot in Mendoza.	
1823			O'Higgins's second plan of government. Earthquake in Valparaiso. O'Higgins resigns.
1824			
1825			
1827	Canning becomes British Prime Minister but dies a few months later.		
1828		Revolution of Juan Lavalle. Independence of Uruguay.	
1829		Rosas dictatorship in Argentina	
1830			

Independence *Movement*, 1808–1830

Gran Colombia	Peru and Bolivia	Mexico
	Chuquisaca audiencia protests loyalty to Ferdinand. Rebel Juntas in La Paz and Quito.	First Mexican uprising. Fall of Iturrigaray.
Bolívar returns from London to Venezuela. Miranda blockades Caracas. Liberal Juntas in Caracas, Nueva Granada, Bogotá, and Cartagena.	Liberals victorious at Suipacha.	Hidalgo rises and gives 'Grito de Dolores'.
First Congress of Venezuelan Republic. Independence declared in Cartagena.	Liberal defeats in Upper Peru.	Hidalgo excommunicated and shot.
Earthquake in Caracas. Miranda appointed dictator, captured, and betrayed. Bolívar's Cartagena manifesto. He goes to Curacao.		
Bolívar's 'War to the Death' decree.		Congress of Chilpancingo. Morelos enunciates independence principles.
Boves forces patriots out of Caracas.	San Martín takes over command from Belgrano.	
	Patriots defeated at Sipe-Sipe.	Morelos anathematized and shot.
Bolívar to Kingston, then Haiti. He fails to invade Venezuela.		
Bolívar invades Venezuela from Haiti.		
Battle of Boyacá. Bolívar proclaims Colombian republic.		
	San Martín begins invasion of Peru.	Plan of Iguala.
Battle of Carabobo seals Venezuelan independence. Congress of Cúcuta. Bolívar elected President of Gran Colombia.	Patriots enter Lima. San Martín proclaimed Protector.	O'Donojú arrives in Mexico. Army of Three Guarantees enters Mexico City.
		Iturbide proclaimed Emperor Agustín I. Guatemala and El Salvador break away.
Last Spanish troops in Venezuela capitulate.		Iturbide exiled.
Battles of Junín and Ayacucho.		Iturbide returns to Mexico and is executed.
Congress of Panama.		
Ocaña convention. Bolívar acclaimed Dictator in Bogotá.		
Bolívar opens Congress in Caracas, and resigns. Death of Bolívar.		

GLOSSARY OF FOREIGN WORDS

Arriero	Cattle drover.
Audiencia	Royal Court established by Spain in the colonies for administrative purposes.
Cacique	Indian chief. Used nowadays for 'boss'. Hence *caciquismo*, 'bossism'.
Caudillo	Commander, chief, leader. Halfcaste or white parallel to *cacique*.
Charro	Mexican cowboy (originally a rough, uneducated man, or churl).
Cholo	Peruvian Indian or half-breed peasant.
Conquistador	Conqueror. Used specifically for the exploring and conquering Spanish soldiers in the New World.
Corregidor	Magistrate.
Corrido	Mexican popular ballad.
Cueca	Chilean folk dance.
Encomienda	A grant of land made by the Spanish Crown to *conquistadores* and bearing with it the responsibility for the care of Indians living in the area.
Gaucho	Argentine cowboy.
Gobernaciones	Governorships.
Hidalgo	Nobleman.
Huaso	Chilean cowboy.
Intendencia	An administrative division in charge of legal and communal affairs, tax collection, the promotion of trade, and organization of the local militia.
Llanero	Plainsman.
Mestizo	Halfcaste. Hence *mestizaje*, 'halfbreedism'.
Mita	Enforced service by Indians.
Poncho	Woollen garment with a slit for head to go through.

Pongo	Indian servant working in feudal conditions.
Regidor	Alderman.
Repartimiento	A system whereby the conquering soldiers shared out Indians to provide labour in fields and mines. Replaced later by the more civilized *encomienda*.
Requerimiento	Obligatory proclamation to be read by *conquistadores* to Indians. It demanded submission to the Pope and the King of Castile.
Roto	Rough Chilean labourer.
Serrano	Hill dweller.
Siesta	An afternoon snooze.
Sombrero	Hat; literally 'shader', hence frequently used to mean specifically a broad-brimmed straw hat.
Unitario	Supporter of centralism as opposed to federalism.

BIBLIOGRAPHY

Alamán, Lucas. *Obras*, 5 vols., V. Agüero, Mexico City, 1900.

Albareda, Gines de, and Garfías, Francisco. *Antología de la Poesía Hispanoamericana*, Biblioteca Nueva, Madrid, 1961, *et seq.*

Alberdi, Juan Bautista. *Bases y Puntos de Partida para la Organización Política de la República Argentina*, Ediciones Estrada, Buenos Aires (no date).

Arciniegas, German (Ed.). *The Green Continent: a Comprehensive View of Latin America by its Leading Writers*, Alfred A. Knopf, New York, 1945.

Barcía Trelles, A. *San Martín en América*. 3 vols., Editor Aniceto López, Buenos Aires, 1943.

Barraclough, Geoffrey. *An Introduction to Contemporary History*, Penguin Books, Harmondsworth, 1967.

Bealunde, Victor Andrés. *Bolívar and the Political Thought of the Spanish American Revolution*, John Hopkins Press, Baltimore, and Oxford University Press, London, 1938.

Bello, Andrés. *Obras Completas*, 20 vols., Ministry of Education, Caracas, 1951 *et seq.*

      Principios de Derechos de Jentes, Facsimile of 1832 (first) edition, Caracas, 1965.

Benson, Nettie Lee (Ed.). *Mexico and the Spanish Cortes 1810–1822*, Institute of Latin American Studies, University of Texas Press, Austin and London, 1966.

Binayán, Narciso (Ed.). *Ideario de Mayo*, Editorial Kapelusz, Buenos Aires, 1960.

Blakeslee, George (Ed.). *Latin America: Clark University Address*, Stechert and Company, New York, 1914.

Bolívar, Simón. *Decretos del Libertador*, 3 vols., Sociedad Bolivariana de Venezuela, Imprenta Nacional, Caracas, 1961.

The Jamaica Letter (Edition in Spanish, English, and French), Ministry of Public Education, Caracas, 1965.

South American Independence, the speech of Bolívar at the act of installation of the Second National Congress of Venezuela, on February 15, 1819, and the Proceedings of the Congress, G. Young, 1819.
(See also under Lecuna, Vicente.)

Bryce, James. *South America, Observations and Impressions*, Macmillan, New York, 1912.

Burke, William. *Additional Reasons for our Immediately Emancipating Spanish America deduced from the New and Extraordinary Circumstances of the Present Crisis: and containing valuable information respecting the late important events both at Buenos Aires and in the Caraccas: as well as with respect to the present disposition and views of the Spanish Americans: being intended as a supplement to 'South American Independence.'* Second edition, J. Ridgway, London, 1808.

Burton, Captain Richard F. *Letters from the Battle-fields of Paraguay*, Tinsley Brothers, London, 1870.

Bustamante, Carlos María. *Resúmen Histórico de la Revolución de los Estados Unidos Mexicanos*, R. Ackermann, London, 1828.

Carr, Raymond. *Spain 1838–1939*, Oxford University Press, London, and New York, 1966.

Carrasco, Ricardo. *Francisco de Miranda, Precursor de la Independencia Hispano-americana, 1750–1792*, Editorial Bell S.A., Buenos Aires, 1951.

Child, Theodore. *The Spanish American Republics*, James R. Osgood, McIlvaine and Co., London, 1892.

Clissold, Stephen. *Latin America: a Cultural Outline*, Hutchinson, London, and Harper & Row, New York, 1965.

Cochrane, Lord. *Adventures Afloat: Extracts from the Autobiography of a Seaman and Services in the Liberation of Chile*, Thomas Nelson and Sons, London, Edinburgh, Dublin, and New York, 1907.

Collier, Simon. *Ideas and Politics of Chilean Independence, 1808–1833* Cambridge University Press, London, 1967.

Bibliography

Connell-Smith, Gordon. *The Inter-American System*, issued under the auspices of the Royal Institute of International Affairs, Oxford University Press, London, 1966.

Constitución de las Provincias Unidas en Sud-América. Sancionada y Mandada Publicar por el Soberano Congreso General Constituyente en 22 de Abril de 1819, seguido del Manifiesto del Mismo Congreso en el que, después de dar una idea general de la revolución, pasos que ha seguido y estado actual de aquellas provincias unidas en república, hace el análisis de la Constitución y operaciones del congreso y del gobierno, Imprenta de la Independencia, Buenos Aires, 1819.

Cosani Sologuren, Armando. *Los Andes, Cuna de una Nueva Civilización*, in *Humanismo*, Nos. 9–12, Mexico City, 1953.

Costeloe, Michael P. *Church Wealth in Mexico: a Study of the 'Juzgado de Capellanías' in the Archbishopric of Mexico 1800–1865*, Cambridge University Press, London, 1967.

Diccionario Enciclopédico U.T.E.H.A. Unión Tipográfica Editorial Hispano Americana, 10 vols., Mexico City, 1953.

Ducoudray Holstein, H. L. V. *Memoirs of Simón Bolívar, President Liberator of the Republic of Colombia and of his Principal Generals, comprising a Secret History of the Revolution, and the events which preceded it, from 1807 to the present time*, 2 vols., Henry Colburn and Richard Bentley, London, 1830.

Echavarría, S. *Orozco*, Planeación y Promoción S.A., Guadalajara, Mexico, 1959.

Edinburgh Review, 1809 (containing a commentary on the Spanish American situation and the *Lettre aux Espagnols-Américains* by the Jesuit Juan Pablo Viscardo y Guzmán).

Edwards, Agustín. *The Dawn, Being the History of the Birth and Consolidation of the Republic of Chile*, Ernest Benn, London, 1931.

Elliott, J. H. *Imperial Spain 1469–1716*, Edward Arnold, London, 1963.

Fitzgibbon, Russell H. (Ed.). *The Constitutions of the Americas*, University of Chicago Press, Chicago, and Cambridge University Press, London, 1948.

Bibliography

Galdames, Luis. *A History of Chile*, University of North Carolina Press, 1941.

Gibson, Charles. *The Aztecs Under Spanish Rule. A History of the Indians of the Valley of Mexico, 1519–1810*, Stanford University Press, Stanford, and Oxford University Press, London, 1964.

Gómez Robledo, Antonio. *Idea y Experiencia de América*, Fondo de Cultura Económica, Mexico City, 1958.

González Casanova, P. *La Democracia en México*, Ediciones Era, Mexico City, Second Edition, 1967.

González Grases, Pedro. *Bello: El Primer Humanista de América*, Ediciones del Trideste, Buenos Aires, 1946.

Tiempo de Bello en Londres y Otros Ensayos, Ministry of Education, Department of Culture and Fine Arts, Caracas, 1962.

and Santa Cruz, Victor. Diamante booklet No. XVI on Bello, published by the Hispanic and Luco-Brazilian Councils, London, 1966.

Graham, Gerald S., and Humphreys, R. A. (Eds.). *The Navy and South America 1807–1823: Correspondence of the Commanders-in-Chief on the South American Station*, The Navy Records Society, London, 1962.

Graham, Maria. *Journal of a Residence in Chile during the year 1822 and a Voyage from Chile to Brazil in 1823*, Longman, Hurst, Rees, Orme, Brown, and Green, London, 184; Frederick A. Praeger, New York, 1969.

Gutiérrez, Juan María. *San Martín en la Historia y en el Bronce. Bosquejo Biográfico del General D. José de San Martín*, published for the Year of the Liberator General San Martín by the Argentine Government, Buenos Aires, 1950.

Guzmán, Nicomedes (Ed.). *Autorretrato de Chile*, Zig-Zag, Santiago, 1957.

Guzmán Blanco, General. *Documentos para la Historia de la Vida Pública del Libertador de Colombia, Perú, y Bolivia*, 2 vols., Imprenta de 'La Opinión Nacional' de Fausto Teodore de Aldrey, Caracas, 1875.

Hall, Basil. *Extracts from a Journal written on the coasts of Chile, Peru, and Mexico in the years 1820, 1821, 1822,* 2 vols., Archibald Constable and Co., Edinburgh, and Hurst, Robinson, and Co., London, 1824.

Hanke, Lewis. *The Spanish Struggle for Justice in the Conquest of America,* University Press, Cambridge, Massachusetts, and Oxford University Press, London, 1945.

Hanson, Simon G. *Five Years of the Alliance for Progress: an Appraisal,* The Inter-American Affairs Press, Washington, 1967.

Hasbrouck, Alfred. *Foreign Legionaries in the Liberation of Spanish America,* Columbia University Press, New York, 1928.

Henao, Jesús María, and Arrubla, Gerardo, *History of Colombia,* University of North Carolina Press, Chapel Hill, 1938.

Henríquez-Ureña, Pedro. *Literary Currents in Hispanic America,* Harvard University Press, Cambridge, Massachusetts, and Oxford University Press, London, 1945.

Hernández, José. *El Gaucho Martín Fierro, and La Vuelta de Martín Fierro,* Ediciones Beuser, Buenos Aires, 1958.

Herring, Hubert. *A History of Latin America,* second edition, Alfred A. Knopf, New York, 1961.

Hidalgo y Costilla, Procesos Inquisitorial y Militar Seguidos a D. Miguel, Instituto Nacional de Antropología e Historia, Mexico City, 1960.

Hippisley, G. *A Narrative of the Expedition to the Rivers Orinoco and Apuré in South America which sailed from England in November 1817 and Joined the Patriotic Forces in Venezuela and Caracas,* John Murray, London, 1819.

Humphreys, R. A. *British Merchants and South American Independence,* in *Proceedings of the British Academy,* vol. 51, 1965.

Liberation in South America 1806–1827: The Career of James Paroissien, University of London, The Athlone Press, London, 1952.

Jane, Cecil, *Liberty and Despotism in Spanish America,* Oxford University Press, London, 1929.

Johnson, J. J. (Ed.). *Continuity and Change in Latin America,* Stanford University Press, Stanford, California, 1964.

Bibliography

Key-Ayala, S. *Vida Ejemplar de Simón Bolívar*, Tipografía Americana, Caracas, 1942.

Lecuna, Vicente (Ed.). *Cartas del Libertador*, 10 vols., Venezuelan Government, Caracas, 1939.
    Proclamas y Discursos del Libertador, 1811–1830, Venezuelan Government, Caracas, 1939.
    Relaciones Diplomáticas de Bolívar con Chile y Buenos Aires, 2 vols., published by Imprenta Nacional under the auspices of the Bolivarian Society of Venezuela, Caracas, 1954.
    Simón Bolívar, Obras Completas, 3 vols., Editorial Lex, Havana, 1950.
    Simón Bolívar, Selected Writings, 2 vols., published by the Bank of Venezuela at the Colonial Press Inc., New York, 1951.

Levene, Ricardo. *Lecciones de Historia Argentina*, 2 vols., nineteenth edition, Editorial Lajouane, Buenos Aires, 1947.

Lillo, Samuel A. *Literatura Chilena*, sixth edition, Editorial Nascimiento, Santiago, 1941.

Lugones, Leopoldo. *Historia de Sarmiento*, Editorial Universitaria de Buenos Aires, Buenos Aires, 1961.

Mancisidor, José. *Hidalgo, Morelos, Guerrero*, Biografía Gandesa, Mexico City, 1966.

Mathison, Gilbert Farquhar. *Narrative of a Visit to Brazil, Chile, Peru, and the Sandwich Islands during the years 1821 and 1822*, Charles Knight, London, 1825.

Medina, José Toribio. *Historia del Tribunal del Santo Oficio de la Inquisición en México*, Santiago, 1905.

Miers, John. *Travels in Chile and La Plata*, 2 vols., Baldwin, Cradock, and Joy, London, 1826.

Miller, John. *Memoirs of General Miller, in the Service of the Republic of Peru*, 2 vols., Longman, Rees, Orme, Brown, and Green, London, 1828.

Miranda, Francisco de. *Archivo del General Miranda*, 22 vols., Tipografía Americana, Caracas, 1930 *et seq.*
El Colombiano de Francisco de Miranda y Dos Documentos Americanistas, Instituto Nacional de Hipódromos, Colección Venezolanista, Caracas, 1966.

O'Leary, Daniel Florence. *Memorias*, 6 vols., Imprenta Nacional, Caracas, 1952.
Orrego Vicuña, Eugenio. *Don Andrés Bello*, Zig-Zag, Santiago, 1949.

Páez, José Antonio. *Autobiografía*, 2 vols., with an introduction by the author, written in New York, April 18, 1867, Venezuelan Ministry of Education, Caracas, 1946.
Parkes, Henry Bamford. *A History of Mexico*, revised edition, Houghton Mifflin, Boston, 1960, Eyre and Spottiswoode, London, 1962.
Parks, E. Taylor. *Colombia and the United States 1765–1934*, Duke University Press, Durham, North Carolina, 1935.
Parra-Pérez, C. *Miranda–Bolívar*, lectures given at the Spanish Institute of the University of Paris, February and March, 1947.
Parry, J. H. *The Spanish Seaborne Empire*, Hutchinson, London, and Knopf, New York, 1966.
Pendle, George. *A History of Latin America*, Pelican Books, Harmondsworth, 1963.
Pérez Vila, Manuel. *Bolívar y Su Epoca: Cartas y Testimonios de Extranjeros Notables*, published by the General Secretariat of the Tenth Interamerican Conference, 2 vols., Caracas, 1953.
Picón-Salas, Mariano. *A Cultural History of Spanish America from the Conquest to Independence*, University of California Press, Berkeley and Los Angeles, 1962.
Pike, Fredrick B. *The Modern History of Peru*, Weidenfeld and Nicolson, London, and Frederick A. Praeger, New York, 1967.
Pilling, William. *The Emancipation of South America*, a condensed translation of *The History of San Martín* by General Bartolomé Mitre, Chapman and Hall, London, 1893.

Restrepo, José M. *Historia de las Revoluciones de la República de Colombia en la América Meridional,* 6 vols., Bibliografica Popular de Cultura Colombiana, Imprenta Nacional, 1945.

Rippy, J. Fred. *Latin America: a Modern History,* University of Michigan Press, Ann Arbor, and Mayflower Press, London, 1959.

Rivas-Vicuña, Francisco. *Las Guerras de Bolívar.* Vol. I (1812–14) published by Editorial Victoria (Manrique y Ramírez Angel), Caracas; and Vol. 2 (1814–17) by Empresa Editorial Norte, Centro y Sud-América, Caracas, no publication date.

Robertson, William Spence. *France and Latin-American Independence,* Johns Hopkins Press, Baltimore, 1939.

History of Latin-American Nations, D. Appleton and Company, New York and London, 1925.

Iturbide of Mexico, Duke University Press, Durham, North Carolina, 1952.

Life of Miranda, 2 vols., University of North Carolina Press, Chapel Hill, 1929.

Rise of the Spanish American Republics as told in the Lives of their Liberators, New York, 1918.

Rodó, José Enrique. *Ariel,* Editores Sarandi 441, Montevideo, 1944.

Rojas, A. *Miranda dans la revolutión française,* Imprimerie et Lithographie du Gouvernement National, Caracas, 1889.

Royal Institute of International Affairs. *The Republics of South America,* Oxford University Press, London, 1937.

Rydjord, John. *Foreign Interest in the Independence of New Spain: an Introduction to the War for Independence,* Duke University, Durham, North Carolina, 1935.

San Martín, José de. Articles on him in *Revista del Instituto Nacional Sanmartiniano,* Buenos Aires, September 1955.

Sarmiento, Domingo Faustino. *Facundo,* Editorial Tor, Buenos Aires (not dated).

Obras de, 38 vols., published

under the auspices of the Argentine Government, Buenos Aires, 1900.

Obras Selectas (Director, Enrique de Gandía), Editorial La Facultad, Buenos Aires, 1944.

Scott Elliot, G. F. *Chile: its History and Development, Natural Features, Products, Commerce and Present Conditions*, T. Fisher Unwin, London, 1907.

Sierra, Justo. *Evolución Política del Pueblo Mexicano*, Fondo de Cultura Económica for La Casa de España en México, Mexico City, 1940.

Street, John. *Artigas and the Emancipation of Uruguay*, Cambridge University Press, London, 1959.

Teja Zabre, Alfonso. *Morelos*, Colección Austral, Espasa-Calpe, Buenos Aires, 1946.

Trend, J. B. *South America*, Oxford University Press, London, 1941.

U.S.A. Archives. *Mexico and Mr. Poinsett: Reply to a British pamphlet*, Philadelphia, December 21, 1829.

Vicuña Mackenna, Benjamín. *La Corona del Héroe*, Santiago, 1872.

Villoro, Luis. *El Proceso Ideológico de la Revolución de Independencia*, Universidad Nacional Autónoma de México, Mexico City, second edition 1967.

Ward, H. G. *Mexico* (during the years 1825, 1826, and 1827), 2 vols., London, Henry Colburn, 1828 and 1829 and Frederick A. Praeger, New York, 1968.

Webster, C. K. (Ed.). *Britain and the Independence of Latin America 1812–1830, Selected Documents from the Foreign Office Archives*, 2 vols., for the Ibero-American Institute of Great Britain by the Oxford University Press, London, 1938.

Foreign Policy of Castlereagh 1812–1822, G. Bell and Sons Ltd., London, 1934.

White, Blanco (under pseudonym of Doblado, Leucadio). *Letters from Spain*, Henry Colburn and Co., London, 1822.

Zea, Leopoldo. *The Latin American Mind*, University of Oklahoma Press, Norman, Oklahoma, 1963.

INDEX

Index

Index